T0114839

TRACING FOOTSTEPS

The Frasers of Scotland to Frazers of Virginia and West Virginia

LILLIAN "SISSY CRONE" FRAZER

authorHOUSE®

AuthorHouse™
1663 Liberty Drive
Bloomington, IN 47403
www.authorhouse.com
Phone: 833-262-8899

Published by AuthorHouse 02/25/2021

ISBN: 978-1-6655-1740-9 (sc)
ISBN: 978-1-6655-1739-3 (e)

Library of Congress Control Number: 2021903312

Print information available on the last page.

"The past is never dead, it's not even past."

William Faulkner

INTRODUCTION

"JE SUIS PREST"
I AM READY

The name "Fraser" became well-known for those who followed the "Outlander," the fictional and historical television drama series starring the well-educated, tall, handsome and natural leader, Jamie Fraser. James Alexander Malcolm MacKenzie Fraser, the fictional dashing character and warrior, entered our homes wearing his Scottish kilt, becoming one who many of us loved instantly.[1] Although this Jamie Fraser and family were historical fiction, the "Fraser" family was a true family of the Scottish Highland Clan Fraser of Lovat and ancestors of our Frazer family. The Frazers of Colonial America may have not worn kilts, but many were handsome, well-educated, prominent and courageous men, fighting for their country and making homes for their families. Gallantry continued in America.

The Scottish Highland Clan Frasers of Lovat have been documented with stories shared in numerous writings. They are strongly associated with Inverness and the surrounding area since the 13th Century. The family members were historically dynamic and dominating in local politics and major military conflicts in Scotland history, known for their fighting spirit. Even today it is said, "Fraser remains the most prominent family name within the Inverness area."[2]

Perhaps the most notorious Clan Chief and rebel was Simon Fraser, the

---

[1] Gabaldon, Diana, 1991, *Outlander*, Book Series 1991-2001 and Starz Historical Drama, 2014.

[2] *Clan Fraser of Lovat Profile scotclans.com*. Retrieved 11 May 2014.

11th Lord Lovat, known as "The Fox." Simon Fraser has been described as a clan chief, spy, traitor, philosopher, and one who changed allegiances. My mother-in-law, Emily Francis (Fran) Cole Frazer, wife of Oscar Wallace Frazer, Jr., described Simon Frazer as a paternal ancestor to my children, which meant he was a family member and a father. His ambition and wit led him into the thick of politics, and he became a legend of his time. Simon Fraser, "The Fox," was the last of the rebel Scottish lords to be executed for treason against the Crown after the Jacobite Rebellion of 1745. At age 80, his sentence was carried out and Simon Fraser was beheaded on April 9, 1747. [3]

[3] Fraser, Sarah, 2012, *The Last Highlander*, p. Prologue xxiii.

While vaguely listening, I recall my children's grandparents speak of the Scottish Highland Fraser ancestors and their descendants as they visited libraries and museums and gravesites, meticulously tracing family lineage. They were adamant about their discoveries but with no computers nor internet nor on-line sources available to them, searches were frequently futile.

One day while visiting us, Fran, then in her senior years, handed over a thin, leather-bonded folder containing several typewritten sheets of paper, the results of her ancestor searches. A smile lightened a compassionate face with spiderweb wrinkles around soft eyes. Short, aged arms wrapped protectively around Nikki, my young pretty and freckled-faced, reddish-blonde-haired daughter, as Fran said primly, "Maybe someday you or John Michael or Nikki will pick up where I left off."

Accepting the papers out of self-preservation, my initial thought was, "No, no way!" as I grimaced at the horrors of dredging through old papers and files and shuddered as I thought of the endless hours of tedious paperwork. I hoped my thoughts were not translated with body language as I loved Fran, who was always inherently kind and thoughtful and far from the dreadful character that is habitually attached to a mother-in-law. In my defense, I was a young mother with two youngsters, and day to day living was a challenge that I cherished. My thoughts were of each day and possibly tomorrow, but yesterday and the prospect of digging up old graves and uncovering family roots were not among them and had no place in my current life. As much as I enjoyed piecing together puzzles and learning local history, I loved my life as it was and had no desire to fill it with yesterdays and tracing footsteps of aged and departed relatives.

As I glanced up at the pure and sweet face of my daughter and the anxious awaiting face of Fran with her polished manners and charm, my original thought faded as I absently echoed her statement, "Perhaps someday."

In years to follow, I recollected comments made of the Frazer family by my mother-in-law, Fran. I had stashed those tidbits in the far recesses of my mind or so I thought. Many, many years later with children grown and now grandchildren, I scanned through Fran's notes, which prompted me to research and seek additional material. The more I explored and probed, the more I wanted to know and to share with my grandchildren and other young generations and friends of the Frazer family.

When at long last, opting to research the Scottish roots of my children and grandchildren after my pivotal indecisiveness, I speculated if my decision was premature. I had no idea the magnitude of history the family had encountered and actively participated in throughout the years, not only in Scotland but in Colonial America. Knowing the availability of what little personal time after years of work that I could carve out would be engulfed in research, laborious tasks, accumulating documents, and traveling to little towns and cemeteries played a major role in that uncertainty.

With my mother-in-law and my children in mind, dutifully, I decided to plunder ahead and explore as I dove head-first into the overwhelming discovery of family, resolving that I would concentrate on the Frazer family of Colonial America. The commitment was there, and the curious nature was abundant so with an unrelenting pace I was determined to learn all I could of this notable family, good and bad, and the threads of history that bind us. The Motto of Clan Fraser of Lovat is "Je suis prest," meaning "I am ready."[4] This became my motto for this writing.

The "Frasers," now known as "Frazers" continued their fighting spirit in these new lands of America. It is from the Fraser ancestors of Scotland that William Frazer came to America, settling in Fredericksburg, Virginia. The many lives of the Frazers in this writing descended from this one man and his wife Frances. As in all families, the characters are human with strengths and weaknesses. Throughout the research and writing, I was astounded at the number of historical events in which the family participated, not as bystanders but as active contributors.

---

[4] Clan Fraser of Lovat Profile, scotclans.com, Retrieved 11 May 2014.

WILLIAM FRAZER

I AM READY – SCOTLAND TO VIRGINIA
THE BEGINNING OF STRANDS OF
FAMILY HISTORY IN AMERICA
LIFE IN FREDERICKSBURG, VIRGINIA

THE FIRST GENERATION

WILLIAM FRAZER, (1701-1734) the Scottish immigrant, born in Scotland about 1701, migrated to America and is the father of the Frazer descendants in this writing and a direct paternal ancestor to my children and grandchildren. William was a member of the Highland Clan Fraser of Lovat.

Historical fiction provides an opportunity to display a physical description and unique behavior and disposition of the character being presented, bringing that personality to lifelike and allowing us the possibilities of a fondness or a dislike for the character. The creativity in historical fiction and at times the fantasy and the plot, though entertaining, may be exaggerated to get and maintain our interest. To write and record our ancestors, the narrative non-fiction style writing and recording is less than whole so to maintain an accurate account. As we cannot know what the character thinks or feels from centuries ago, it is difficult to portray the character objectively and accurately in a three-dimensional form. Dates and names may be attached but that tells little about the ancestor and for myself as a reader leaves the character as a cold and empty shell, the person's name of which I have forgotten almost as soon as I have read it. But, at times, our discoveries enlighten us with a view, a tiny glimpse or two, of the true character, not a fictional one. That fast peek, the fleeting look, the few descriptive narratives, along with family tales, allow us to draw a shadow of the person. The geographical and historical and authentic view of the day allows us to envision the life of the time. All leave us to draw our own conclusions, if only partial ones, knowing the full picture is lost in history that no one took the time to record. It is the less popular nonfiction that I tell of William and the Frazer family because my purpose is to leave an accurate account of our ancestors, defining details with perhaps the fleeting glimpses discovered during our research. You may use your imagination to fill in the blanks.

The name Fraser has been spelled in various ways, including Frasier, Frazier, Frasher, Frisales, Frisels and Frazer as it is now known. The Scottish Clan Fraser has been researched and written, stories passed down of castles and brave countrymen and movies depicting the many turmoil's, but not much is written of the various family members who immigrated to America.

Little has been uncovered on William, our family's first-generation Frazer known in America. His date of arrival is not documented in records, which is not unusual, as during the early 1700s, it was not required to maintain ship passenger records. Many names that were recorded were of passengers exiled and sent to the Colonies by the government for religious, political, or criminal reasons. Some documented passengers arrived as apprentices or as indentured servants, sold for years of service. William Frazer's name was not among any of the recorded lists, but this does not exclude him from those categories as complete lists were not maintained. It is possible that he, as many did during the early 1700s, traveled and disembarked without any required documentation. Discontent with the land system and the devastation caused by the wars and Jacobite risings, motivated a large number of Scottish settlers to migrate, searching for a better life in the Colonies or to escape the conflicts of their current life. The desire to savor life more fully and the courage and curiosity to face a new life and a new beginning brought many to America, a land young and full of promise and possibilities.

There continues to be many mysteries and undocumented facts in history. Tracing William's footsteps was difficult because of the lack of census and passenger lists, so we reverted to the oral tradition that supports and is popularly told that William Frazer was born in Scotland and arrived at the port of Norfolk, Virginia as a young man, living in the Norfolk vicinity for a few years before moving to Fredericksburg, Virginia. William was able to write his name, as documented in court records.

As stated in *Tyler's Quarterly Historical and Genealogical Magazine*:

William Frazer (1701-1734) immigrated to Virginia from Scotland the place of his nativity, being a descendant of the ancient highland clan of Fraser of Lovat. Tradition states that he arrived at the port of Norfolk and lived a few years in that vicinity before moving to Fredericksburg in Spotsylvania county, Virginia. He was living in Spotsylvania county by September 1, 1724 when he made a deposition regarding an Indian in which he states he is aged about 23 years.

William Frazer died in March 1734 and on April 3, 1734 his widow Frances Frazer was appointed to administer his estate. John Gordon and Susannah Livingston, both of Fredericksburg, were her securities. By deed dated August 6, 1734 Benjamin Berryman of King George county conveyed to Frances Frazer, widow, and James Frazer, her son, of Fredericksburg, lot number 50 in the said town. By deed dated July 7, 1752 Isaac Darnall and Frances his wife, late Frances Frazer, and James Frazer, her son, sold lot number 50 to James Hunter.[5]

During the turn of the century, what would become Spotsylvania County was then the territory of other counties in the colony of Virginia. The House of Burgesses passed an Act authorizing the formation of a new county, which was composed of territories of the counties of Essex, King William, and King and Queen, and, thus, the heritage of Spotsylvania County began in 1721. This new county was named in honor of the Lieutenant Governor of the Colony, Alexander Spotswood. William Frazer arrived in Spotsylvania County during these formative years.

The years 1722-1734 encompass the period when Spotsylvania was a giant parent county stretching to the middle of the Valley. By the separation of Orange in 1734

---

[5] *Genealogies of Virginia Families*, Tyler's Quarterly Historical and Genealogical Magazine, p. 757.

it was reduced to its present size. But for the twelve years from 1722 to 1734 it contained within its bounds the present Piedmont counties of Orange, Culpeper, Madison, Rappahannock and Greene as well as the Valley counties of Rockingham, Page and Warren. [6]

What is now the commercial core of Fredericksburg was the first grid plan drawn up in 1721.[7]

> Be it enacted, by the Lieutenant Governor, Council, and Burgesses, of this present General Assembly, and it is hereby enacted, by the Authority of the same, that within six Months after the passing of this Act fifty Acres of Land, Parcel of a Tract of Land belonging to John Royston and Robert Buckner, of the County of Gloucester, situate, lying and being upon the South Side of the River Rappahannock aforesaid in the County of Spotsylvania commonly called or known by the Name of the Lease Land, shall be surveyed and laid out, . . . And when the said Town shall be so laid out the said Directors and Trustees shall have full Power and Authority to sell all the said Lots by publick Sale or Auction, from Time to Time, to the highest Bidder, so as no Person shall have more than Two Lots; . . . [8]

---

[6] *Spotsylvania County Road Orders*, 1722-1734, Pawlett, Nathaniel Mason, Faculty Research Historian, Virginia Highway & Transportation Research Council, Virginia Department of Highways & Transportation and the University of Virginia, p. 2.
[7] Fredericksburg, Virginia, *Settlement to Society* (1607-1750).
[8] *The History of the City of Fredericksburg, Virginia*, Quinn, S.J., The Hermitage Press, Inc., 1908, p.39.

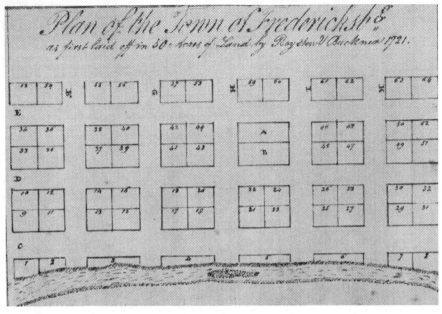

Map from the University of Mary Washington Library
(Lot 50 located on the corner of Princess Ann
and Amelia Streets that Frances and son
James Frazer purchased after William's death.)

Fredericksburg, nestled along the banks of the Rappahannock, became a haze of history and adventure. The town knew birth and death, love and war, and tears and fury, and William played his part in this history. By September 1, 1724, William lived in Spotsylvania County, documented by a deposition he made in court regarding an Indian, and in it, he states that he (William) "is aged about 23 years." William's deposition in court was prior to Fredericksburg having officially been chartered.

These early times in Colonial Virginia were 50-plus years prior to America gaining independence. The site of what would become the town of Fredericksburg in Spotsylvania County was known by the name "Lease Land." The settlement served as a trading post and was considered a place of importance, but it had not been chartered until 1727, at which time the settlement of Fredericksburg received an official charter from the House of

Burgesses. The City of Fredericksburg was established in 1728 by an act of the Virginia General Assembly.[9]

In William's deposition of 1724, he stated that he worked for Alexander Spotswood as an aide. He was also described as a tailor and a protégé. The incident with Sawney Indian occurred at Spotswood's mansion at Germanna, located in present-day Orange County about 20 miles west of Fredericksburg. Spotswood, out of a strong sense of power and wealth, established the German settlement of Germanna on the Rapidan River and built his home, colloquially known as "The Enchanted Castle" (a name given by William Byrd II that was noted in Byrd's private journal). The huge, stone and brick Georgian-style mansion, elaborately designed and decorated and described as something out of a fairytale, was built in 1718 and destroyed by fire in the 1750s. A rich meadow surrounded the house with shady lanes and a winding river. It was here at Germanna that William resided.

Spotswood, who served as the Lieutenant Governor for Spotsylvania County, had been recalled from the Lieutenant Governorship in 1722. He returned to London to attempt to get back into good graces, and in 1724/25 married while in England. While gone, Spotswood left his cousin in charge of his ironworks in Germanna. Upon Spotswood's return to America in 1729 to his home in Germanna, he was unhappy with the management of his property while in London. Many of the German indentured servants had fulfilled their indenture contracts and had left Germanna. William worked for Spotswood in 1724, the length of time of service is unknown, but William lived in Fredericksburg by 1727 according to other court records, so he would not be at Germanna at Spotswood's return.

An account of William Frazer's disposition of the incident that occurred at Spotswood's home was taken from the writings of *The Frazer Family from Scotland to America:*

> It seems that Sawney, a Sapony Indian, was given two
> letters from Governor Burnett of New York to carry to
> Governor Drysdale of Virginia regarding Indian affairs.
> While he was traveling through Spotsylvania County on
> his way to Williamsburg and the Governor, he stopped at

---

[9] *History of Fredericksburg, Fredericksburg, Virginia,* www.fredericksburgva.gov/202.

an ordinary where he became very drunk. Sawney fired his gun, without harm, at a resident, and then taking off his clothes, he struck another with the butt of his gun. After creating havoc in the town, Sawney went to former Governor Alexander Spotswood's house and asked to see Katina, an Indian maid, so that he might kiss her goodbye. William happened to be in charge of the house that day while Spotswood's housekeeper was away. When Sawney demanded to come into the house, William refused saying that he would send Katina out if she desired to see him. Then, Sawney cursed William and tried to enter the house through a window. William barred his way and threatened to give him a good knock on the head with a banister from the stairway. Sawney then swore by God that he would tear up the Governor's letters as he wasn't Governor now anyway. William replied that if he did he would be hanged. Eventually, a captain of the local militia took charge of Sawney and escorted him out of town. When the now sober Sawney reached Williamsburg, he complained bitterly to Governor Drysdale about his treatment by the townspeople. The governor called for an investigation of the matter, and witnesses were called to the September 1724 session of court.[10]

A deposition taken on September 1, 1724 of John Lee, a witness to the incident of Sawney states:

> The Deposition of John Lee aged ab't 25 years taken before the Court of Spotsylvania the 1st Day of September 1724. Who being Duly sworn and Examined Deposeth and saith that on the fryday the 28th of Aug't last, he heard an Indian man called Sawny say that he fear'd not Gov'r Drisdal that he was an Irish son of a bitch. That he and all the Indians feared Coll'n: Spotswood but that he was no Gov'r now, this Deponent further saith that he saw

---

[10] Frazer, Lyle and Loretta, *The Frazer Family from Scotland to America*, 2015, p.24.

three or four Letters in s'd Indians Custody, and further
saith that the sd Indian when sober, did say severall times
that the Canada Indians did design to come down on
the Inhabitants of this Colony for they feared no Gov'r
now Col'o Spotswood was gone, and that they were stout
fellows though did not care to fight fairly. John Lee.

In researching Katina, the Indian maid, it was discovered that
Katina was a Sioux Indian princess who was captured somewhere near
Williamsburg and given to Governor Alexander Spotswood. Katina served
Spotswood's family until his death in 1740, at which time he willed his
treasured servant to the Thornton family of Fall Hill in Fredericksburg.
Katina, much loved by the Thornton family, cared for three generations
of the family until she died in 1777. Some say Katina remains constant
at the old estate on Fall Hill as many have had Katina encounters long
after her death. It is said that Katina is buried under "massive oaks at Fall
Hill," marked by a granite stone with no inscription. She is somewhat of
a local legend. Katina is also found in the first chapter of *In the Ghosts of
Fredericksburg* by L.B. Taylor. In an article, *Katina: Ghost Nanny at Fall
Hill* by Donna Chasen states:

> Katina was a Sioux Indian princess who was given as a
> gift to Gov. Alexander Spotswood while he was living in
> Williamsburg. When Spotswood moved to the Germanna
> settlement, he brought Katina along with his family. At
> his death, she was passed on to the Thorntons, whose
> family had intermarried with the Spotswoods.
>
> The Thorntons had settled in Fredericksburg where
> they built a small home named The Falls, located where
> the George Washington Executive Center now stands on
> Princess Anne Street. They soon built Fall Hill, where
> they were living when Katina joined the family, raising
> three generations of the family's children during her long
> life.
>
> . . . Families come and go, some spend generations
> at the grand old house, but time passes on, and only

Katina remains constant. She still serves the owners of this old estate, never ending in her role as caregiver and comforter to the young or ill who live or visit there. There is a sense of safeness and comfort that encompasses the house and surrounding land that is directly associated with her presence. She is the true mistress of Fall Hill.[11]

Another account of the incident with Katina and Sawney in which William Frazer was deposed in court, as stated by the same article *Katina: Ghost Nanny at Fall Hill* states:

Spotsylvania County court records confirm another bit of legend about the Indian maiden. In 1724, Sawney, an Indian whose job was to take mail from the Colonial capital in Williamsburg to Gov. Spotswood in Germanna, arrived there with some letters.

Sawney had evidently stopped for refreshment along the way and was feeling no pain when he arrived at Spotswood's door. He demanded to see Katina, from whom he wanted a kiss. Spotswood was away, but his aide (William Frazer) refused to admit Sawney in his impaired condition. Sawney called the aide a fool and took a swing at him. In his rage, he also tore up the letters that he had been sent to deliver. This landed him in the Spotsylvania court, where the incident is documented to this day.[12]

During our travels to Fredericksburg to learn more about William, we walked the streets of this historical town trying to capture a spirit of a time gone by, a time when our relatives walked these same lands almost 300 years ago. Having lived in Fredericksburg previously, I had traveled these same streets many times to visit shops and restaurants, not realizing that past relatives had once lived here. Today, as I strolled the streets, I viewed my surroundings with awareness, unconsciously looking for William and

---

[11] Chasen, Donna, freelance writer, "Katina, Ghost Nanny at Fall Hill," Oct. 26, 2002, Fredericksurg.com.

[12] Ibid.

a nostalgic sweetness of yesterday. We stood on the banks of the river. Had William once stood here? Questions scrambled through my mind. If only we could hear the faded echoes of voices whispering to us. Voices unheard, we continued wandering and scanning the streets and the town with curiosity and a dash of fascination of a world that once existed and the part that the Frazer family played in the early life and history of the town. It was entertaining to speculate about that early life.

In years to follow 1724, William appeared often in court documents in Fredericksburg. In 1727, he served as an administrator, defendant, plaintiff, or on a jury and as jury foreman of other proceedings. In 1728, William served as a witness for the administering of William Norvell's estate by Thomas Grame.[13] In 1730, William served as administrator of David Mitchell's deed with John Gordon and James Roy as witnesses.[14]

Sometime about 1727, after William left employment with Spotswood, he moved to Fredericksburg. He married Frances (last name unknown). They had one child, James Frazer, born about 1729.

William's profession was referred to as a tailor. No records were located listing him in an apprenticeship as a tailor. It is unknown if he learned the trade in Scotland prior to coming to America or if he learned the trade after arriving in the Colonies. As noted in the following court record, William is listed as a "taylor" (sic).

> Sept. 6, 1733. Henry Fitzhugh of Stafford Co., Esqr., to Susannah Livingston of Spts. Co., widow, lease of 100 a. in Spts. Co. "To Susannah Livingston, Thomas Matthews, her servant, and James Frazier, son of William Frazier, taylor," etc.; on Fest. of St. Luke, Oct. 18th, 500 lbs. of tobacco, etc., yearly rental, etc. Witnesses: Sarah Fitzhugh, Lettice Lee. Kecd.[15]

In 1732, five years after Fredericksburg was officially established by law, Col. William Byrd visited Germanna and Alexander Spotswood.

---

[13] William Frazer, Spotsylvania County Records, November 7, 1728, p. 55.
[14] William Frazer, Spotsylvania County Records, October 6, 1730, p. 56.
[15] Spotsylvania County Court, Deed Book B, 1722-1734, March 5, 1733-1734, p. 129 as listed on ancestraltrackers.net.

While visiting, Byrd had a tour of Fredericksburg with Colonel Henry Willis, and he wrote a description of the beginning of the new town of Fredericksburg. He notes, as shown below, that there was a tailor. Would William Frazer be the referred tailor?

> Colonel Willis walked me about his new town of Fredericksburg. It is pleasantly situated on the south shore of the Rappahannock river, about a mile below the falls. . . . The only edifice of stone yet built is the prison, the walls of which are strong enough to hold Jack Sheppard (notorious English thief and prison escapee of 18th-century London), if he had been transported thither. Though this be a commodious and beautiful situation for a town, with the advantages of a navigable river, and wholesome air, yet the inhabitants are very few. Besides Colonel Willis, who is the top man of the place, there are only one merchant, a tailor, a smith, an ordinary-keeper, and a lady, Mrs. Livingston, who acts here in the double capacity of a doctress and a coffee-woman. It is said the courthouse and the church are going to be built here, and then both religion and justice will help to enlarge the place.[16]

Also, in 1732, Alexander Spotswood sued William Frazer for seven pounds seventeen shillings for the balance due on account. William paid the amount, including attorney fees. As mentioned, Spotswood had spent five years in England, and upon his return, he was unhappy with the management of his estate, suing some of his former employees and some prior indentured servants.

A couple of years later in March 1734, William Frazer died as a young man of 33 years old. His son James was five years old. His widow Frances "Frazier" was appointed administrator to his estate on April 2, 1734.[17] John Gordon and Susannah Livingston were her securities.

---

[16] Quinn, S.J., *The Project Gutenberg eBook*, The History of the City of Fredericksburg, Virginia, Dec. 10, 2012, eBook #41597, p.43.

[17] William Frazer, Spotsylvania County Court Order Book 1730-1738, p. 300.

> On Petition of FRANCES FRAZIER for administration
> of her late Husband, WILLIAM FRAZIER deced Estate,
> is granted; she having taken the Oath as the Law directs and
> entered into Bond with SUSANNAH LIVINGSTON &
> JOHN GORDON her Securitys and acknowledged the
> same in Court, And ordered that JAMES ROY, THOS.
> HILL, RICHARD TUTT & JAMES WILLIAMS or
> any two of them (being first sworn before a Majestrate of
> this County) do appraise all such of the said deceds Estate
> as shall be produced & shewn there by the said Admrx,
> And make report of their proceedings to the next Court.[18]

After William's death and by deed, on August 6, 1734, "Benjamin Berryman of King George County conveyed to Frances Frazer, widow, and her son, James Frazer, of Fredericksburg, lot number 50 in Fredericksburg."[19] Lot 50 was located at the corner of Princess Ann and Amelia Streets.

No records indicated what was located on that Lot during the 18 years Frances lived there. Today on Lot 50 in Fredericksburg, is the following home.

---

[18] William Frazer and Frances Frazer, Spotsylvania County, Virginia Order Book, 1734-1735.

[19] *Tyler's Quarterly Historical and Genealogical Magazine*, "Genealogies of Virginia Families," p. 757.

Lot 50, Fredericksburg (Located in the Historical District)
The current home was built in 1888. (Over
130 years after Frances sold the lot.)
Photo taken by Lillian Frazer, August 2020

We are unsure how Frances financially survived as a widow in colonial days with a young child of five other than selling what was among William's estate. There were no known relatives to assist, but without knowing her last name that would be difficult to uncover. Frances remarried in 1735, the year following William's death, to Isaac Darnall, a small landowner. Frances and Isaac had two sons, Henry and Nicholas. In 1752, eighteen years after Frances and son James purchased Lot 50, Frances, Isaac, and James sold Lot 50 as shown below:

July 7, 1752. Isaac Darnal and Frances, his wife, late Frances Frasher, and James Frasher, her son, of Spts. Co., to James Hunter of Fredericksburg, Mercht. Lbs53 15s. curr. Lot No. 50, in Town of Fredksbg. No witnesses.[20]

On April 13, 1770, Mrs. Frances Frazier (Frazer), widow, is shown in Virginia Marriage Records, Norfolk County Marriage Bonds, 1770-1850[21] as marrying Dickerson Pryor in Norfolk County, Virginia. Had Isaac Darnall died? No other records were located on this marriage with Dickerson Pryor.

William, the young man who left his home country and his way of life with the awareness of possibilities to start a new life, arrived in Norfolk at about age 20, moving on at age 23 to play his role in what would become Fredericksburg, Virginia. William met and married his wife Frances, the beginning of generations of Frazers in America. A decade later, at age 33, William's life was cut short, but he left a son James to carry on his legacy. Much is still a mystery about William, but he was the beginning of strands of history for our family in America. He was a brave young man, daring and respectable.

---

[20] Frances Frasher (Frazer) and James Frasher (Frazer), Virginia, Spotsylvania County Records, 1721-1800, Deed book E. 1751-1761.

[21] Frances Frazier (Frazer), Virginia County Records, Quarterly Magazine, Vol. VI. September 1909, p. 253.

JAMES BENJAMIN FRAZER

FARMER AND TOBACCO PLANTER
SPOTSYLVANIA, VIRGINIA

THE SECOND GENERATION

JAMES BENJAMIN FRAZER (abt. 1729-1774/1775), the only child of William and Frances Frazer, was born about 1729 in Spotsylvania County, Virginia. He was five years old when his dad, William, died in 1734 at the young age of 33. William left no Will, so on April 2, 1734, Frances filed with the court for Administrator of his Estate, which was granted.

On August 6, 1734, four months after Frances filed for Administrator of William's Estate, she and her five-year-old son, James, purchased Lot 50, land among the first grid plan of Fredericksburg at the corner of Princess Ann and Amelia Streets. We were unable to locate what home was on this property at the time. In the previous chapter, we included a picture of the current home that sits on the property, built in 1888, after Frances and James sold the property.

Susannah Livingston had several connections with William and Frances Frazer and son James. Susannah is the lady William Byrd speaks of in his description of Fredericksburg as "there are only one merchant, a tailor, a smith, an ordinary-keeper, and a lady, Mrs. Livingston, who acts here in the double capacity of a doctress and a coffee-woman."[22] We know William worked as a tailor and was in Fredericksburg during these years. If William was the "tailor" referred to by Byrd, William and Susannah

---

[22] Barbara Crookshanks, Librarypoint Blogs, "Coffee Houses: A Tradition Dating to Colonial Times," from The Westover Manuscripts, September 5, 2018.

Livingston were among the first businesses in Fredericksburg. Susannah also acted as security to Frances Frazer while administrator of William's Estate. Was this coincidental or was there a friendship between Susannah Livingston and William and Frances? Could Susannah or her deceased husband William Livingston have been a relative of either William or Frances? These are unknown questions.

We do know Susannah Livingston was the wife of William Livingston. *The Rappahannock Gazette* stated:

> There were many "key" people to the settlement of the region, but prior to 1730 seven or eight individuals stand out from the rest – Royal Lt. Gov. Alexander Spotswood, Lawrence Smith, Robert Taliaferro, John Bucker, Thomas Royston, Larkin Chew, William Livingston and Henry Willis.[23]

Among these "key" people who stand out from the rest, Spotswood was once the employer of William Frazer, father of James. Robert Taliaferro and his son Robert Taliaferro were the maternal grandfather and great grandfather of James Frazer's wife Elizabeth, respectively. William Livingston was the husband of Susannah Livingston.

> William Livingston and his wife Susannah had leased 50 acres from Royston/Buckner and as of 1726 was operating a small farm in the area across from the current "Barefoot Green's" on Lots 27 & 28 on Amelia Street. . .
>
> In 1727 he (William Livingston) was running an ordinary that his wife would continue running after his death in 1729. In that year Susannah also opened a "public roleing (rolling) house" on lots 29 and 31 (a tobacco warehouse). Fredericksburg now had one real resident, a rolling house and an ordinary.[24]

---

[23] *The Rappahannock Gazette,* Newsletter of the Rappahannock Colonial Heritage Society, Inc., Volume 6 Number 1, Winter 2003, p. 1.
[24] Ibid.

On September 6, 1733, Susannah Livingston, who was a widow, leased 100 acres of land in Spotsylvania County along with her servant, Thomas Matthews, and James Frazier (Frazer), son of William Frazier (Frazer), with 500 pounds of tobacco paying the yearly rental.[25] This occurred about six months prior to William Frazer dying. Why lease the land with James, the five-year-old son of William? Was William already sick and wanting to be assured that his wife and son would have a source of income? There could be other reasons. The answer is unknown, but this indicates there was a connection between Susannah Livingston and either Frances or the Frazer family.

Frances, mother of James, remarried after William's death to Isaac Darnall. James had two younger half-brothers, Henry and Nicholas, from this marriage. Isaac was a small landowner, likely farming the land. Frances, James, and Isaac maintained ownership of Lot 50 at the corner of Princess Anne and Amelia Streets in Fredericksburg for 18 years, selling the home and lot on July 7, 1752. James was about 23 years old at this time and considered a master carpenter.

About the same year in 1752, James married Elizabeth "Betty" Foster (abt. 1729/1733 - abt. 1791/1796), daughter of Anthony and Martha Taliaferro Foster of Spotsylvania County. Anthony Foster, a prominent landowner, came to Spotsylvania County from St. Anne's Parish in Essex County, Virginia. Martha Taliaferro Foster, Elizabeth's mother, as mentioned above, was the daughter of Robert Taliaferro and granddaughter of Robert Taliaferro, one of the "key people" of Fredericksburg mentioned in the article in *The Rappahannock Gazette.*

There was little information about James in court records or printed documents other than the buying and selling of land. James Frazer was a farmer and tobacco planter. Tobacco grew best in uncultivated soils, so the landowner had to spend considerable time when necessary in clearing the land before planting if the land was not already farmland. Tobacco was a successful cash crop in Colonial Virginia, but as tobacco drained the land of nutrients and only allowed for about three growing seasons, it was necessary to have significant acreage. After planting several seasons, the land would have to sit for several years before planting tobacco again.

---

[25] James Frazier (Frazer), Virginia, Spotsylvania County Records, March 5, 1733-4, p. 129.

This created a huge drive for the tobacco grower to purchase new farmland. Eventually, many farmers switched to other crops.

James and Betty had their first child, a son, in 1754, naming him after Betty's father, Anthony. Anthony Foster was pleased with this, and in 1755, he deeded 234 acres of land to his daughter Betty Frazer and her husband James Frazer. Anthony Foster also left his daughter Elizabeth "Betty" and son-in-law James Frazer a legacy in his Will, which was proved in 1763. Among the witnesses to this Will was Isaac "Darnal." By 1756, James and Betty had their second son, John. Soon after, James joined the Virginia Regiment.

Among "A Necessary Roll of Captain Thomas Waggener's Company on the South Branch, Dec. 4, 1757" of the Virginia Regiment, commanded by Colonel George Washington, Fort Loudoun, December 1, 1757, was James Frazer.[26]

The third son of James and Betty, named after his father, was born in 1758, and son William was born in 1761. James had assured that the Frazer family name would continue for a future generation. Their only daughter Martha was born by 1763. Little is known about Martha.

On March 4, 1764, James and Elizabeth purchased 323 acres of land in Spotsylvania County, on which they lived, from Betty's brother John Foster. James purchased an additional 120 acres on June 12, 1766 from John Waller of Spotsylvania County, and on July 5, 1766, he purchased another 183 acres from John Rouzie. On August 1, 1767, James "Frasher" purchased all "Goods and Chattels" from his stepfather Isaac Darnall with William Mastin as a witness. On November 6, 1771, James and Betty sold 332 acres of land in Spotsylvania County to John Mastin.

James' and Betty's last child, Reuben, was born in 1767. About seven years later, James Frazer died sometime in 1774-1775 but before February 16, 1775, at age of almost forty-six. His oldest son, Anthony, who was about 20 at that time, was the administrator of his Estate with Edward Herndon and Stapleton Crutchfield as seconds.[27] Sons John, James, and William were ages 18, 16, and 13. Martha was age 11, and his youngest child Reuben was seven years old. On February 18, 1779, "Betty Frasher"

---

[26] *Colonial Soldiers of the South*, 1732-1774, p. 482.

[27] Anthony Frazer, Virginia, Spotsylvania County Records, 1721-1800, Will Book E, p.65.

was appointed the legal guardian to children William, Reuben, and Martha "Frasher." Elizabeth "Betty" Frazer died about 1791/1796.

James and Elizabeth "Betty" Foster Frazer had six children (more information on children below):

B.1.   ANTHONY FRAZER (March 22, 1754 – March 4, 1804)

B.2.   JOHN FRAZER (1756 - November 28, 1793)

B.3.   JAMES FRAZER II (December 23, 1758 – December 20, 1798)

B.4.   WILLIAM FRAZER (March 1, 1761 – March 19, 1819)

B.5.   MARTHA FRAZER (abt.1763 - Unknown)

B.6.   REUBEN FRAZER (1767-1832)

B.1.   **ANTHONY FRAZER** (March 22, 1754 – March 4, 1804) (Son of JAMES BENJAMIN FRAZER, WILLIAM FRAZER) (See chapter on **ANTHONY FRAZER**.) Anthony is direct lineage to Oscar Frazer II.

B.2.   **JOHN FRAZER** (1756 - November 28, 1793) (Son of JAMES BENJAMIN FRAZER, WILLIAM FRAZER) John was born in Spotsylvania County, Virginia, the second son of James and Elizabeth "Betty." He was about 18 years old when his dad, James, died. John was well-educated and said to have attended The College of William and Mary.

John was an officer in the Continental Army.[28] Spotsylvania County Court Order Book 1774-1782, page 175 under court proceedings of Feb. 20, 1782 records:

> John Frazer is recommended as Lieutenant in the Room of Thos. Miller having resigned his commission and B. Robinson, Ensign in Capt. Legg's Company.[29]

On January 16, 1783, John married Elizabeth Polly Fox (1762-1795). Elizabeth was the youngest child of Thomas Fox and his first wife Philadelphia Claiborne. After the Revolutionary War, John Frazer and

---

[28]   John Frazer, *U.S.*, Revolutionary War Rolls, 1775-1783.

[29]   John Frazer, Spotsylvania County Court Order Book 1774-1782, page 175.

Elizabeth moved to Fredericksburg where they leased the "Old Eagle Tavern."[30] This was a well-used stagecoach stop located on the main route from lower Virginia to the Washington D.C. area. Today, the house known as "The Rising Sun Tavern" is preserved as a shrine by the Association for the Preservation of Virginia Antiquities. The tavern is located at 1304 Caroline Street in Fredericksburg.

This historical property was built in approximately 1762 for Charles Washington, youngest brother of General George Washington who "purchased Lots 87 and 88 from Warner Lewis, who acquired the land in 1759 when the General Assembly of Virginia enlarged the town of Fredericksburg, laying out new streets and lots on the northern side of town."[31] The one and one-half story building was built to be Charles Washington's private residence. This property was visited several times by George Washington while visiting his brother Charles. In 1786, Charles Washington and his wife sold the property to their son George Augustine Washington and wife Francis. George and Francis owned the property for five years before selling it to Larkin Smith in 1791. In 1792, Smith sold the property to Gustavus Brown Wallace. In that same year, Wallace began to rent out the property. On September 29, 1792, John Frazer occupied the property, opening a tavern known as "The Golden Eagle Tavern."[32]

It was not until 1822 that the tavern became known as "The Rising Sun Tavern." The tavern offered both dining and sleeping accommodations. Later, the building was renovated and opened as a museum. It is on the *National Register of Historic Places* and continues to be open as a historic location.

---

[30] John Frazer, Fredericksburg Deed Book A, p. 404.

[31] Historic Structure Report, Rising Sun Tavern, Conducted by University of Mary Washington Historic Preservation Student, Kracen, Emilie, HISP461, Fall 2010, p. 5.

[32] Ibid.

RISING SUN TAVERN

BUILT ABOUT 1760 BY CHARLES,
THE YOUNGEST BROTHER OF
GEORGE WASHINGTON.

OWNED BY THE ASSOCIATION
FOR THE PRESERVATION OF
VIRGINIA ANTIQUITIES.

Photo taken by Lillian Frazer, Summer 2020

John and Elizabeth Frazer both died in the prime of life. John Frazer died in 1793 at about age 37 in an upstairs bedroom of what was then called the "Old Eagle Tavern." Their daughter Ann died the year before at age four. Elizabeth had four children, ages 10 through one to care for after John's death. She continued to run the tavern until 1795, and she died at about age 33. Elizabeth left behind four orphan children, ages 12 to three. On January 5, 1796, Anthony Frazer was named as guardian to Thomas Frazer and John Frazer, orphans of John Frazer (Anthony's brother), with William Frazer and Reuben Frazer, seconds.

(See "**The Ghost at The Rising Sun Tavern**" on the following pages.) John and Elizabeth Polly Fox Frazer had five children.

B.2.1.　**THOMAS FOX FRAZER** (1783-1841) (Son of JOHN FRAZER, JAMES BENJAMIN FRAZER, WILLIAM

FRAZER) Thomas married Margaret "Peggy" Magee.[33] They had three children. Mary was the second child.

MARY ELIZABETH FRAZER CHANDLER (1821-September 9, 1881) (Daughter of THOMAS FOX FRAZER) Mary married Thomas Coleman Chandler (his second wife). Mary is buried at Berea Christian Church Cemetery, Spotsylvania Courthouse, Spotsylvania, Virginia (Site has her name as "Frazier").[34]

B.2.2. **JOHN FRAZER** (1786-1819) (Son of JOHN FRAZER, JAMES BENJAMIN FRAZER, WILLIAM FRAZER)

B.2.3. **ANN FRAZER** (1788-1792) (Daughter of JOHN FRAZER, JAMES BENJAMIN FRAZER, WILLIAM FRAZER) Ann died at age four.

B.2.4. **ELIZABETH FRAZER** (1790-1873) (Daughter of JOHN FRAZER, JAMES BENJAMIN FRAZER, WILLIAM FRAZER)

B.2.5. **PHILADELPHIA CLAIBORNE FRAZER TURNER** (1792-1831) (Daughter of JOHN FRAZER, JAMES BENJAMIN FRAZER, WILLIAM FRAZER) Philadelphia married George Turner in 1828.[35] After Philadelphia's death, George Turner married Philadelphia's cousin Martha Frazer, daughter of Reuben and Frances Herndon Frazer, in 1832.[36]

B.3. **JAMES FRAZER II** (December 23, 1758 – December 20, 1798) (Son of JAMES BENJAMIN FRAZER, WILLIAM FRAZER) James Frazer II was the third son of James and Elizabeth Foster Frazer. James had a distinguished Revolutionary War record,

---

[33] Marriage of Thomas Fox Frazer and Margaret "Peggy" Magee, Virginia, Compiled Marriages, 1740-1850.

[34] Mary Elizabeth Frazer Chandler, U.S., Find A Grave Index, 1600s-Current, Memorial ID 27125142.

[35] Marriage of Philadelphia Claiborne Frazer and George Turner, Dodd, Jordan R., et. al., *Early American Marriages: Virginia to 1850*.

[36] Marriage of Martha Frazer and George Turner, Virginia, *Select Marriages*, 1785-1940.

serving in a company of Light Dragoons. His horse, "Rainbow," was killed under him at the Battle of Cowpens, a battle during the Revolutionary War fought near the town of Cowpens, South Carolina in 1781.[37] James was about 22 years old. He was also at the surrender of Lord Cornwallis in 1781 at Yorktown, Virginia. For his services, James received a grant of 400 acres in Kentucky on June 10, 1784.

> Moreover, Certificate #100 was granted by Benjamin Winslow, County Lieutenant, for a gun belonging to James Frazer, of the Spotsylvania Militia, 17 May 1781.[38]

On June 6, 1787, James was appointed ensign of the County Militia. James also owned 420 acres of land known as the "Red House Tract" located near the courthouse in Spotsylvania County, Virginia.[39] Upon the settlement of his estate, an article was printed in the *Virginia Herald of Fredericksburg*, January 11, 1799 issue:

> By virtue of authority to us given by the legatees of the Estate of James Frazer, deceased, to be sold – 420 acres of land lying within one mile of Spotsylvania Court House and known by the name of the Red House Tract. There is a dwelling house with three rooms below and two above (the stairs), an orchard. . .[40]

James married Sarah Herndon about 1783. Sarah's sisters Hannah and Philadelphia married James' brothers Anthony and William, and her niece, Fannie, married James' brother Reuben. Sarah was the daughter of Edward Herndon and Mary Duerson Herndon. She lived only a year or two after her marriage to James. With all the marriages within the two

---

[37] James Frazer II, U.S., Sons of the American Revolution Membership Applications, 1889-1970.

[38] Herndon, Goodwin, John, *The Herndon Family of Virginia*, p.85.

[39] General Index of Deeds, Deeds of Trust, Release Deeds and Wills, etc., Spotsylvania County, Virginia, p. 111.

[40] *Virginia Herald of Fredericksburg*, January 11, 1799.

families, the Herndons and Frazers had close family ties. James and Sarah had no children.

James married his second wife, Sarah Kenyon Thomas, about 1786. Sarah died six years later, in 1792, at the birth of her daughter Sarah Kenyon Frazer. James and Sarah had three children.[41]

B.3.1. **ELIZABETH FRAZER FRAZER** (1787-1846) (Daughter of JAMES FRAZER II, JAMES BENJAMIN FRAZER, WILLIAM FRAZER) Elizabeth married her first cousin, James Frazer, son of Anthony Frazer and Hannah Herndon Frazer.

B.3.2. **MARTHA "BETSY" FRAZER** (b. abt. 1789) (Daughter of JAMES FRAZER II, JAMES BENJAMIN FRAZER, WILLIAM FRAZER)

B.3.3. **SARAH KENYON "SALLIE" FRAZER HANSFORD** (February 10, 1792 – September 3, 1888) (Daughter of JAMES FRAZER II, JAMES BENJAMIN FRAZER, WILLIAM FRAZER) Sarah married Felix Gilbert Hansford (1795-1867) in Greenbrier County in 1821. Sarah and Felix are buried at Hansford Cemetery, Hansford, Kanawha County, West Virginia.[42] Felix was born at Paint Creek, West Virginia

James married his third wife Lucy Smith (1750-1799) on December 2, 1794.[43] They had two children.

B.3.4. **JAMES FRAZER** (b. abt. 1794) (Son of JAMES FRAZER II, JAMES BENJAMIN FRAZER, WILLIAM FRAZER) James married Sarah Long, daughter of Richard Long of Spotsylvania.

B.3.5. **WILLIAM SMITH FRAZER** (November 10, 1795 – January 27, 1850) (Son of JAMES FRAZER II, JAMES BENJAMIN

---

[41] Herndon, Dudley L., *The Herndons of the American Revolution*, pp. 85-86.

[42] Sarah Kenyon "Sallie" Frazer Hansford, U.S., Find A Grave, 1600s-Current, Memorial ID 174280958.

[43] James Frazer, Crozier, William Armstrong, ed. *Virginia County Records, Spotsylvania County Records*, 1721-1800.

FRAZER, WILLIAM FRAZER) William was born at "Red House," Spotsylvania.[44] William married Ann Burrus (February 28, 1800 – April 11, 1877) in June 1819.[45] He died at his home at "Waverly," Orange County, Virginia.

On December 3, 1799, Anthony and William Frazer were named guardians to their brother's children Elizabeth, Patsey (Martha), and Sarah Frazer with John Crutchfield and Joseph Herndon, Jr. as seconds.[46]

An excerpt from the Daughters of the American Revolution National Number 122466 about Nelle Elizabeth Frazer states:

> William Smith Frazer, son of James Frazer II and Lucy Smith was three years of age when his father died and less than five at his mother's death. His half-sister Sarah Kennon married Felix Hansford and it is from her daughter Mrs. Hansford Middleton that we have direct record of James Frazer II. In a written statement she said that three of the sons, Anthony, John and James were in the Revolutionary War.[47]

(Marriages and children names were taken from *The Herndons of the American Revolution*, pp. 85-86.)

B.4. **WILLIAM FRAZER** (March 1, 1761 – March 19, 1819) (Son of JAMES BENJAMIN FRAZER, WILLIAM FRAZER) William Frazer was the fourth child of James and Elizabeth Foster Frazer of Spotsylvania County, Virginia. William was a Revolutionary soldier as were his brothers Anthony, John, and James.

In 1784, 1785, 1786 and 1789, William Frazer was the "Collector of

---

[44] William Smith Frazer, 1850 United States Federal Census, YEAR: 1850, Census Place: Orange, Virginia; Roll: 967; Page: 237A.

[45] Marriage of William Smith Frazer and Ann Burrus, Virginia Select Marriages, 1785-1940.

[46] Anthony Frazer and William Frazer, *Spotsylvania County Records*, Virginia Court Records, Guardians Bonds, Will Book F, p. 83.

[47] James Frazer II, Daughters of the American Revolution National Number 122466.

Tax" for Spotsylvania County.[48] In 1787, he was the deputy sheriff for his district. He married Philadelphia Herndon (October 6, 1770- September 23, 1830) on April 17, 1788. Philadelphia was the daughter of Edward Herndon and Mary Duerson Herndon and sister of the wives of William's brothers James and Anthony.

On January 7, 1789, William's brother-in-law, John Herndon, was named as security on his tax bond. William and Philadelphia were living in Berkeley Parish in Spotsylvania County in 1792. They lived there until 1810. In October of 1810, William, Philadelphia, and their children, along with Philadelphia's brother John Herndon and his wife, Judith Hampton Herndon, and children left Spotsylvania in a caravan to Clark County, Kentucky.[49]

William and family lived in Clark County, Kentucky, living in Winchester for only a few years. His son, Dr. Warren Frazer, married Laura Brooking of Winchester and they continued to live there for several years. William and his family moved to Lexington, Fayette County, Kentucky where they stayed for the remainder of their lives. William's home was on the Winchester Pike and was named "Forkland." William founded a hemp business, which became an extensive business.

William died March 19, 1819. His widow, Philadelphia, lived until September 23, 1830. He and his wife Philadelphia were devout Episcopalians and were buried in the same tomb in the Old Episcopal Third Street Cemetery[50] (also known as Christ Church Cemetery), 251 East 3rd Street, Lexington, Kentucky.

Philadelphia and William had reputed 13 children, 11 identified by Bible, court, and graveyard records. A twelfth died in infancy. The other is unknown.[51]

B.4.1. **REBECCA FRAZER** (1788 – October 22, 1851) (Daughter of WILLIAM FRAZER, JAMES BENJAMIN FRAZER, WILLIAM FRAZER) Rebecca was born in Spotsylvania

---

[48] Herndon, John Goodwin, *The Herndon Family of Virginia*, Volume 2, p. 93.
[49] Ibid.
[50] William Frazer, U.S., Find A Grave Index, 1600s-Current, Memorial ID 197719452.
[51] Herndon, John Goodwin, *The Herndon Family of Virginia*, Volume 2, p. 95-96.

County, Virginia. She is buried at Old Episcopal Third Street Cemetery (also known as Christ Church Cemetery, Episcopal Burying Ground, 251 East 3rd Street, Lexington, Kentucky. [52]

B.4.2. **MARY DUERSON FRAZER** (1790-1842) (Daughter of WILLIAM FRAZER, JAMES BENJAMIN FRAZER, WILLIAM FRAZER)

B.4.3. **MARTHA D. FRAZER** (1792-1851) (Daughter of WILLIAM FRAZER, JAMES BENJAMIN FRAZER, WILLIAM FRAZER)

B.4.4. **DR. ROBERT FRAZER** (1795-1833) (Son of WILLIAM FRAZER, JAMES BENJAMIN FRAZER, WILLIAM FRAZER) Robert attended Transylvania University. He was a medical doctor. His first marriage was to Mary Bledsoe, and his second marriage was on July 5, 1821 to Nancy Chryses Gordon Bledsoe,[53] niece of his first wife.

B.4.5. **WILLIAM FRAZER** (January 26, 1797 – 1880) (Son of WILLIAM FRAZER, JAMES BENJAMIN FRAZER, WILLIAM FRAZER)

B.4.6. **LUCY M. FRAZER BARTLETT** (1798 - March 6, 1842) (Daughter of WILLIAM FRAZER, JAMES BENJAMIN FRAZER, WILLIAM FRAZER) Lucy married July 16, 1828 in Lexington to Thomas H. Bartlett of Henry County, Kentucky. Lucy is buried at Old Episcopal Third Street Cemetery (also known as Christ Church Cemetery, Episcopal Burying Ground, 251 East 3rd Street, Lexington, Kentucky.[54]

B.4.7. **PHILADELPHIA HERNDON FRAZER** (1802-1819) (Daughter of WILLIAM FRAZER, JAMES BENJAMIN FRAZER, WILLIAM FRAZER) Philadelphia died at 17 years old, unmarried.

B.4.8. **DR. WARREN FRAZER** (October 6, 1805 - November 16,

---

[52] Rebecca Frazer, U.S., Find A Grave Index, 1600s–Current, Memorial ID 16414467.

[53] Marriage of Dr. Robert Frazer and Nancy Chryses Gordon Bledsoe, Kentucky, Compiled Marriages, 1802-1850.

[54] Lucy M. Frazer Bartlett, U.S., Find A Grave Index, 1600s-Current, Memorial ID 16318729.

1884) (Son of WILLIAM FRAZER, JAMES BENJAMIN FRAZER, WILLIAM FRAZER) Warren was educated at Transylvania University. He studied medicine with his elder brother Robert Frazer, M.D. He practiced at Winchester for 25 years and took care of the extensive hemp business founded by his father. He married Laura Brooking (abt. 1818 – January 18, 1885) of Kentucky. Warren and Laura are buried at Lexington Cemetery, 833 W. Main St., Lexington, Fayette County, Kentucky.[55]

B.4.9. **JOHN PEACHY FRAZER** (1810-1819) (Son of WILLIAM FRAZER, JAMES BENJAMIN FRAZER, WILLIAM FRAZER)

B.4.10. **VIRGINIA K. FRAZER** (Unknown - June 8, 1859) (Daughter of WILLIAM FRAZER, JAMES BENJAMIN FRAZER, WILLIAM FRAZER) Virginia is buried at the Old Episcopal Cemetery, Third Street, Lexington, Kentucky.[56]

B.4.11. **ELIZABETH JANE GARNETT FRAZER NOLAN** (1814 – May 30, 1852) (Daughter of WILLIAM FRAZER, JAMES BENJAMIN FRAZER, WILLIAM FRAZER) Elizabeth attended Lafayette Female Academy in Lexington, Kentucky in 1825. Elizabeth married Dr. John Tilghman Nolan, a graduate of Transylvania University in 1831. Dr. John Nolan and his second wife, Elizabeth "Jane" Garnett moved to Yazoo City, Mississippi, living near Benton, close to the plantation of his brother James Harnesberger Nolan. Elizabeth was named executrix of the Will of her oldest brother Robert Frazer when he caught the cholera epidemic in 1833 after he had taken care of those stricken. "Jane" died at age 38 in West Baton Rouge. She is buried at the Old Episcopal Cemetery, Third Street, Lexington, Kentucky.[57]

---

[55] Dr. Warren Frazer, U.S., Find A Grave Index, 1600s-Current, Memorial ID 99330223.

[56] Virginia K. Frazer, U.S., Find A Grave Index, 1600s-Current, Memorial ID 16318751.

[57] Elizabeth Jane Garnett Frazer Nolan, U.S., Find A Grave Index, 1600s-Current, Memorial ID 16414568.

B.4.12. **EDMUND FRAZER** (Unknown) (Son of WILLIAM FRAZER, JAMES BENJAMIN FRAZER, WILLIAM FRAZER) Edmund died in infancy.

B.4.13. **CHILD FRAZER** (Unknown) (Child of WILLIAM FRAZER, JAMES BENJAMIN FRAZER, WILLIAM FRAZER)

(Child information is taken from "The Herndons of the American Revolution," Vol. Two, Part II, Edward Herndon and his known descendants, Herndon, John Goodwin, 1951, p. 94-97 and U.S. Find A Grave.)

B.5. **MARTHA FRAZER** (b.1763 - Unknown) (Daughter of JAMES BENJAMIN FRAZER, WILLIAM FRAZER) .

B.6. **REUBEN FRAZER** (1767-1832) (Son of JAMES BENJAMIN FRAZER, WILLIAM FRAZER) Reuben was the youngest child of James and Elizabeth. He married Frances "Fanny" Herndon (niece to his brothers' wives) of Spotsylvania County, Virginia. Reuben and Fanny had three known children:

B.6.1. **FREDERICK FRAZER** (1807-1863) (Son of REUBEN FRAZER, JAMES BENJAMIN FRAZER, WILLIAM FRAZER) Frederick married Mary B. Holliday (Holladay) on November 8, 1825 in Louisa County, Virginia.[58] In 1837, he is listed as the Postmaster at the Lewis Store in Spotsylvania, Virginia[59] and in the 1860 census he is listed as a farmer.[60]

B.6.2. **MARTHA FRAZER TURNER** (1811 – July 2, 1876)) (Daughter of REUBEN FRAZER, JAMES BENJAMIN FRAZER, WILLIAM FRAZER) Martha married George Turner (1793-1880) in 1832. George was married previously to Philadelphia Claiborne Frazer, daughter of John and

---

[58] Marriage of Frederick Frazer and Mary B. Holliday (Holladay), Virginia, Select Marriages, 1785-1940.

[59] U.S., Appointments of U.S. Postmasters, 1832-1941.

[60] Frederick Frazer, 1860 United States Federal Census, St. Georges Parish, Spotsylvania, Virginia, p.392, Family History Library Film: 805380.

Elizabeth Fox Frazer. Martha died in Bethany, Brooke County, West Virginia[61] and Martha and George are buried at Campbell Cemetery, Bethany, West Virginia.[62]

B.6.3. **CASSANDRA FRAZER** (Unknown) (Daughter of REUBEN FRAZER, JAMES BENJAMIN FRAZER, WILLIAM FRAZER)

(James Frazer's children's names were taken from Genealogies of Virginia Families, Tyler's Quarterly Historical and Genealogical Magazine, Volume I, Genealogical Publishing Co., 1981, and from U.S., Find A Grave.)

---

[61] Death of Martha Frazer Turner, West Virginia, Deaths Index, 1853-1973.

[62] Martha Frazer Turner, U.S., Find A Grave Index, 1600s-Current, Memorial ID 63671507.

* * * * *

The Ghost at The Rising Sun Tavern

Current picture of "The Rising Sun Tavern Museum." The
front porch that spans the tavern was not on the original home
but was added during a major restoration that took place in
the 1930s. Pictured below is the current backyard patio of
the tavern. Photos taken by Lillian Frazer, August 2020

While living in Fredericksburg over twenty years ago, I heard a radio announcement for the Rising Sun Tavern and the Ghost of John Frazer. As I chuckled, I gave my son whose name is also John Frazer a phone call inviting him down to visit the Rising Sun Tavern. Fresh out of college, he laughed, responding quickly with a humorous remark that escapes me now but typical of both him, his father, and his granddad and uncles. Each had a sense of humor and a fast wit that brought friendly snickers to those on the receiving end. He passed on the invite, escaping on the pretext of other plans as I responded, "But he may be related to you."

He quickly retorted with jesting in his voice, "Don't let him follow you home!" Well, it seems John Frazer was related.

Recently, we attempted to visit "The Rising Sun Tavern" several times in 2020, anxious to see the interior and hear the tales of ghosts and bygone days. With the COVID19 virus restrictions during most of the year, we were only able to view the exterior of the building with a mental note to visit the tavern again later. As we stood on the outside of the building, my thoughts went to yesterday and the many people who walked this same patch of land and passed through these walls with stories and histories. It was a mystical, timeless place. If only the tavern could whisper the tales and share the secrets it had heard bounced off its walls, I would anxiously pepper it with questions and stir up ghosts.

Today, the Rising Sun Tavern Museum provides a lively interpretation of tavern life in the 18th century. Costumed guides claim that the ghost of the tavernkeeper, John Frazer (son of James Benjamin Frazer and grandson of William Frazer as mentioned above), at times, even over 220 years later, can be felt in this tavern. A year after John and his wife Elizabeth opened the tavern known then as the "Old Eagle Tavern," John, still a young man, took ill. He died on November 28, 1793 in an upstairs bedroom of an illness that no one knows what it may have been. It is said that his spirit never left the tavern and that he pulls plugs out of walls, opens doors, makes postcards fly off a rack, and, on occasion, holds onto the skirts of the tavern wenches who give tours.

"But he does respond to scolding," she (tavern manager Jo Atkins) said.

"We've had wenches say, 'OK, John, that's enough.' Then usually, the mischief will stop."[63]

"I hate to say it's like 'bump in the night' but that's the way it is around here sometimes," said Katie King, the site's manager.[64] In the same article in *The Free Lance-Star*, Cathy Jett states:

> Frazer had served as an officer in the Continental Army during the American Revolution before he and his wife, Elizabeth Fox Frazer, began running what was then called the Eagle Tavern in 1792. If the name Frazer has a familiar ring, it's the same Scottish Highland clan of the fictional Jamie Fraser in the popular Starz TV series "Outlander."
>
> In fact, John Frazer's grandfather, William Frazer, was a descendant of Clan Fraser of Lovat, and emigrated from Scotland to Virginia. He's known to have been living in the Fredericksburg area by 1727. William Frazer died young, and his only son, James Frazer, was a tobacco planter in Spotsylvania County. He was wealthy enough to send John Frazer to The College of William & Mary.
>
> King said she's always wondered how a man with Frazer's level of education ended up running a tavern in what had been built as the home for Charles Washington, George Washington's youngest brother. The Wallace family purchased it in 1792, and it operated as a tavern, stagecoach stop and Fredericksburg's post office for the next 35 years.
>
> Whatever Frazer's reason for becoming its first tavern keeper, he apparently had a playful nature that time has not diminished.
>
> There's the story of the tavern guide who decided his ghost was having great fun unplugging the lights in an

---

[63] Gross, Edie, *The Free Lance-Star, Fredericksburg, Virginia*, "Who's Haunting Your Haunts," Oct. 17, 2011.

[64] Jett, Cathy, *The Free Lance-Star, Fredericksburg, Virginia*, "Rising Sun Tavern to Highlight Ghostly Prankster on John Frazer Night," October 26, 2017.

upstairs room, and was getting tired of plugging them back in. She finally cried out, "Come on now, stop it!"

John did, but not without playing one more trick. He pulled the rug out from under her as she was leaving the room.[65]

All agree that the ghost of the Rising Sun Tavern is a playful apparition and that it is the spirit of John Frazer, once the tavernkeeper when a tavern was a stagecoach stop, a post office, and the center of colonial life.

---

[65] Ibid.

* * * * *

"Stonewall" Jackson and the Chandler Plantation
Home of Thomas and Mary Elizabeth Frazer Chandler

John (son of James Benjamin Frazer and grandson of William Frazer) and Elizabeth Fox Frazer's first child, Thomas Fox Frazer, married Margaret "Peggy" Magee, and they had three children. Their second child, a daughter, Mary Elizabeth Frazer (1821- September 9, 1881) married Thomas Coleman Chandler (1798 - February 1890), a wealthy man.[66] Thomas' first wife, Clementina Alsop Chandler, died young in life in 1844. After her death, Chandler purchased "Fairfield" Plantation in Caroline County, Virginia in 1845.[67]

About 1847, Thomas married twenty-six-year-old Mary Elizabeth Frazer, who was considerably younger by twenty-three years. Mary and Thomas made their home on the Fairfield plantation near Guinea Station. The entrance of the plantation was lined with lush and sprawling trees. The original family home was located near the railroad line. During our research, we visited the site of Fairfield, noting that the train track ran much nearer the plantation home site than I had imagined. Having grown up in a small home near a railroad track, I could almost hear the grinding steel of the trains as they pulled to a stop. Personally, I loved hearing the sound of the train coming and going, bringing life to our little town. I wondered if Mary and Thomas shared my feelings or if they thought of it as a nuisance?

The Chandler estate of Fairfield was 740 acres and Mary Elizabeth Frazer Chandler, described as a Southern hostess, loved their home, raising their family there in the upcoming years. It was said Fairfield was a small village within itself with the estate home and other buildings necessary to run a plantation of this size. During these colonial days before the Civil War, slaves were used for working the fields and grounds and maintaining the plantation home, making Fairfield one of the more prosperous plantations in the county.

Today, Guinea is an unincorporated community about 8.5 miles from Bowling Green, Virginia in a rural and peaceful setting. In the years of

---

[66] Mary Elizabeth Frazer Chandler, Virginia, Deaths and Burials Index, 1853-1917.
[67] Mackowski, Chris and White, Kristopher D., *The Last Days of Stonewall Jackson: The Mortal Wounding of the Confederacy's Greatest Icon*, 2013.

the Civil War, Guinea Station was a bustling supply base. Confederate supplies came into the station by train and dispersed to the camps. The clatter of the trains and the hustle and bustle as the train stopped to unload and load supplies and passengers made what was a remote and peaceful rural farmland into a busy and noisy place. The clatters and vibrations of the train and the hectic comings and goings of the Confederate officers picking up supplies would not be the only changes in this serene setting. The Chandlers opened their plantation to Andrew Jackson who for a time made his headquarters at Fairfield during the Fredericksburg Campaign of 1862, camping on the land.

On May 2, 1863, Thomas J. "Stonewall" Jackson was mistakenly shot by one of his men during the Civil War at the Battle of Chancellorsville. The wound necessitated the amputation of his left arm. Robert E. Lee wanted Jackson transported to a safe place well behind friendly lines to recuperate. Jackson had camped at the Chandler plantation of Fairfield earlier in the year and the Chandlers were kind to him, developing a friendship between them. Lee decided Jackson would be taken to Fairfield at Guinea Station by train, but the tracks were torn up by the Union cavalry. So, they had to make the 27-mile trip by land, arriving at the Chandler plantation on May 4.[68]

Thomas J. "Stonewall" Jackson

---

[68] Ibid.

Earlier in 1863, Thomas Chandler was already feeling the effects of the war and sold the Fairfield Plantation. The war and battles were close by and many of the slaves Chandler maintained for the plantation labor had left. Maintenance of the plantation was difficult. However, Mary Chandler was not in a rush to move from their beloved home at Fairfield. Before the Chandlers had an opportunity to move, Jackson arrived.

Office Building on the Chandler Plantation of "Fairfield"
Place of General Thomas "Stonewall" Jackson's Death
Photo taken by Lillian Frazer, Summer, 2020

Jackson was taken to the office plantation building, located across from the home, rather than the Chandler's home. The doctors felt this building offered more privacy and a quieter location as the plantation home was too busy. It was said:

> The house already held other wounded Confederates, including several soldiers who were suffering from erysipelas, a highly contagious skin disease. McGuire would not allow Jackson to be exposed to the infected

men and instead moved his patient to a small separate building on the grounds that had been used as an office.[69]

The Chandler Plantation home once stood on this property. This view looks out from the office building, the only building standing today. Photo taken by Lillian Frazer, Summer, 2020.

The Chandlers prepared the building for Jackson's arrival, using the same bedframe and one of the same blankets exhibited today in the building. A clock was also placed on the mantle. The same clock, donated by Lucy Chandler Pendleton, daughter of Thomas and Mary Frazer Chandler, sits in the building today, ticking as it did at Jackson's death. When Jackson's wife, Mrs. Mary Anna Jackson, and her young daughter, Julie, arrived at Guinea Station, they lodged in the Chandler home.[70] Jackson appeared to be improving, then he caught what the doctors diagnosed as pneumonia. Jackson died on May 10, 1863.[71]

---

[69] *America's Civil War Magazine,* "America's Civil War: Stonewall Jackson's Last Days," *Haines, Jr., Joe D.*
[70] National Military Park, Virginia, Fredericksburg & Spotsylvania, "Stonewall" Jackson Death Site.
[71] Ibid.

Lucy Chandler (1851-1943), the 11- or-12-year-old daughter of Thomas and Mary Frazer Chandler and her 15-year-old brother, James Chandler, were at Fairfield during Jackson's passing. Even behind the enemy line, it would have to be disconcerting for the Chandler family, as it was for so many other families, knowing battles could be fought in their backyard and the fear of retribution for harboring the Confederate soldiers and the strength of character needed to support their home and beliefs in the constant struggle surrounding them. In heartbreaking circumstances, Mary Frazer Chandler accompanied Mrs. Jackson and the body of General Jackson to Richmond after his death to comfort and support Mrs. Jackson. As written by Mary Anna Jackson:

> A special car had been set apart for us, in which were Mr. Lacy and the staff-officers, while Mrs. Hoge and Mrs. Chandler were my attendants, and proved themselves the kindest of friends and comforters.[72]

The Chandlers remained on the property of Fairfield until March 1865. During and after the war, the plantation fell into despair. The Chandlers no longer had slaves for labor after the Civil War. It is unknown what became of the slaves as many had fled to safety once the war began. According to census records, some remained with the Chandlers but no longer as slaves. All would have to come to the realization that life as they knew it would not be the same. The Chandlers left behind the horrors of war and with a heavy heart moved on with their lives and their new home. Before the Chandlers moved from the plantation, Ulysses S. Grant visited the area in 1864, stopping by Fairfield.

> That respect for Jackson in the Union army extended all the way up to commander Ulysses S. Grant who, during his stopover at Fairfield in May of 1864, expressed his esteem for Jackson to Mrs. Chandler. (Mary Elizabeth Frazer Chandler) .

While researching other Frazer family members, I discovered

---

[72] Life and Letters of "Stonewall Jackson" by His Wife, Mary Anna Jackson.

19-year-old Major Philip Foulke Frazer,[73] son of James Addison Frazer and grandson of James A. Frazer and great grandson of Anthony Frazer, among the same Frazer family as Mary Chandler. Philip served in the 27th Virginia Infantry Regiment under General Thomas "Stonewall" Jackson. After General Jackson's death, Philip was one of a five-man committee who petitioned the War Department to officially name the First Brigade, as it was known, to the "Stonewall Brigade."[74]

When the time came to finally leave Fairfield, Thomas and Mary Frazer Chandler moved to Lake Farm, a plantation just down the road from Fairfield, staying there only five years before moving on to a new home christened "Ingleside," less than three miles from Fairfield. Here is where they spent the remainder of their lives.

In 1909, the RF&P Railroad acquired the property of Fairfield and pulled down the main house and restored the farm office, calling it the "Jackson Shrine," donating it to the National Park Service in 1937. Today, this building is part of Fredericksburg & Spotsylvania National Military Park. All that remains of the once-sprawling prosperous plantation in Caroline County is the office building where Jackson had spent his final days.

Mary Elizabeth Frazer Chandler died at age 62 in 1881,[75] and Thomas Chandler died in 1890 at age 92.[76] Thomas Coleman Chandler and his first wife Clementina Alsop Chandler and his second wife Mary Elizabeth Frazer "Frazier" Chandler are buried at Berea Christian Church Cemetery, Spotsylvania Courthouse Road, Spotsylvania County, Virginia.[77] This church was built under the supervision of Samuel Alsop, father to Clementina Alsop Chandler, who was Thomas Chandler's first wife. Samuel Alsop was considered one of the foremost builders of his time.

During the battle of Spotsylvania Court House, the Berea Christian Church was used as a hospital as battles raged nearby. A few days later,

---

[73] *Civil War Soldiers and Sailors System*, National Park Service, 27th Virginia Infantry.
[74] Virginia Military Institute, VMI Archives Digital Collections, Virginia Military Institute, Lexington, VA.
[75] Mary Elizabeth Frazer Chandler, Virginia, Deaths and Burials Index, 1853-1917.
[76] Mary Elizabeth Frazier (Frazer) Chandler, U.S. Find A Grave Index, 1600s-Current, Memorial ID 27124811.
[77] Ibid.

the church was used as headquarters of General Jubal Early. On May 13th, the area was under artillery fire from Federal lines. A large artillery shell passed through the front doors and became hidden in one of the walls.[78] This church building located near the Spotsylvania County Courthouse, which once heard prayers of the sick and fearful, no longer serves as a church. The old cemetery remains.

Palmer and I made a day trip to the courthouse area, visiting the old cemetery where several Frazer family members are laid to rest. It was a day when the sky was layered with clouds. I glanced up as the sun was trying to poke its way through the puffy layer overhead. Having passed this little church almost every day when living in the area, I often peered over at the neat brick structure knowing it had offered comfort and hope to many in a troubled world of yesterday. Little did I know that the Frazer family members were among those. We walked the small cemetery, amazingly recognizing names of those discovered through the family research. I felt almost as if I had once known them. To my delight, there happened to be a few people at the church building who graciously offered me to enter and take pictures. The church is closed to the public but appears to have private functions on occasion. The Spotsylvania County Museum did fantastic in restoring the cemetery and the historical church, maintaining traces of bygone days of those who have departed, leaving us evidence of their footsteps in our history. Below are pictures of Berea Church in 2020.

---

[78] Spotsylvania County Department of Economic Development and Tourism, Historic District, "Crossroads of the Civil War."

Photos taken by Lillian Frazer, Summer 2020

Unaware of the history of our Frazer ancestors, I once owned property and a home near Po River, about two miles from the courthouse in Spotsylvania County. At time of purchase, I was told that the Confederate Army camped on the land and the surrounding land in the small subdivision during the battles at the courthouse. A neighbor kindly gave me a tour of his property; trenches of the Civil War remained on the land. It was such a lovely and peaceful area, which tugged at me for the purchase initially.

Viewing the land with the history in mind, it was difficult to conjure up visions of nearby bloody battles and ghosts of young, daring, and fearless men as well as those with twinges of fear of who laid in wait in the nearby trees and bushes. A splash of reality hit me. Would their enemies be waiting for them over the crest? Or perhaps the campsite brought them a feeling of peace and safety if only for the evening, as night crept in among the quiet darkness and thick spread of trees. Men, many who had only meager possessions themselves, camped there, ready for battle to support and protect their families and homes and a life they loved. Men on both sides of this War Between the States suffered but were guided by duty, honor, love, and pride. These men awoke the next morning, grass still damp with dew, as they, with weariness, faced another day of battles. Years later, I sold that property but always loved the serenity it brought me. I hope this same land had provided a haven to those soldiers who camped there, if only for a few hours.

ANTHONY FRAZER

OVERSEER AT BELVEDERE PLANTATION, REVOLUTIONARY SOLDIER, FARMER, TAX COMMISSIONER AND DEPUTY SHERIFF FRERICKSBURG AND SPOTSYLVANIA, VIRGINIA

THE THIRD GENERATION

ANTHONY FRAZER (March 22, 1754 – March 4, 1804), the oldest child of six of James Benjamin Frazer and Elizabeth Foster Frazer and grandson of William Frazer, was born on March 22, 1754 in Spotsylvania County, Virginia. He is a direct ancestor to my children. Anthony's parents, farmers and tobacco planters, were profitable enough to afford their children a suitable education, an important quality during these years.

In researching family while weeding through and critically examining document after document, I learned most are not celebrated for extraordinary accomplishments. To discover any historical record that navigated to Anthony brought joy to my tired and bloodshot eyes as I hunched over my computer. Each layer of breakthrough added confidence to my explorations. I discovered the date Anthony was born, located who he married, uncovered his life as a tobacco planter and farmer, learned he spent time as a deputy sheriff in Spotsylvania County, served as a tax commissioner and a tobacco inspector, and was appointed Clerk of the Vestry of St. George's Parish (today known as St. George's Episcopal

Church). I discovered the names of his children and when he died. Anthony began to materialize, and as my interest piqued, I liked what I saw.

While once living in Spotsylvania County, our home was near where Anthony spent most of his life. We traveled the same land. The distance merely centuries in time. We decided to take another day journey to the county, following the familiar quiet calmness of what once was a rural road. It was a beautiful day, spring bursting loose, full of color and scent. The dusty roads Anthony traveled on horseback or with horse and carriage gave way to paved roads and cars and houses that sprung up here and there. If we had been of the same century, we may have passed each other during our journey. His life had no city buzz but laborious work as a farmer with rituals and routines.

Farmers I knew loved their land and farming, the sun on their face, a light breeze, and the pride and satisfaction of the finished product they produced. Anthony, born into the tobacco and farm life, chose to follow that path in adulthood, perhaps as an expression of himself. Anthony was ambitious as well, obvious in his other dealings as deputy sheriff, tax commissioner, and tobacco inspector. Anthony joined the Virginia Militia as a young man, serving in the Revolutionary War as did three of his brothers. Slowly, Anthony emerged becoming a person, not just another name on my list of ancestors but a young hard-working man, caring for and protecting his family and his home that he loved.

The trail to the Frazer family led us from Virginia to Lewisburg, West Virginia and the National Historical Society of Greenbrier County. Many thanks to their historian, librarian, and staff for assisting us in our research. Not expecting to find information on Anthony in Lewisburg, it was a delightful find to discover links to him. Among the books referencing the Frazer family was one by Lyle and Loretta Frazer, *The Frazer Family from Scotland to America*. This was a tremendous source in comparing their findings with our own, secretly wishing I had discovered their book earlier. It was gratifying to know that our ancestor findings agreed. Their book led us to another link to Anthony in a journal written by an indentured servant who worked on a well-known Virginia plantation. We had visited this plantation many times in current days, taking our younger folks for hayrides and pumpkins, unknowing that there was any family involvement in years gone by. Naturally, I went in search of the printed journal, finding it informative of the early adult life of Anthony during 1775-1776. Following the footstep trail of the family to Lewisburg, West Virginia brought us to a charming and passionate but possibly sad young love of a romantic past in history in Fredericksburg, Virginia.

The journal was that of a young Scottish merchant, John Harrower, who with a failing business in the Shetland Islands and ruined by the panic of 1772, came to America to seek work, leaving his wife and children at home with plans to send for them once he had saved enough money. Upon arriving in America, he signed over the only negotiable talent he had, a literacy that was in demand in the Colonies. Harrower signed a four-year indenture as a schoolmaster. Colonel William Dangerfield (in his Journal written as "Daingerfield" so I will use that spelling) bought Harrower's indenture and Harrower became the tutor for Daingerfield's children and neighboring planters. Harrower, who kept a daily diary from 1773 to 1776, giving detailed accounts of life and people at and near the plantation, "Belvidera," today known as Belvedere, died before his indenture was completed.

What was of extreme interest to us were the journal notes referencing Anthony Frazer who was hired as overseer at the plantation. Anthony started work on February 21, 1775 at 21 years old, nearly 22, and became the roommate of John Harrower at the schoolhouse. James, Anthony's dad, died in 1774 or early 1775. Anthony, the administrator of his dad's estate and the oldest child, may have sought work to assist with the family farm or small plantation as it may have been called until the estate had been finalized. On February 16, 1775, Anthony's brother James, at 17 years old, apprenticed himself to John McCalley with his mother's consent.[79] Unlike Harrower, Anthony was not serving an indenture contract, nor was he serving as an apprentice, but was hired, allowing him more freedom.

---

[79] James Frazer, Virginia, Land, Marriage, and Probate Records, 1639-1850.

Belvedere Plantation, currently a 645-acre working farm on the Rappahannock River in Fredericksburg, Virginia was built by Colonel William Daingerfield about 1770.[80] The plantation was then 1,300 acres, land inherited to Daingerfield's wife Sarah from her father Lawrence Taliaferro. Martha Taliaferro, sister of Lawrence, was the maternal grandmother to Anthony, so there was a family connection between Anthony and Sarah. The plantation included the main home, a separate kitchen, schoolhouse, smokehouse, cabins for slave quarters, barns, corn cribs and stables. Today this heritage farm, no longer owned by the Daingerfield family, continues as a working farm with corn, wheat, soybeans, and pumpkins, open in the spring and fall for special events.

In the diary of John Harrower, Scotch tutor at "Belvidera," he writes:

This day the Coll. on finding more wheat left among the straw then should be blamed Mr. Lewis the Overseer for his carelessness, upon which Mr. Lewis seem'd verry much enraged for being spoke to and verry sawcily threw

---

[80] Belvedere Plantation, 2014, "History of Belvedere Plantation,", retrieved August 2020.

up all the keys he hade in charge and vent off, upon which
the Coll. sent for me and delivered me the keys of the Barn
and begged I would assist him in his bussiness until he got
another Overseer. (Tuesday, February 14th, 1775)[81]

Colonel Daingerfield went in search of another overseer, soon to
become Anthony Frazer. By Monday, February 27, 1775, the following
was written: "*Col. Daingerfield engaged a young man named Anthony Frazer
as an overseer.*"[82]

On Monday, February 27, 1775, Mr. Harrower writes:

This day Mr. Fraser (Frazer) came here and entered to
take his charge as Overseer, and he is to have his bed in
the school with me. He appears to be a very quiet young
man and has had a tolerable education. His grandfather
came from Scotland.[83]

Labor for plantations in the Colonial Period was mostly performed by
slaves and indentured servants. It is distressing that the casual acceptance
of any slavery ever existed. My paternal ancestors came to America as
indentured servants, working on a farm in nearby Richmond, Virginia,
unable to marry or have children until their indenture contracts were
honored but at some time the contracts were fulfilled unlike the slaves.

The fertile land in Fredericksburg attracted many wealthy planters.
This also added a social life to the town with horse racing, concerts, and
balls, making Fredericksburg a vocal point of cultural life. However, life at
Belvidera was one with little time for visitors or banquets but one of work.
Harrower, the 40-year-old Scottish once-merchant and now the plantation's
tutor, spoke of day-to-day activities at the plantation. He attended church
in Fredericksburg or Carolina County along with Anthony Frazer, the
young housekeeper Lucy, and others, riding by horseback when saddles

---

[81] Riley, Edward Miles, *The Journal of John Harrower, An Indentured Servant in the
Colony of Virginia*, 1773-1776, 1963, p.84.
[82] Ibid.
[83] *Genealogies of Virginia Families*, Tylers Quarterly Historical and Genealogical
Magazine, p. 757.

were available. Anthony owned his own horse and saddle so was able to go more freely than the others. The schoolhouse was cleaned by a young black maid. Harrower described the schoolhouse as being " . . .right above the Warff so that I can stand in the door and pitch a stone onboard of any ship or Boat going up or coming doun the river." Their meals were taken at the main plantation house along with the Daingerfield family and the housekeeper Lucy. In a letter to his wife, Harrower told her, *"I never lived a genteel regulare life until now."* Harrower was happy with his treatment by Colonel Daingerfield.[84]

> The plantation home of Belvidera was described as:
>
> Belvidera was a rectangular, brick, two-story house of the simple design characteristic of rural dwellings in the Tidewater. . . On the first floor the central passageway opened into a parlor and a dining room on the one side, and on the other into "the Chamber", which served as the master bedroom, linen storage room, office, and family room. A walnut stairway led from the passage to three bedrooms and a nursery on the upper floor. Except for the room occupied during Harrower's time by Lucy Gaines, the housekeeper, the bedrooms were used by the children of the family. (The interior arrangement of the house is taken from the Inventory and appraisal of Colonel Daingerfield's estate which listed the personal property by rooms. Spotsylvania County Will Book E, 1772-1798, 590-592.)[85]

Harrower gave a detailed description of planting corn and the splendid job Anthony did as overseer. Overseer of a plantation of this size would have been demanding and challenging, especially for such a young man. Harrower speaks of Anthony often going up to the country to see his mother and family and friends. On occasions, Anthony's brothers John or James returned to the plantation with him.

---

[84] Riley, Edward Miles, *The Journal of John Harrower, An Indentured Servant in the Colony of Virginia*, 1773-1776, 1963, p.84-172.
[85] Ibid.

Anthony and Harrower, both of Scottish descent, became friends, even with the 18 years difference in age, often socializing together after work or on weekends. As time progressed, Anthony and the young housekeeper Lucy became more than friends. Harrower, missing his own family, gave accounts of Anthony and Lucy's courtship and nocturnal fun. Harrower followed the friendship and love affair of Anthony and Lucy Gaines, giving advice to both young people, perhaps from his friendship and liking both Anthony and Lucy, both people seemingly amiable and good-natured.

Lucy, a vibrant young woman with a flow of emotions, wanted marriage. Anthony felt he was too young and not financially prepared for a wife and children. Harrower encouraged the marriage, saying Lucy was a *"genteel, cliver, weel looked girle & of a good temper, and that I wou'd be greatly deceived in her if she did not make an extream good wife."* This put a strain on the friendship between Harrower and Anthony. Anthony left the plantation more often, visiting his mother and family.

One night in the schoolhouse while Harrower spoke with Anthony about the love affair, Harrower noted the following in his journal as Anthony's response:

> He (Anthony) answered me that he had a great many thoughts. That he was young & cou'd hardly maintain himself. That it was a Daningerous situation & ought to be well considered of. That he hade a fickle Master to do with & was uncertain of his time here. That at any rate he was determined not to stay above another year here, if he staid that. (Sunday, February 25, 1776)[86]

Soon after, Anthony distanced himself from Lucy. He was not ready for marriage. Lucy contacted her mother and begged to be able to leave the plantation and return home as she could not bear to stay there.

About this time, Harrower made an important notation in his journal of a historical matter. On Wednesday, July 10, 1776, Harrower writes:

> At 6 pm went to Mrs.Battaile's & teach'd until sunset and then returned home & soon after hea(r)d a great many

---

[86] Ibid.

Guns fired towards Toun (sic). About 12 pm the Colo. Despate(h)ed Anthy. Frazer there to see what was the cause of (it) who returned, and informed him that there was great rejoicings in Toun on Accott. of the Congress having declared the 13 United Colonys of North America Independent of the Crown of great Britain.[87]

On July 23, 1776, shortly after Anthony returned to Belvidera with this news that had just reached Fredericksburg, Lucy resigned as the housekeeper at Belvidera. It is unknown what became of her after she returned home to her mother. She is thought to be the daughter of Robert and Ursula Gaines, her father having died in 1763. She had a sister Alice, who married John Robinson of the Wilderness in Orange County. One source noted that Lucy died later in 1776, but no documents nor verbal testimonials substantiated this statement that we could locate. Had Lucy died that same year?

It is unknown when Anthony left the employ of Daingerfield as Harrower died before completing his indenture and the journal writings ceased. The last entry was July 28, 1776, and Anthony continued to be employed at Belvidera. By March 1, 1777, Anthony became an officer in the Continental Army. He was a 2nd Lieutenant, 1st Regiment, Revolutionary War soldier, serving in the Twenty-first Infantry.[88] "Anthony Frazer was commissioned Ensign in the First Virginia State Regiment 1 March 1777, and promoted to a Second Lieutenancy 29 May 1777. He served in the Battles of Germantown and Monmouth and resigned 12 February 1778."[89]

---

[87] Ibid.

[88] Anthony Frazer, U.S. Compiled Revolutionary War Military Service Records, 1775-1783.

[89] Herndon, John G., *The Herndon Family of Virginia*, Volume II, 1947-1952.

The Battle of Germantown in which Anthony participated was fought on October 4, 1777 at Germantown, Pennsylvania between the British Army and the American Continental Army under George Washington.[90] The British defeated the American Continental Army at Germantown and the Continental Army retreated to the winter camp of Valley Forge. Anthony was among them.

It was stated in The *Herndon Family of Virginia* that Anthony served in the Battle of Monmouth, but that battle was fought on June 28, 1778 near the Monmouth Courthouse in New Jersey. Anthony, among the sick, resigned on February 12, 1778, so it seems unlikely that he fought in the Battle of Monmouth.

The Muster Roll for Valley Forge Legacy lists 2nd Lieutenant Anthony "Frazier," ID: VA11296, 1st Virginia Regiment, 5th Division in Brigadier General Peter Muhlenberg's Brigade, Capt. John Camp Company, DARA041942, was at the winter encampment at Valley Forge in December

[90] Anthony Frazer, U.S., Sons of the American Revolution Membership Applications, 1889-1970.

1777. Anthony resigned on February 12, 1778. Valley Forge encampment had shortages of food, clothing, water, and medicine and the soldiers were sick from diseases, hunger, and exposure to the cold and wet winter. The damp wind iced the men through to the bones. Many soldiers did not have shoes as their shoes had worn out on the long march to the camp and others lacked decent coats. Blankets were scarce and they were plagued with rainy weather. The soldiers lived in crude huts they built on the plateau, and in the glittery light of the sun they searched for straw to use as bedding as they watched their breath puff out from the cold and their stomach ached from hunger.

The 1st Virginia Regiment entered Valley Forge with 237 men assigned and 94 fit for duty as part of Greene's Division.[91] In February 1778, when Anthony resigned, only 283 men from all Regiments assigned under Muhlenberg's Brigade were fit for duty out of 1,246 at Valley Forge.[92] Common diseases killed many of the men and made others too sick to fight. Among those diseases were influenza, typhus, typhoid, smallpox, and dysentery.[93]

---

[91] Valley Forge Legacy, The Muster Roll Project, The Encampment.
[92] Ibid.
[93] Ibid.

Recently, I ordered from the Valley Forge Park Alliance an official Muster Roll Certificate of Service for Anthony Frazier (Frazer) during the Valley Forge Winter Encampment of 1777-1778 as shown below:

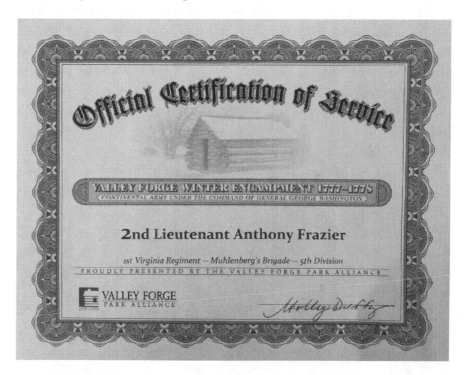

Anthony returned home from the Continental Army to a city ravished by war and to a life not as he had left it. But, then again, having sparred back and forth during the battles and endured the hardships of Valley Forge, Anthony would not have returned the same man as when he left. Like others, he would have to deal with the losses that all sustained from the demons of war with all its ugliness and horror. Unlike many of the soldiers, Anthony recovered from his illness. On November 19, 1778, he finalized the administration of his dad, James Frazer's, estate.[94]

Almost two years later, at age 26, on April 13, 1780, Anthony married Hannah Herndon (November 22, 1760 – February 3, 1824), the daughter of Edward Herndon III and Mary Duerson. There was a friendship between the Herndon and Frazer families. Two of Hannah's sisters, Sarah

---

[94] Anthony Frazer, *Virginia, Spotsylvania County Records*, 1721-1800.

and Philadelphia, married Anthony's brothers, James and William, and her niece, Frances (Fanny), married Anthony's brother Reuben.

As Anthony was a farmer and tobacco planter, he showed up often in land records. Virginia Land Records indicate that on November 19, 1782, Anthony purchased 20.5 acres of land in Berkeley Parrish, Spotsylvania County.[95] On March 6, 1787, the records indicate Anthony had 9.25 acres also in Berkeley Parrish.[96] On April 17, 1787, Anthony Frazer and John Chew, Jr. recorded 258 acres of land in Spotsylvania County conveyed to them by Harry and Sarah Bartlett for standing security for them.[97] On May 10, 1789, land totaling 450 acres was recorded to Anthony Frazer in Berkeley Parrish, Spotsylvania.[98] On March 2, 1790, Anthony Frazer and John Chew acted as grantor of 500 acres of land in Spotsylvania County, Virginia to Thomas Duerson.[99] On November 17, 1796, Thomas Crutcher of Nelson County, Kentucky, conveyed to Anthony Frazer, James Frazer, William Frazer, and Reuben Frazer of Spotsylvania County, 300 acres whereon Crutcher lived in Kentucky. On July 4, 1797, Anthony, along with John Steward, acting as executors of the Will of John Wright, sold 86.5 acres of land in Berkeley Parrish, Spotsylvania County.[100]

Anthony served as the deputy sheriff in Spotsylvania County in 1778, at age 24, under Sheriff Edward Herndon, and in 1780, at age 26, under Sheriff John Lewis. Anthony was listed as "Commissioner in the County of Spotsylvania from 1st May 1786 to 1st May 1787," and at age 32 he served as tax commissioner for his district.[101] In 1791, at age 37, Anthony was appointed inspector of tobacco at Royston Warehouse by Governor Edmund Randolph.

Hannah and Anthony were members of St. George's Parish in Fredericksburg. The first church building was a wooden structure built in the 1730s. The present building of St. George's was built in 1849.[102] The

---

[95] Anthony Frazer, *Virginia, Land, Marriage, and Probate Records*, 1839-1850.

[96] Ibid.

[97] Ibid.

[98] Ibid.

[99] Ibid.

[100] Anthony Frazer, *Virginia County Records – Spotsylvania County*, 1721-1800, Volume 1, edited by William Armstrong Crozier.

[101] Anthony Frazer, Virginia Genealogical Society Quarterly, Volume 7, No. 4, p. 95.

[102] St. George's Episcopal Church, Fredericksburg, Virginia, "History."

first wooden building was the one that George Washington and family attended and was the one that Anthony and Hannah attended. During the Colonial Period, St. George's was responsible by law for the welfare of widows, orphans, and the needy. In 1783, at about age 29, Anthony was appointed Clerk of the Vestry of St. George's Parish.

John, Anthony's brother, died in 1793. On January 5, 1796, Anthony Frazer was named guardian to Thomas Frazer and John Frazer, orphans of John Frazer (Anthony's brother), with William Frazer and Reuben Frazer, seconds. Two years later, in 1798, Anthony's brother James died. On December 3, 1799, Anthony and William Frazer were named guardians to James' children Elizabeth, Patsey, (Patsy), and Sarah Frazer with John Crutchfield and Joseph Herndon, Jr. as seconds.[103]

On March 4, 1804, Anthony died in Virginia of consumption, known today as tuberculosis. He was 49 years old, young by today's standard. The *Virginia Herald* on March 9, 1804 announced his death: "Died – In this county, on Sunday last, Mr. Anthony Frazer, a gentleman much esteemed by his neighbors and acquaintances."[104]

The Herndon Family of Virginia states that Anthony and Hannah had ten children. Nine children were verified, but we were unable to locate information on a tenth child. At time of Anthony's death, his oldest child, Mary, had died as a young child. His daughter Elizabeth preceded his death by just three months, having died as a teenager. This must have been emotionally trying for Hannah having lost a daughter and a husband in such a short span of time. Anthony's oldest son James was 21 years old and his youngest known child was three years old when Anthony died.

After Anthony's death, his wife Hannah continued farming their land. In 1815, she is listed as an owner of land on Glady Run where they had lived. This land is supposedly six miles West from the Spotsylvania Courthouse. Thinking of Glady Run, it conjured up vague memories of a little stream called Glady Run. With our curious nature and my grinding desire to be accurate, during one of our day trips to Spotsylvania, Palmer and I drove the surrounding area of the courthouse, enjoying the history and enchantment of the land. We were unable to identify with certainty

---

[103] Anthony Frazer and William Frazer, *Spotsylvania County Records*, Virginia Court Records, Guardians Bonds, Will Book F, p. 83.
[104] Anthony Frazer, *Genealogies of Virginia Families*, p. 758.

what was once home to Anthony and Hannah, although we did locate Glady Run stream. Hannah Frazer died on February 3, 1824 at age 63.

Known children of Hannah Herndon Frazer and Anthony Frazer (more information on children below):

C.1.   MARY LEWIS FRAZER (1781-1786)

C.2.   JAMES A. FRAZER (June 7, 1783 – February 11, 1854)

C.3.   EDWARD FRAZER (February 4, 1785 – July 25, 1863)

C.4.   ELIZABETH FRAZER (February 13, 1787 – December 3, 1803)

C.5.   GEORGE FRAZER (March 3, 1790 – November 13, 1830)

C.6.   HERNDON FRAZER (August 20, 1792 – July 10, 1877)

C.7.   MARGARET "PEGGY" FRAZER (abt. 1795/1799 – January 9, 1828)

C.8.   JOSEPH ADDISON FRAZER (May 22, 1798 – March 31, 1886)

C.9.   ANTHONY FRAZER (abt. 1801 – February 14, 1839)

C.10. UNKNOWN CHILD

C.1.   **MARY LEWIS FRAZER** (1781-1786) (Daughter of ANTHONY FRAZER, JAMES BENJAMIN FRAZER, WILLIAM FRAZER) Mary died at five years of age.

C.2.   **JAMES A. FRAZER** (June 7, 1783 – February 11, 1854) (Son of ANTHONY FRAZER, JAMES BENJAMIN FRAZER, WILLIAM FRAZER) James was born in Spotsylvania County, Virginia. He married his first cousin, Elizabeth Frazer, daughter of Sergeant James Frazer (brother to Anthony) and James Frazer's second wife Sarah Kenyon Thomas Frazer (August 1, 1781 - December 14, 1846). James was an early hotel proprietor in Lewisburg, West Virginia.[105] He died of pneumonia in Lewisburg on February 11, 1854.[106] He had a plantation named Harmony Hill, which at the time of death he left to his five children. He also

---

[105] Herndon, John Goodwin, *The Herndon Family of Virginia*, Volume II, No. 772.

[106] Death of James A. Frazer, West Virginia, Deaths Index, 1853-1973, Lewisburg, West Virginia.

owned a tavern and inn, among other investments that he left to his children. Elizabeth and James are buried at Old Stone Presbyterian Church Cemetery, Lewisburg, West Virginia.[107] We visited the gravesites, but their headstones were damaged by natural elements and difficult to find unless instructed. See chapter on **JAMES A. FRAZER**.

C.3. **EDWARD FRAZER** (February 4, 1785 – July 25, 1863) (Son of ANTHONY FRAZER, JAMES BENJAMIN FRAZER, WILLIAM FRAZER) Edward was born in Spotsylvania County, Virginia. He married his first cousin, Elizabeth Frazer (June 24, 1790 – May 10, 1873) on December 13, 1816.[108] Elizabeth was daughter of John Frazer (brother to Anthony) and Elizabeth Fox. He died on July 25, 1863. Edward and Elizabeth are buried at Lexington Cemetery, Fayette County, Kentucky.[109]

C.4. **ELIZABETH FRAZER** (February 13, 1787 – December 3, 1803) (Daughter of ANTHONY FRAZER, JAMES BENJAMIN FRAZER, WILLIAM FRAZER) Elizabeth died at age 16. She was unmarried.

C.5. **GEORGE FRAZER** (March 3, 1790 – November 13, 1830)[110] (Son of ANTHONY FRAZER, JAMES BENJAMIN FRAZER, WILLIAM FRAZER)

C.6. **HERNDON FRAZER** (August 20, 1792 – July 10, 1877) (Son of ANTHONY FRAZER, JAMES BENJAMIN FRAZER, WILLIAM FRAZER) Herndon received his education at Washington College (now Washington and Lee University). He was a Baptist clergyman. Herndon married his first wife who was his first cousin, Huldah Herndon[111] (1798-1843/1845), daughter of Joseph Herndon and Lucy Duerson, in 1817. In 1848, he married

---

[107] James A. Frazer, U.S., Find A Grave Index, 1600s-Current., Lewisburg, West Virginia, Memorial ID 106295267, Section B-1.

[108] Edward Frazer, Virginia Compiled Marriages, 1740-1850, Spotsylvania County, Virginia.

[109] Edward Frazer, U.S., Find A Grave Index, 1600s-Current, Lexington, Kentucky, Memorial ID 51302488.

[110] George Frazer, U.S., Find A Grave Index, 1600s-Current.

[111] Herndon Frazer, Virginia, Select Marriages, 1785-1940.

his second wife, his cousin, Martha Lucetta Rawlings, daughter of Richard Rawlings and Lucy Scott Herndon.[112]

It is said that Herndon was a man of "uncommonly fine physique and would arrest the eye of a stranger in any gathering. His dress was always carefully considered, and his carriage would suggest that he had been a student of military movements."[113]

"He had his academic training in such schools as were at that day accessible to the sons of the well-to-do, and then went to Washington College, now Washington and Lee University."[114] After college he devoted some years to teaching. He loved books and reading. In 1841, he was ordained to the gospel ministry at Mount Hermon Church on August 14. He wrote in his diary:

> On this day I (a poor sinner) was ordained to the arduous, solemn, and responsible work of the gospel ministry, by a Presbytery consisting of our pastor, James L. Powell, and Elders John C. Gordon and Jacob W. Herndon, invited by the church to aid in this business. Lord, help me to fulfil the expectations of my friends, for without Thee I can do nothing good, since in me, that is in my flesh, there dwelleth no good thing. Lord, hear my prayer and grant that I may never be guilty of conduct incompatible with the office to which I have been called by Thy permissive Providence. May it have been with Thy approbation, and may the few days that I have to spend on earth be employed in efforts to promote Thy glory? Amen and Amen.[115]

Herndon and his first wife Huldah Herndon had no children. Herndon and Martha L. Rawlings had two children: Herndon (1849 – December

---

[112] Herndon, John Goodwin, *The Herndon Family of Virginia*, Volume II, No. 776.
[113] Herndon Frazer, *Virginia Baptist Ministers*, 3ʳᵈ Series, Taylor, George Braxton, 1912, p. 259-263.
[114] Ibid.
[115] Ibid.

24, 1876), who was called Don, and Huldah Frazer (September 6, 1852 – March 10, 1940). Don died of typhoid fever before reaching manhood. He is buried at North Pamunkey Cemetery, Orange, Virginia. In earlier days, his (Herndon) home had been that of "the country gentleman with the air of amplitude and refinement and bespeaking always a hospitality that made everything the property of its guests." After the war he was left with but scant comforts.[116]

Herndon's preaching career connected with the Goshen Association. The churches he served were: "Mount Hermon, Zion, Antioch, Lower Gold Mine, Mount Pisgah, Trinity, Mechanicsville, and Elk Creek. "[117]Herndon is buried at North Pamunkey Cemetery, Orange, Virginia.[118]

C.7. **MARGARET "PEGGY" FRAZER** (abt. 1795/1799 – January 9, 1828) (Daughter of ANTHONY FRAZER, JAMES BENJAMIN FRAZER, WILLIAM FRAZER) Margaret was known as "Peggy." She was born in Spotsylvania County, Virginia. She died of "consumption" (tuberculosis) and is buried at Old Stone Presbyterian Church Cemetery, Lewisburg, West Virginia.[119] There is no grave marker for her.

C.8. **JOSEPH ADDISON FRAZER** (May 22, 1798 – March 31, 1886)[120] (Son of ANTHONY FRAZER, JAMES BENJAMIN FRAZER, WILLIAM FRAZER) See chapter on **JOSEPH ADDISON FRAZER**. Direct ancestor of Oscar Wallace Frazer, Jr.

C.9. **ANTHONY FRAZER** (abt. 1801 – February 14, 1839) (Son of ANTHONY FRAZER, JAMES BENJAMIN FRAZER, WILLIAM FRAZER) Anthony was born in Spotsylvania County, Virginia. Anthony was unmarried. He moved to Lewisburg, West Virginia. He is buried in Old Stone Presbyterian Church Cemetery,

---

[116] Ibid.

[117] Ibid.

[118] Herndon Frazer, U.S., Find A Grave Index, 1600s-Current, Memorial ID 188211102.

[119] Margaret "Peggy" Frazer, U.S., Find A Grave Index, 1600s-Current, Memorial ID 106294957.

[120] Joseph Addison Frazer, U.S., Find A Grave Index, 1600s-Current, Memorial ID 21460189.

Lewisburg, West Virginia. Cause of death was consumption (tuberculosis).

C.10.   **UNKNOWN CHILD** (No information was located on a tenth child, if one.)

(Names and dates of children of Anthony Frazer and Hannah Herndon Frazer were taken from *The Herndon Family of Virginia*. Dates and additional information were verified from *Ancestry.com* and *Find a Grave*. Documents or information to verify accuracy on several of the children listed above were unable to be located.)

JAMES A. FRAZER

TAVERN AND STAGECOACH INN PROPRIETOR
"THE POLISHED OLD HOTEL-KEEPER
WHO FIGURED SO PROMINENTLY IN THE
EARLY HISTORY OF LEWISBURG."

THE FOURTH GENERATION

JAMES A. FRAZER (June 7, 1783 – February 11, 1854) (Son of ANTHONY FRAZER, JAMES BENJAMIN FRAZER, WILLIAM FRAZER) was born on June 7, 1783[121] in Spotsylvania, Virginia, the second child and first son of Anthony and Hannah Herndon Frazer and among the fourth-generation family in America. James was one of a large family who grew up on a crop and tobacco farm, or small plantation as it may have been called. His family was not wealthy but had worked diligently to establish a respectable and profitable farm. Each generation in America were hard-working men, and each generation to this point died early in life compared to today's standards. His dad served in the Revolutionary War, worked primarily as a farmer, and believed in education for his children. James' dad died in 1804, when James was 21 years old. James was not a direct ancestor to my children but was a sixth-generation uncle.

James married his first cousin, Elizabeth Frazer, (August 1, 1781 – December 14, 1846), daughter of Sergeant James Frazer and James Frazer's second wife Sarah Kenyon Thomas Frazer. Elizabeth's mother Sarah died

---

[121] James A. Frazer, U.S., Find A Grave Index, Old Stone Presbyterian Church Cemetery, Lewisburg, West Virginia, Memorial ID 106295267.

at the birth of Elizabeth's sister Sarah in 1792 when Elizabeth was 11 years old. Elizabeth's dad remarried Lucy Smith in 1794.[122] Several years later, in December 1798, Elizabeth's father died.[123] Her stepmother moved from the area to live with her family. A year later, on December 3, 1799, Anthony and William Frazer (brothers of James Frazer) were named guardians to their brother's children Elizabeth, Patsey (Patsy), and Sarah. Elizabeth was almost 17 or 18 years old when she went to live with either her Uncle Anthony's family or William's family.

In 1810 or possibly earlier, as a young man of 27 years old, James along with his wife Elizabeth migrated to White Sulphur Springs to join his Uncle William Herndon. Also, in 1810, their first child Richard was allegedly born. The Herndon and Frazer families had many connections. James' mother was a Herndon as were wives of three of his uncles. At the time James joined his uncle, White Sulphur Springs was part of Virginia, later becoming West Virginia. What was White Sulphur Springs Resort is now known as The Greenbrier Resort. The springs received its name from the famous mineral springs that became renowned for its healing powers.

According to legend, the first reported healing at the springs was in 1778 when Amanda Anderson, suffering from rheumatism, was brought to the springs on a sling carried between two horses, and after a few weeks of treatment, she left riding horseback. Her family had heard from the Indians that the strong-smelling springs had healing powers. The news of Amanda spread and brought others to the springs, camping in tents and primitive cabins, seeking the healing powers of the springs. Growing around the springs, a small town formed known as "Old White" and incorporated as White Sulphur Springs in 1909.[124]

Modern analysis shows the water at the springs to be rich in sulfate, calcium, and other minerals.

Michael Bowyer, who had legal title to the springs and 950 surrounding acres, is credited with hacking out the site of a potential spa. The primeval resort of the Sulphur Spring was known as Bowyer's Sulphur Spring, many referred to it as simply "Sulphur Spring." Boyer

---

[122] Marriage of James Frazer and Lucy Smith, Virginia, Land, Marriage, and Probate Records, 1639-1850.

[123] U.S., Sons of the American Revolution Membership Applications, 1889-1970.

[124] Conte, Robert S., *The History of The Greenbrier America's Resort*, 2000, p. 8-11.

died in 1808. The year he died, he commenced construction of a tavern with a dining room and a few guest rooms on a hill just above the springs. This original tavern stood on what today is the croquet court for The Greenbrier Resort.[125] This structure as well as the cabins, barn, stable, and mills were deeded to his eldest son James Bowyer in 1809, and the land was divided equally among his seven children, with a small portion held in common. His son-in-law, James Calwell, a Baltimore merchant who married Bowyer's daughter Mary "Polly" Bowyer, had his eye on running the springs business, but he was shuttling back and forth from Baltimore with his established business there and had little time for the springs business until later.[126]

Illustration of Michael Bowyer's original tavern,
which stood on the site of what today is
the croquet court of The Greenbrier Resort.[127]
Illustrated by John McFarland

---

[125] Ibid.
[126] Ibid.
[127] Ibid.

In 1810, William Herndon leased the operation of the springs with a clause that required Herndon to build ten log buildings, eighteen- by-twenty-two-feet, finished with shingle roofs and brick chimneys[128]. This was the first of a style that would come to dominate the grounds. The cottages were strung in a row with each row with its own name. Herndon hired his 27-year-old nephew, James Frazer, to be the superintendent.[129] Soon, additional cottages were built. As stated in the book, *The Greenbrier Resort*:

> In 1808, the year of Bower's death (In 1778, Mrs. Anderson, a wife of a Greenbrier County settler, recovered from chronic rheumatism after bathing in a hollowed log filled with water from a spring. News of the healing powers of the spring spread. Michael Bower obtained legal title to the spring in Greenbrier County and 950 surrounding acres in 1783), construction began on a large tavern at what had become known as Bower's (Bowyer's) Sulphur Spring. His family leased the operation to a Mr. Herndon, and a clause in the lease directed the new manager to build "ten new cottages, each 18 x 20 feet, with brick chimney and shingled roof." Begun in 1810, the cottages were finished by July 20, 1811, and were soon augmented by additional cabins. In 1816 a visitor described the cabins as "built of square log, whitewashed, and disposed in a range just on the skirts of a little lawn, so that they have all the air of a rural village."*[130]*

Another source states the following of White Sulphur Springs:

> The massacre of the Carpenters (Nathan Carpenter patented the land on which sits White Sulphur Springs, building his cabin near the spring, and brought his family

---

[128] Ibid.

[129] Ibid.

[130] Chambers, Jr., S. Allen, *The Greenbrier Resort*, West Virginia, White Sulphur Springs,

there in 1774. Soon they were attacked by Indians and he and all his family were murdered except for his wife Kate and an infant child who escaped to a high mountain.) did not deter others from settling near the site of the bloody tragedy, and soon after came William Herndon, the first to open the Springs as a public resort, he having leased the property from James Caldwell for a period of ten years.[131]

Having grown up in a small coal town located only an hour from White Sulphur Springs, as a child I experienced love at first sight when I encountered The Greenbrier Resort. I was the youngest of the seven children of a coal mining family. Our large family was unable to afford vacations other than an occasional visit to family, and travel outside our surrounding area was rare. On one of those rare trips, Mom, Dad, and I were returning home on a passenger train from Northern Virginia after visiting my older brothers who lived and worked outside of Washington, D.C. Usually, our views of trains were from the outside of the monstrous black trains that rolled through our area loaded with cherished coal that's mere existence allowed work that provided for home and comforts of a coal mining family. Today, we were seated on the inside, looking out of the soiled and dirt-covered train windows. This little girl was still tingling with excitement from the train trip. The mighty train pulled to a roaring stop as steel grinded against steel in the little town of White Sulphur Springs. Looking out of the grimy train window, I was in awe. A horse drawn carriage sat waiting for its prince and princess dressed in their fineness. It was an enchanted fairytale, glamorous and untouchable, close, and yet so far out of my reach. It was a young girl's princess castle come to life, but it was not my life. It was not our vacation. I looked at my own clothes, clean and sensible but far from being a princess. Not envious but just wishful, perhaps someday, I thought. With age, I discovered other fabulous resorts that were among our vacations, but none astounded me as that childhood love. It was not until many years later that those old childhood daydreams were fulfilled as we visited The Greenbrier Resort. Part of me will always be that small coal-town girl with the childhood love of the Greenbrier Resort with its "Old World"

---

[131] Greenbrier County, WV Early History, White Sulphur Springs.

grace and charm and romantic past rooted in time. I could not imagine how many hands grasped the rails of that fascinating resort or walked across their floors. Its long and glamorous history cannot be erased. James Frazer played his part in the early history of this enchanting resort, and for that, I was thrilled.

The Greenbrier Resort in current day.

The earliest known advertisement for "The White or Bowyers Sulphur Springs" appeared in an issue of the *Washington, D.C. National Intelligencer* on July 4, 1810. The advertisement spoke of James Frazer, as follows:

> *The White or Bowyers Sulphur Springs, Greenbrier County, Virginia.*
> *These highly and justly celebrated waters, together with the buildings and a part of the landed estate appertaining thereto, have been leased by the subscribers; who mean to exert their utmost power to prepare for the reception and comfortable accommodation of as many as a want of health, or a wish to preserve it, may induce to visit these well-known Fountains of Health, the salutary effects of which they hope and believe will be much increased by the additional comforts*

in the accommodation which the subscribers mean to afford. The season will commence on the First day of July, 1810; but a good Tavern will at all times be kept open for the reception and accommodation of Travellers and others, under the care of Mr. James Frazer, a most respectable man, for whose good conduct the subscribers pledge themselves. William Herndon & Co.[132]

James and Elizabeth's second son, James Addison Frazer, was born in 1812 in Greenbrier County. Death records indicate James Addison Frazer was born in 1813.[133] By 1814, James Frazer purchased 1,212 acres of land from Robert Henning, described as "lying near the Town of Lewisburg and being the same through which the road from Bowyers Sulphur Spring to Lewisburg run."[134] This is the property that became home to James Frazer, known as Harmony Hill, located on Washington Street, East in Lewisburg. Below is a current picture of the home that sits on the property. This land was located near White Sulphur Springs, being convenient for James to the Springs.

---

[132] Conte, Robert S., *The History of The Greenbrier America's Resort*, 2000, p. 10.

[133] James A. Frazer, "West Virginia Deaths, 1853-1970." Index. FamilySearch, Salt Lake City, Utah, "Death Records."

[134] Deed Book 6, "Henning to Frazer, 1814," Lewisburg, West Virginia, Greenbrier County Courthouse County Clerk, p. 134.

Today this is a privately owned home on the
property that once was Harmony Hill
and is no longer in the Frazer family. Photo
taken by Lillian Frazer, Summer 2020

In 1815, James and Elizabeth had their first daughter, Hannah Herndon.[135] Their son William Herndon was born in 1817, living only until age eight, dying of dysentery, an infection of the intestines.[136]

We are unsure how long William Herndon and James Frazer managed Bowyer's Sulphur Springs, but James Calwell moved his family to White Sulphur Springs permanently by 1818. By 1820, the day-to-day management of the resort was conducted by William Calwell, son of James Calwell, and no records indicate that William Herndon or James Frazer were active in the operations after this time. Years later, one of James Calwell's sons married one of James Frazer's daughters.

This property continued to change. Throughout the years, the resort

[135] Hannah Herndon Frazer, U.S., Find A Grave Index, Old Stone Presbyterian Church Cemetery, Lewisburg, West Virginia, Memorial ID 107787957.
[136] William Herndon Frazer, U.S., Find A Grave Index, Old Stone Presbyterian Church Cemetery, Lewisburg, West Virginia, Memorial ID 106294892.

had various names, and since 1913, what was called the Sulphur Springs became the current historic resort known as The Greenbrier Resort. What has not changed throughout the years has been the surrounding mountains, the soothing waters of the springs, and the resort's past romantic history.

In 1820, James and Elizabeth had a daughter Sarah Thomas.[137] Records indicate that another child Thomas was born in 1820, having died in 1850, but no other information was located on the son Thomas. We are unsure if this record is correct. In 1826, they had their seventh child, Margaret Carter[138] and in 1829, they had their last child, a daughter, Elizabeth "Bettie."

Once William Herndon's lease at Sulphur Springs was completed and it was time for him and James Frazer to leave, James was living at Harmony Hill near Lewisburg. Lewisburg, set in a small valley amid the foothills of the Allegheny Mountains, boasted celebrated springs from nearby White Sulphur Springs, rich pasture and farmland with estates devoted to livestock and fine horses as well as hogs and sheep. James had grown up on a crop and tobacco farm, and he continued to be a farmer as well as a hotel keeper. He maintained livestock and grew wheat and corn.[139] The town's local economy remained agricultural, but its mark of distinction was its position as a judicial center. In 1824, the James River and Kanawha Turnpike was completed, expanding trade from Virginia to the West and ran through the middle of Lewisburg. This brought travelers, goods, stagecoaches, and freight wagons to town, supporting merchants and taverns.

A quotation from Joseph Martin printed in *Gazetteer of Virginia* on the public services in Lewisburg in 1835 states Lewisburg had the following (Lewisburg was in Virginia during these years.):

> 6 mercantile stores, 1 printing office issuing a weekly
> paper, 2 tan yards, 3 saddlers, 4 blacksmith shops, 2

---

[137] Sarah Thomas Frazer, U.S., Find A Grave Index, Old Stone Presbyterian Church Cemetery, Lewisburg, West Virginia, Memorial ID 107232931.

[138] Margaret Carter Frazer Calwell, "West Virginia Deaths, 1853-1970," Index. FamilySearch, Salt Lake City, Utah, "Death Records."

[139] Will Book 3, "Frazer Estate," Lewisburg, West Virginia, Greenbrier County Courthouse, County Clerk, pp. 96-98.

coppersmiths and tin plate workers, 3 brick layers, 4 house carpenters, 4 tailor shops, 2 cabinet makers, and 3 hotels (taverns) --- population about 750 persons of whom 7 are attorneys and 3 regular physicians. The town contains 101 dwelling houses, 3 houses of public worship, 1 academy, 1 common school, and 3 Sunday schools.

During the Frazer family research, I discovered that James Frazer owned and operated a tavern in Lewisburg, a town I had been to numerous times as I grew up in the neighboring county. I briefly recalled on occasion mention of early stagecoach inns and taverns scattered throughout the counties but paid little attention. I envisioned old stone buildings that followed the Old Midland Trail. Now I was relentless in my search of the tavern owned by James Frazer. Suddenly, there it was in front of us the entire time. Part of my confusion was James Frazer owned two different taverns, not hidden from us but located amid town .

James opened a tavern in downtown Lewisburg at the intersection of Lafayette and Washington Streets. The tavern was thought to have been built before 1823. It was a popular stop for early stagecoaches. James opened the tavern under the name of "Frazier's Tavern" (Frazer's). Henry Clay was celebrated at Frazer's Tavern while journeying to White Sulphur Springs. [140] While researching James Frazer and his part at White Sulphur Springs when he assisted his Uncle William Herndon and had managed the White Sulphur Springs Resort, I discovered the friendship between Henry Clay and James Calwell and family. Possibly, James Frazer became acquainted with Henry Clay during Clay's many visits to the springs. James later sold his tavern in Lewisburg to John Mays. [141] The original main building no longer stands, said to have been torn down for "name of progress." The "western part" of the tavern currently stands on 113 Washington Street, East. The building was later known as Bell Tavern. [142] The two-story building, today painted white, serves as a real

[140] Shepherd, Sarah, *200 Years at the North House, The History of a House and its People,* Greenbrier Historical Society, 2020, p.46.

[141] Ibid.

[142] James E. Talbert, *Historic Lewisburg's Sixty-Four Original Lots,* 1872-2001, (Lewisburg, West Virginia Greenbrier Historical Society, 2001, p. 143.)

estate company. During our visit to Lewisburg, we walked the streets of the historical town, excited to have found a trail to a Frazer ancestor. (Throughout our research, we noted in Lewisburg that James Frazer's name was spelled both as "Frazer" and/or "Frazier" when in print.)

Current photo of what was once part of "Frazier's Tavern" managed by James Frazer.
Photo of restored building taken in Summer 2020, operating as a real estate company.

In 1834, James Frazer constructed a two-story brick building as a library and study for use by the judges and clerks of the Supreme Court of Virginia.[143] The building was located adjacent to the North House. James leased this building to the Supreme Court of Appeals of Virginia. This splendid structure had two rooms on the first floor and twin fireplaces with carved mantels. A stairway at the west end led to the one room second floor with another pair of fireplaces. The court sessions ended in 1864, after West Virginia was established. During the Civil War, the building served as a military hospital. In 1941, the building was dedicated as the

---

[143] J.V. Dotson, *Masonic Sketches of Greenbrier Lodge No. 49, Fort Union Lodge No. 42*, and *Greenbrier Lodge No. 42* in Lewisburg, 1796-1939, 3.

Greenbrier County Library and Museum. The second floor of the building was used as a museum until 1976, when the need for more space led the Greenbrier Historical Society to move to the North Building. In 1972, the building was listed on the *National Register of Historic Places*.[144]

> "Before the war, the Virginia Supreme Court of Appeals met there regularly in the first red brick building built west of the Alleghenies. Next door was Frazer's famous Star Tavern."[145]

Greenbrier County Library and Museum, Architect: James "Frasier"
Built in 1834 and known as "Supreme Court Library Building"
Photo taken by Lillian Frazer, Summer 2020

In 1836, James Frazer purchased the John A. North House.[146] The exquisite house was built in 1820 in Lewisburg, thought to be built by John Dunn. The property was owned by Henry B. and Elizabeth Hunter. In 1821, the home was sold to the prominent local lawyer, John A. North

---

[144] *National Register Information System, National Register of Historic Places*, National Park Service, 2010.
[145] Amick Partisan Rangers, Old Stone Church, Lewisburg, Emmick, David.
[146] Deed Book 13, 1836, WV Greenbrier County Courthouse, "North to Frazer," 647-648.

and his wife Charlotte. The home was quite lavish. This building became one of Lewisburg's first two-story brick homes built on Washington Street. John A. North was appointed Clerk of the Greenbrier District Court of Chancery and Clerk of the District of Virginia Supreme Court of Appeals. The home, originally a two-story "L-shaped" home, featured a double portico with heavy columns. The North family lived in the home for about thirteen years, then sold this home to James Frazer.[147]

After James Frazer purchased the John A. North home, he opened an inn and tavern, calling the inn, "The Star Hotel." He added two wings to the home. This allowed him the space to establish a local restaurant and inn. The inn was available to travelers and lawyers and jurists who attended Court in the courthouse adjacent to the tavern. This inn was also a "rest stop" for travelers along the James River and the Kanawha Turnpike. A June 1854 advertisement stated that the property had an orchard, vegetable garden, fifty-horse stable, servants' cabins, kitchens, meat-house, dairy and cellars.[148] It was said his business was good as he catered to court sessions, and the new roads being built brought travelers to the various nearby resorts.

"This account reveals the importance of the Star Hotel as a prestigious destination for the wealthy and powerful men of the era." [149]

> On August 15, 1838, President Martin Van Buren, his Secretary of State Joel R. Poinsett, and Congressman Andrew Beirne, traveled through Lewisburg, and after the bustle of introduction subsided, about sixty persons sat down to a scrumptious dinner, prepared for the occasion by our worthy and esteemed James Frazer, Esq.[150]

Much information gathered on the North House and those who lived

---

[147] National Register Information System, *National Register of Historic Places*, National Park Service, July 9, 2010.

[148] Great Sale of Real and Personal Property in Lewisburg, Virginia, *Greenbrier Era*, June 3, 1854.

[149] Shepherd, Sarah, *200 Years at the North House, The History of a House and its People*, Greenbrier Historical Society, 2020, p.47.

[150] "The President of the United States at Lewisburg," *The Richmond Inquirer*, August 28, 1838.

in the home throughout the years, including the North and Frazer families, and the people who lived and worked on the premises, was due to the Greenbrier Historical Society and their efforts to preserve the history. They were extremely gracious and helpful to us in identifying the properties and the Frazer ancestors in Greenbrier County. Sarah Shepherd and the Greenbrier Historical Society, due to their diligent research, shared their findings in a marvelous and informative book published in 2020, *"200 Years at the North House: The History of a House and its People."*

North House with a view of the addition on the left side,
and on the right side of the house is a view of the
Law Library. James Frazer purchased the home from John A. North,
opening an inn and tavern known as "The Star Hotel." Today the
building serves as home to the Greenbrier Historical Society.
Photo taken by Lillian Frazer, Summer 2020

The North House
Once owned by James Frazer and served as a tavern and inn.
Today the building is owned by the Greenbrier Historical
Society. Photo taken by Lillian Frazer, Summer 2020

Interior views of the rstored North House
Photos taken by Lillian Frazer, Summer 2020

Interior views of The North House
Photos taken by Lillian Frazer, Summer 2020

Elizabeth died on December 14, 1846[151] of consumption, today known as tuberculosis. James Frazer died at 71 years old on February 11, 1854 listed as pneumonia.[152] James and Elizabeth are buried at the Old Stone Presbyterian Church Cemetery, Lewisburg, West Virginia. James died before the Civil War and his only living son James died in 1860, just a year before the Civil War. Lewisburg, until the Civil War years, was a part of Virginia. The war not only divided the North and the South, but the western and eastern portions of Virginia also split. Lewisburg, by 1863, became part of the state of West Virginia, and although the state supported the Union, many people in these surrounding areas were also split, most men in Greenbrier County supporting the South.

Although James Frazer nor son James Addison Frazer fought in the War Between the States, James Addison had three sons that enlisted in the Greenbrier Rifles of the 27th Virginia Infantry Regiment. Greenbrier County was one of the wealthiest counties in Western Virginia and had no desire to split from Virginia. It became part of the newly formed State of West Virginia for strategic reasons and the County remained southern sympathizers with 81 percent of the men, over 2000 men, enlisting with the Confederate Army.[153]

James, at death, left debts for his estate to pay off. Considering his various business adventures, it would be understandable there may be outstanding debt and according to his Will he anticipated funeral and debts to be paid from his estate.

A portion of the Last Will and Testament of James Frazer in part is as follows:

> I James Frazer of the town of Lewisburg, Greenbrier County, Virginia, do hereby make my Last Will and

---

[151] Elizabeth Frazer Frazer, U.S., Find A Grave Index, Old Stone Presbyterian Church Cemetery, Lewisburg, West Virginia, Memorial ID 106295374.

[152] Death of James Frazer, West Virginia, Deaths Index, 1853-1973, Lewisburg, West Virginia.

[153] Local History, Blue Sulphur Spring, Civil War, Greenbrier County, Greenbrier Historical Society, "The Civil War in Greenbrier County: An Overview," July 1, 2013.

Testament in the manner and form following, that is to say

First, after my death to be entered in the burial ground in Lewisburg by the side of my dear departed wife, and all my funeral expenses paid, also all my just debts paid from the sale of any portion of my personal estate to be designated by my executors.

2ⁿᵈ I give and bequeath to my five children my plantation known by the name of Harmony Hill, to be laid off and divided as follows. To my son James A. Frazer, all the land lying north of the turnpike road, adjoining the land of E. Callison, Thos. B. Reynolds, Matthew Gregory & others for his part.

To my daughter Hannah H. Thompson, that part of the land on which she now lives and bounded as follows, beginning at the corner of Joseph F. Calwell's & Samuel S. Smith's and running with Smith's line (which he purchased of Pleasant Wade) to the turnpike road and with the said turnpike to the mouth of the lane where the gate now stands & continue that lane to the draw bars, and thence commencing at the north corner of the bars and with a straight line through the field to the corner between J. F. Calwell & myself and with that line to the beginning for her part.

To my daughter Sarah Thomas, the Harmony Hill house and two hundred acres of the land to be laid off as follows, beginning at the top of the hill on the turnpike near the gate that leads to the house, thence running down the turnpike until it strikes the line of H. B. Hunter, and with Hunter's line as far as will be necessary to give the two hundred acres, by thence running until it strikes the Cary road (as it is called) and with the Cary road or lane, to the beginning on the turnpike, or in order to make it better understood, after it strikes the Cary road, to run a straight line to the mouth of the lane & with that lane, to the beginning on the turnpike for her part.

The balance of the land I wish divided into two equal
parts agreeable to situation and quality, one part of which
I give to my daughter Margaret, and the other part I give
to my daughter Elizabeth. . .[154]

James left the tavern and the two acres of land, which he purchased
from John A. North, along with the buildings, to his son James. He left the
brick building and the log house on the three-fourth acres of land opposite
the tavern jointly to his three daughters, Sarah Thomas, Margaret, and
Elizabeth for them to occupy, rent or sell.[155] He left slaves to his various
children, short-lived as the Civil War was approaching. In 1860, six years
after James Frazer died, Greenbrier County, which at the time was part of
Virginia, shows 1525 slaves (more than 10 percent of the total population
for the county) counted during the census.[156] Greenbrier County was the
fourth county in what becomes the State of West Virginia with the greatest
number of slaves.

In a letter written to Mary Emaline Reynolds Lewis on February
13, 1854, James Frazer's death is mentioned, and the writer of the letter
(from and to a non-member of the Frazer family) expects there to be
some bitterness between the settlement of the estate; however, no specific
reasons are mentioned so this may be speculation. With adult children
who married and became multiple families staying under one roof, friction
could occur for various reasons. It was stated that Sarah and her sister-
in-law Sophia (James Addison Frazer's wife) had a strained relationship
even after James Addison Frazer's death,[157] which could be the cause of
the friction between Sarah and her brother James. Sophia also had bad
feelings with James' sister Elizabeth Taylor Beirne, according to the same
book as stated by Mary Taylor (granddaughter of James Addison Frazer),
"some sort of bad feeling between our house and the house of Beirne."[158]

---

[154] West Virginia, Wills and Probate Records, 1724-1985, "James Frazer," Vol 2-3,
1825-1863, pp.345-347.

[155] Ibid.

[156] Steelhammer, Rich, *The Charleston Gazette-Mail*, "Exhibit explores slavery's
presence in Greenbrier County's past," August 1, 2020.

[157] Shepherd, Sarah, *200 Years at the North House, The History of a House and its
People*, Greenbrier Historical Society, 2020, pp. 59, 63-64, 71.

[158] Ibid.

Sarah, still unmarried, lived at home with her father in 1750, and was highly likely still unmarried at the time of her father's death as in his Will he refers to her as "Sarah Thomas," and he left her the Harmony Hill house. She married before 1758, when she had her first child. Her sisters were married at the time of their father's death.

Records often show James Frazer as old Mr. Frazer; I think this is to identify which James Frazer as he had both a son James Frazer and a grandson James Frazer. Mr. Frazer is mentioned in a letter written to Mary Emeline Reynolds Lewis:

> You will scarcely be surprised to hear that old Mr. Frazer was buried today; he took to his bed this day week ago & died Saturday night; I presume his lungs were almost gone for some time; his last sickness was pleurisy attended with paralysis. His children were all with him, but Margaret (She married Bedford Calwell in 1848, an heir to the White Sulphur Springs resort, today known as The Greenbrier Resort.) who was in Richmond on a visit. They are a very distressed family; the members have not agreed for some time; indeed Sarah (daughter who married Harry H. Harrison, a civil engineer of Greenbrier County) & James came to an open rupture, & Sarah left the house for several weeks, & stayed with Margaret; I expect there will be some bitterness, in the settlement of the Estate.[159]

James Addison Frazer, the son, attempted to sell the inn at one point after his father's death but was not successful. He and his wife turned the inn into a private residence. I located no records to indicate why the son James did not continue the business tavern and inn. Again, we can only speculate the reason. Perhaps he was not the businessman as was his father. Perhaps once the debt of his father's estate had been paid, and once the land, farm, and business had been divided among the children, the finances would not warrant the continuation of the tavern and inn. It was

---

[159] Letters from Lewisburg, written to Mary Emeline Reynolds Lewis (1828-1911) of Lewisburg, West Virginia, and Osceola, Missouri, Edited by Caroline S. Miller, 2013. pp. 183-184.

also said that James, the son, was an excessive alcohol drinker. Whatever reason, the house once again became a private residence. James Addison died in 1860, just six years after his dad died. His cause of death was labeled as "intemperance" or lack of moderation in excessive indulgences, especially in alcohol.[160] If James was an excessive user of alcohol, this may be a cause of ill feelings between him and his sister Sarah.

In 1871, his wife Sophia sold the tavern and inn to Colonel Joe McPherson, who purchased the property for his daughter and son-in-law, and the property was made again into a private home. By the turn of the century, the home was sold to Dr. Robert L. Telford. Dr. Tedford was the pastor of the Old Stone Church in Lewisburg and later became the first president of the Lewisburg Female Institute (Greenbrier College for Women). In 1925, renovations began on the home. The house changed hands several other times. Since 1975, the Greenbrier Historical Society operated the North House Museum out of the home, and in 1994, the Historical Society officially owned the building. In 2020, this building was 200 years old.[161]

In an obituary of Sarah Harrison, daughter of James, who died in 1891, James Frazer was described as *the polished old hotel-keeper who figured so prominently in the early history of Lewisburg.*[162] After our research, I feel this an appropriate description of James Frazer.

The Herndon Family of Virginia, Volume II by John Goodwin Herndon reports that James and Elizabeth had eight children. We were unable to verify all the names and dates from other sources. The additional two children mentioned died at young ages and unmarried. Therefore, I have included Richard and Thomas as children. Names of grandchildren, in part, were taken from the Greenbrier Historical Society records, verified through Ancestry and Find a Grave. Statements of Mary Henry Taylor Randolph, daughter of Elizabeth Frazer Taylor, were taken from Mary's memoirs as printed in *200 Years of the North House: The History of a House and its People.*

---

[160] Morgan Donnally Bunn, *Marcellus Zimmerman's Survey of the Old Stone Church Cemetery*, ed.

[161] Greenbrier Historical Society, Lewisburg, West Virginia, "The Greenbrier Historical Society is Celebrating the 200th Birthday of the North House!"

[162] *Staunton Spectator*, "Death of Mrs. Harrison," April 8, 1891.

Known children of James A. Frazer and Elizabeth Frazer (more information on children below):

C.2.1.   RICHARD FRAZER (1810-1831)

C.2.2.   JAMES ADDISON FRAZER (July 6, 1812 – March 27, 1860)

C.2.3.   HANNAH HERNDON FRAZER THOMPSON (February 5, 1815 – January 23, 1889)

C.2.4.   WILLIAM HERNDON FRAZER (April 22, 1817 – August 9, 1825)

C.2.5.   THOMAS FRAZER (1820) (Unsure if this child is correct. We could not verify any information.)

C.2.6.   SARAH THOMAS FRAZER HARRISON (August 1, 1820 – March 3, 1891)

C.2.7.   MARGARET CARTER FRAZER CALWELL (August 1, 1826 - March 20, 1896)

C.2.8.   ELIZABETH "BETTIE" TAYLOR FRAZER BEIRNE (February 22, 1829 – November 10, 1908)

C.2.1.   **RICHARD FRAZER** (1810-1831) (Son of JAMES A. FRAZER, ANTHONY FRAZER, JAMES BENJAMIN FRAZER, WILLIAM FRAZER) No other information located.

C.2.2.   **JAMES ADDISON FRAZER** (July 6, 1812 – March 27, 1860) (Son of JAMES A. FRAZER, ANTHONY FRAZER, JAMES BENJAMIN FRAZER, WILLIAM FRAZER) James was born on July 6, 1812 at White Sulphur Springs, Greenbrier County, West Virginia. He attended Lewisburg Academy and moved to St. Louis, Missouri for business, where he met Sophia Foulke. James married Sophia Foulke (1817-1885) sometime before 1839. In 1850, James, Sophia and their family were living with his father at Harmony Hill. At his father's death, James inherited the Frazer's Star Hotel, which he turned into a private residence for his family. James died March 27, 1860 at age 47 according to Find A Grave and death records indicate he died on May 27, 1860.[163] His cause of death was listed as "intemperance" or lack of moderation in excessive indulgences such as alcohol. James is

---

[163] James Addison Frazer, West Virginia, Deaths Index, 1853-1973.

buried at Old Stone Presbyterian Church Cemetery, Lewisburg, West Virginia.[164] Known children of James and Sophia:

C.2.2.1. **WILLIAM O. FRAZER** (1839-1889) (Son of JAMES ADDISON FRAZER, JAMES A. FRAZER, ANTHONY FRAZER, JAMES BENJAMIN FRAZER, WILLIAM FRAZER) William served in Virginia 27th Infantry during the Civil War. He moved to St. Louis.[165] William married Anne Taffe.

C.2.2.2. **ELIZABETH FRAZER TAYLOR** (1841-1870) (Daughter of JAMES ADDISON FRAZER, JAMES A. FRAZER, ANTHONY FRAZER, JAMES BENJAMIN FRAZER, WILLIAM FRAZER) Elizabeth married George Edmund Taylor in 1858.[166] She was 17 and he was 34. George joined the Confederate Army when war broke out and was captured and imprisoned until the end of the war. George was the manager of the Montgomery White Sulphur Springs Resort located in Christiansburg in 1860 before the war broke out, and he worked there again after the war as well as other hotels.[167] During the nineteenth century, this resort was a holiday destination for its hot springs. During the Civil War, the resort served as a Confederate hospital. The resort closed in 1904, closure accelerated by a flash flood, now reverted to farmland.[168] The Montgomery White, while open, boasted a three-story hotel with over 200 rooms and over 30 cottages. After Elizabeth died in 1870, George left their children in Lewisburg to stay with their grandmother Sophia. According to her daughter, Mary Henry Taylor Randolph,

---

[164] James Addison Frazer, U.S., Find A Grave Index, 1600s-Current, Memorial ID 106295129.

[165] William O. Frazer, U.S. 1870 Census, St. Louis, Missouri, population schedule, Ward 4, p. 118.

[166] Marriage of Elizabeth Frazer Taylor and George Edmund Taylor, "West Virginia Marriages, 1853-1970," Index. FamilySearch, Salt Lake City, Utah, 2008, 2009.

[167] Ibid.

[168] Historic Sites, Montgomery White Sulphur Springs, Southwest Virginia, Blue Ridge Highlands.

Elizabeth is buried at Montgomery White Sulphur Springs Resort in an unmarked grave by the Confederate Soldier Cemetery (Montgomery White Confederate Cemetery), Christiansburg, Montgomery County, Virginia.[169]

MARY HENRY TAYLOR RANDOLPH (1859-1935)[170]. (Daughter of ELIZABETH FRAZER TAYLOR, JAMES ADDISON FRAZER, JAMES A. FRAZER, ANTHONY FRAZER, JAMES BENJAMIN FRAZER, WILLIAM FRAZER) Mary married Isham Randolph in 1882. Isham had an impressive civil engineering career, including chief engineer of the Chicago and Western Indiana Railway, chief engineer of the Chicago Sanitation and Ship Canal, gold medal awardee at the Paris Expo of 1900, one of six engineers invited by President Roosevelt to advise design plans for the Panama Canal.[171] Mary wrote her memoir called *Long-Long-Ago*. We have been unable to locate a copy as it appears to be no longer in print. After her mother's death in 1870, her father brought her and her siblings to Lewisburg to live with her grandmother Sophia at what was once Frazer's Star Hotel, then converted into the family home. Mary is buried at Old Chapel Cemetery, Millwood, Clark County, Virginia.[172]

WILLIAM FRAZER TAYLOR (1861-1863)[173](Son of ELIZABETH FRAZER TAYLOR, JAMES ADDISON FRAZER, JAMES A. FRAZER, ANTHONY FRAZER, JAMES BENJAMIN FRAZER, WILLIAM FRAZER)

---

[169] Randolph, Mrs. Islam, *Long-Long-Ago*, Columbia, Mo. E.W. Stephens Company, 1937, pp. 62-63.

[170] Illinois Deaths and Stillbirths Index, 1916-1947.

[171] Ibid.

[172] Mary Henry Taylor Randolph, U.S., Find A Grave Index, 1600s-Current, Memorial ID 18567272.

[173] Randolph, Mrs. Islam, *Long-Long-Ago*, Columbia, Mo. E.W. Stephens Company, 1937, pp. 12-13.

HEYWARD GIBBONS TAYLOR (1865-1931) (Son of
ELIZABETH FRAZER TAYLOR, JAMES ADDISON
FRAZER, JAMES A. FRAZER, ANTHONY FRAZER,
JAMES BENJAMIN FRAZER, WILLIAM FRAZER)
In 1931, at 65 years old, Heyward married Amanda Sprunt
in North Carolina.[174] He is buried at Oakdale Cemetery,
Wilmington, North Carolina.[175]

GEORGE EDMUND TAYLOR (b. 1867) (Son of
ELIZABETH FRAZER TAYLOR, JAMES ADDISON
FRAZER, JAMES A. FRAZER, ANTHONY FRAZER,
JAMES BENJAMIN FRAZER, WILLIAM FRAZER)

JULIE EDMOND TAYLOR (b. 1869) (Daughter of
ELIZABETH FRAZER TAYLOR JAMES ADDISON
FRAZER, JAMES A. FRAZER, ANTHONY FRAZER,
JAMES BENJAMIN FRAZER, WILLIAM FRAZER)

C.2.2.3.   **JAMES FRAZER** (b. 1843) (Son of JAMES ADDISON
FRAZER, JAMES A. FRAZER, ANTHONY FRAZER,
JAMES BENJAMIN FRAZER, WILLIAM FRAZER)
James married Martha N. Bush in October 1865.[176]

C.2.2.4.   **MAJOR PHILIP FOULKE FRAZER** (December
22, 1844 – May 5, 1864) (Son of JAMES ADDISON
FRAZER, JAMES A. FRAZER, ANTHONY FRAZER,
JAMES BENJAMIN FRAZER, WILLIAM FRAZER)
Philip attended Virginia Military Institute. When the
Civil War began, he as well as his two brothers, joined the
Greenbrier Rifles. He joined as 2nd Lieutenant Company
of the Virginia 27th Infantry Regiment in 1861 at just 16
years old under General Thomas "Stonewall" Jackson.[177]

---

[174] Heyward Gibbons Taylor, North Carolina County Registers of Deeds, 1741-2011.
[175] Heyward Gibbons Taylor, U.S., Find A Grave Index, 1600s-Current, Memorial No. 27000556.
[176] Marriage of James Frazer and Martha N. Bush, West Virginia Marriages Index, 1853-1970.
[177] Soldier Details, The Civil War, National Park Service, "Frazer, Philip F."

He became Captain in 1862, and later that year, was wounded. He then fought at Chancellorsville and was praised for conduct. He was promoted to Major in 1863. Philip died on May 5, 1864, at the Wilderness Battlefield, Spotsylvania County, Virginia at age 19. Like so many other young men, he gave his life for his home and beliefs. He is buried at Hollywood Cemetery, 412 South Cherry Street, Richmond, Virginia.[178]

C.2.2.5. **JULIA FRAZER EDMOND** (1847-1898). (Daughter of JAMES ADDISON FRAZER, JAMES A. FRAZER, ANTHONY FRAZER, JAMES BENJAMIN FRAZER, WILLIAM FRAZER) Julia married George Edmond in 1867.[179] Julia and George are buried at Christ Church Episcopal Cemetery, Saint Michaels, Talbot County, Maryland.[180] Known children:

DAVID EDMOND (1868-1952) (Son of JULIA FRAZER EDMOND) David married Cornelia V. Sutton. David and Cornelia are buried at Mount Olivet Cemetery, Saint Michaels, Maryland.[181]

ROBERT P. EDMOND (b. 1869/1870) (Son of JULIA FRAZER EDMOND)

PHILIP EDMOND (b. 1870) (Son of JULIA FRAZER EDMOND) Philip married Mary E. Barkman.[182]

---

[178] Major Philip Foulke Frazer, U.S., Find A Grave Index, 1600s-Current, Memorial ID 6794123.

[179] Marriage of Julia Frazer and George Edmond, West Virginia, Marriages Index, 1785-1971.

[180] Julia Frazer Edmond, U.S., Find A Grave Index, 1600s-Current, Memorial ID 105217242.

[181] David Edmond, U.S., Find A Grave Index, 1600s-Current, Memorial ID 115877659.

[182] Philip Edmond, Year: 1930; Census Place: Saint Michaels, Talbor, Maryland; Pag 3A; Enumeration District: 0008; FHL microfilm: 2340614.

MARY (MAE) EDMOND BRIDGES (1872-1945) (Daughter of JULIA FRAZER EDMOND) Mary married Richard Thomas Bridges. She is buried at Mount Olivet Cemetery, Saint Michaels, Maryland.[183]

JULIAN EDMOND (b. 1874) (Son of JULIA FRAZER EDMOND)

MATTIE EDMOND GUTHRIE (1878-1955) (Daughter of JULIA FRAZER EDMOND) Mattie married Wade H. Guthrie.[184] She is buried at Evergreen Burial Park, Roanoke, Virginia.[185]

BESSIE EDMOND (b. 1879) (Daughter of JULIA FRAZER EDMOND)

JOHN DUCAS EDMOND (abt. 1885) (Son of JULIA FRAZER EDMOND) John is buried at Christ Church Episcopal Cemetery, Saint Michaels, Maryland.[186]

C.2.2.6. **MARTHA FRAZER (AGNES HERNDON) JESSEL ANDRUS** (1853-1920)[187] (Daughter of JAMES ADDISON FRAZER, JAMES A. FRAZER, ANTHONY FRAZER, JAMES BENJAMIN FRAZER, WILLIAM FRAZER) Martha moved to St. Louis, Missouri to study drama and become an actress.[188] She traveled with her own company

[183] Mary Edmond Bridges, U.S., Find A Grave Index, 1600s-Current, Memorial ID 115877996.

[184] Mattie Edmond Guthrie, Virginia, Death Records, 1912-2014.

[185] Mattie Edmond Guthrie, U.S., Find A Grave Index, 1600s-Current, Memorial ID 102346507, Section 14, Lot 271N.

[186] John Ducas Edmond, U.S., Find A Grave Index, 1600s-Current, Memorial ID 105217302.

[187] Martha Frazer (Agnes Herndon) Jessel Andrus, "West Virginia Births," Index, 1804-1938.

[188] Gale Research Company, Detroit, Michigan, Accession Number: 2043774, Notable Names in the American Theatre, Clifton, NJ: James T. White & Co., 1976.

by the stage name of Agnes Herndon. Martha was described as "very lovely with beautiful white skin and a quantity of glorious red hair."[189] She first married Joseph A. Jessel, her manager.

On January 16, 1891, *The New York Herald* printed the following:

AGNES HERNDON DIVORCED. OTHER MARRIED COUPLES TO WHOM THE MATRIMONIAL YOKE PROVES GALLING. Judge Dugro, of the Superior Court, has granted Agnes H. Jessel, the actress, known upon the stage as "Agnes Herndon," a divorce from her husband, Joseph A. Jessel, to whom she was married in May, 1878. The case was tried before A. Vanderpoel as referee, the actress charging infidelity on the part of her husband. The Judge granted the decree in her favor upon the report of the referee.[190]

Her second marriage was to her new manager, Albert A. Andrus in 1894.[191] Agnes performed in many shows on Broadway, some of which were: "La Belle Marie," "A Trip to Chinatown," and "Lights and Shadows."

---

[189] Randolph, Mrs. Islam, *Long-Long-Ago,,* Columbia, Mo. E.W. Stephens Company, 1937, p. 69.

[190] Agnes Herndon (Martha Frazer), *The New York Herald*, January 16, 1891.

[191] Martha Frazer (Agnes Herndon) and Albert A. Andrus, New York, New York, Extracted Marriage Index, 1866-1937.

Agnes Herndon (Martha Frazer), 1890s[192]

---

[192] Agnes Herndon (Martha Frazer), Photos New York Public Library.

The Famous Mittenthal Brothers, Theatrical Producers and Managers state:

> By the spring of 1896, the elaborate "The Great Brooklyn Handicap" show had proven too expensive for extended touring and was disbanded. Instead, Aubrey and Harry went on to manage Agnes Herndon, one of America's leading actresses during the late nineteenth century. Outfitted with a rail car full of scenery, The Mittenthal Brothers took her company on a national tour and played to full and gracious houses throughout the Eastern Seaboard.
>
> But all that glittered wasn't gold for the Mittenthal brothers. Agnes Herndon had to be discharged from her second tour with the Mittenthals for being "disagreeable," and in the spring of 1899, Sam found himself in the midst of a lawsuit in Kalamazoo over his violation of a local ordinance banning theatrical entertainment on Sundays.[193]

Agnes apparently had a hobby of collecting shoes, according to an article in Ann Arbor, Ann Arbor District Library, February 23, 1894, regarding Agnes Herndon (in public domain):

> Martha died December 31, 1920.[194] Agnes Herndon Frazer Andrus' burial was listed at Fresh Pond Crematory and Columbarium, Middle Village, Queens County, New York and remains interred at Christ Church Episcopal Cemetery, Saint Michaels, Maryland.[195]
>
> Among her other performing and appearances, Martha, as stage name Agnes Herndon, appeared on the cover of Gypsy Queen Cigarettes trading cards by

---

[193] Kalamazoo Public Library, New York Public Library, "The Mittenthal Bros. of Kalamazoo."

[194] Death of Marth Frazer "Agnes Herndon," New York City Department of Records & Information Services, New York City Death Certificates; Borough: Queens; Year: 1920.

[195] Martha Frazer "Agnes Herndon," U.S., Find A Grave Index, 1600s-Current, Memorial ID 193494120 and Memorial ID 175321363.

Goodwin & Co, New York and on 1890's Sam'L A Pitts Smyra Rug, Victorian Card F, Thomas H. Hall Tobacco and others. These cards are now inexpensive collectibles but difficult to locate. I recently purchased one of her cards for the family collection.

C.2.3. **HANNAH HERNDON FRAZER THOMPSON** (February 5, 1815 – January 23, 1889) (Daughter of JAMES A. FRAZER, ANTHONY FRAZER, JAMES BENJAMIN FRAZER, WILLIAM FRAZER) Hannah was born on February 5, 1815 at White Sulphur Springs, Greenbrier County, West Virginia. She married Col. Samuel Singleton Thompson (March 28, 1801 – March 3, 1877).[196] Samuel worked as a farmer and horse breeder at times. The title Colonel was allegedly given to him by his friends. Hannah died on January 23, 1889, and she and her husband Samuel are buried at Old Stone Presbyterian Church Cemetery, Lewisburg, West Virginia.[197] Hannah had no known children.

C.2.4. **WILLIAM HERNDON FRAZER** (April 22, 1817 – August 9, 1825) (Son of JAMES A. FRAZER, ANTHONY FRAZER, JAMES BENJAMIN FRAZER, WILLIAM FRAZER) William was born April 22, 1817, in White Sulphur Springs, Greenbrier County, West Virginia. He died on August 9, 1825 at age eight. He is buried at Old Stone Presbyterian Church Cemetery, Lewisburg, West Virginia.[198]

C.2.5. **THOMAS FRAZER** (abt.1820) (Son of JAMES A. FRAZER, ANTHONY FRAZER, JAMES BENJAMIN FRAZER, WILLIAM FRAZER) No other information was located on Thomas other than in *The Herndon Family of Virginia*. Sarah

---

[196] Marriage of Hannah Herndon Frazer and Samuel Singleton Thompson, Vital Research Records-Marriage, 1812, West Virginia Department of Arts, Culture, and History.

[197] Hannah Herndon Frazer Thompson, U.S., Find A Grave Index, 1600s-Current, Memorial ID 107787957, Section B-1.

[198] William Herndon Frazer, U.S., Find A Grave Index, 1600s-Current, Memorial ID 106294892.

Thomas was born in 1820 so it is possible that there was no Thomas Frazer or perhaps Thomas died at birth.

C.2.6. **SARAH THOMAS FRAZER HARRISON** (August 1, 1820 – March 3, 1891) (Daughter of JAMES A. FRAZER, ANTHONY FRAZER, JAMES BENJAMIN FRAZER, WILLIAM FRAZER) Sarah was born on August 1, 1820 in Lewisburg, Greenbrier County, West Virginia. She married Major Harry Heth Harrison (1820 – August 11, 1893). Harry graduated from U.S. Naval Academy at Annapolis, Maryland, serving in the Navy.[199] At her father's death, Sarah inherited the Harmony Hill house and 200 acres of land. Sarah and Harry are buried at Old Stone Presbyterian Church Cemetery, Lewisburg, West Virginia.[200] Known children:

C.2.6.1. **KITTY HETH (HEATHER) HARRISON** (1858-1944) (Daughter of SARAH THOMAS FRAZER HARRISON) Kitty is buried at Old Stone Presbyterian Church Cemetery, Lewisburg, West Virginia.[201] Records list her as single.

C.2.6.2. **MARGARET CARTER HARRISON** (1860-1937)[202] (Daughter of SARAH THOMAS FRAZER HARRISON) Death Index lists Margaret's occupation as retired nurse and single.[203]

C.2.7. **MARGARET CARTER FRAZER CALWELL** (August 1, 1826 - March 20, 1896) (Daughter of JAMES A. FRAZER, ANTHONY FRAZER, JAMES BENJAMIN FRAZER, WILLIAM FRAZER) Margaret married Bedford Calwell (abt. 1813-1902) son of James Calwell, an early owner and manager of The White Sulphur Springs Resort on February 23, 1848

---

[199] *Greenbrier Independent*, "Death of Maj. H.H. Harrison, August 17, 1893.

[200] Sarah Thomas Frazer Harrison, U.S., Find A Grave Index, 1600s-Current, Memorial ID 107232931, Section B-1.

[201] Kitty Heth (Heather) Harrison, U.S., Find A Grave Index, 1600s-Current, Memorial ID 107233215, Section B-1.

[202] Margaret Carter Harrison, West Virginia, Births Index, 1804-1938.

[203] Death of Margaret Carter Harrison, West Virginia, Deaths Index, 1853-1973.

in Greenbrier County, Virginia (later became West Virginia).[204] Margaret and Bedford lived with his family at the early White Sulphur Spring Resort in their early marriage. Bedford was past the age of enlistment for the Civil War so did not serve. Margaret died at age 70 on March 20, 1896 in White Sulphur Springs, Greenbrier County, West Virginia.[205] Known children:

C.2.7.1. **MARY ELIZABETH CALWELL YOUNG** (1849 - 1878)[206] (Daughter of MARGARET CARTER FRAZER CALWELL) Mary married Edgar Mantlebert Young in 1871.[207] Mary is buried at Fredericksburg Cemetery, (City Cemetery), Washington Avenue, Fredericksburg, Virginia. Find A Grave lists her name as Mary Constance Calwell Young.[208]

C.2.7.2. **JAMES LEWIS CALWELL** (1852-1895)[209](Son of MARGARET CARTER FRAZERCALWELL) James married Sophia E. Hilleary in 1877.[210]

C.2.7.3. **FANNY BEDFORD CALWELL** (b 1855)[211] (Daughter of MARGARET CARTER FRAZER CALWELL)

C.2.7.4. **SARAH CALWELL** (b. 1856)[212] (Daughter of MARGARET CARTER FRAZER CALWELL)

C.2.7.5. **WILLIAM B. CALWELL (Son** of MARGARET CARTER FRAZER CALWELL)

---

[204] Marriage of Margaret Carter Frazer and Bedford Calwell, West Virginia, Marriages Index, 1785-1971.

[205] Margaret Carter Frazer Calwell, West Virginia, Deaths Index, 1853-1973.

[206] 1860 Census Place, Greenbrier, Virginia, p. 278.

[207] Marriage of Mary Elizabeth Calwell and Edgar Mantlebert Young, West Virginia, Marriages Index, 1785-1971.

[208] Mary Elizabeth Calwell Young, U.S., Find A Grave, Fredericksburg, Virginia, Memorial ID 75533211, Section 9, Lot 105, Stone 23.

[209] U.S., Sons of the American Revolution Membership Applications, 1889-1970, Volume: 279.

[210] Marriage of James Lewis Calwell and Sophia E. Hilleary, West Virginia, Marriages Index, 1785-1971.

[211] Fanny Bedford Calwell, West Virginia, Births Index, 1804-1938, FHL Film No. 595033.

[212] Sarah Calwell, West Virginia, Births Index, 1804-1938, FHL Film No. 595033.

C.2.8. **ELIZABETH "BETTIE" TAYLOR FRAZER BEIRNE**
(February 22, 1829 – November 10, 1908) (Daughter of JAMES
A. FRAZER, ANTHONY FRAZER, JAMES BENJAMIN
FRAZER, WILLIAM FRAZER) James Frazer left land and
other items to his daughter Elizabeth. She married Andrew
Beirne (1830-1888). Elizabeth and Andrew are buried at Old
Stone Presbyterian Church Cemetery, Lewisburg, Greenbrier
County, West Virginia.[213] Known children:

C.2.8.1. **BEDFORD CALWELL BEIRNE** (1852-1907) (Son of
ELIZABETH "BETTIE" TAYLOR FRAZER BEIRNE)
Bedford married Virginia Watkins Ford. He is buried at
Old Stone Presbyterian Church Cemetery, Lewisburg,
West Virginia.[214]

C.2.8.2. **PATRICK BEIRNE** (Son of ELIZABETH "BETTIE"
TAYLOR FRAZER BEIRNE)

C.2.8.3. **HARRY HEATH BEIRNE, SR.** (1857-1910) (Son of
ELIZABETH "BETTIE" TAYLOR FRAZER BEIRNE)
Harry married Blanch Scott.[215] He and Blanch are buried
at Old Stone Presbyterian Church Cemetery, Lewisburg,
West Virginia.[216]

C.2.8.4. **GORDON O. BEIRNE** (1860-1907) (Son of
ELIZABETH "BETTIE" TAYLOR FRAZER BEIRNE)
Gordon is buried at Old Stone Presbyterian Church
Cemetery, Lewisburg, West Virginia.[217]

---

[213] Elizabeth "Bettie" Taylor Frazer Beirne, U.S., Find A Grave Index, Memorial
ID 88174847.

[214] Bedford Calwell Beirne, U.S., Find A Grave Index, Memorial ID 106663324,
Section B-1.

[215] U.S., Find A Grave Index, Memorial ID 89255618.

[216] Harry Heath Beirne, Sr., U.S., Find A Grave Index, Memorial ID 35565958,
Section B-1.

[217] Gordon O. Beirne, U.S., Find A Grave Index, Memorial ID 106662710,
Section B-1.

JOSEPH ADDISON FRAZER

STAGECOACH STAND AND TAVERN PROPRIETOR, FARMER, JUSTICE OF THE PEACE AND SHERIFF GREENBRIER COUNTY, WEST VIRGINIA

the FOURTH GENERATION – BROTHER TO JAMES A. FRAZER

JOSEPH ADDISON FRAZER (May 22, 1798 – March 31, 1886) (Son of ANTHONY FRAZER, JAMES BENJAMIN FRAZER, WILLIAM FRAZER) was born on May 22, 1798 in Spotsylvania County, Virginia, the eighth child of Hannah Herndon Frazer and Anthony Frazer. Joseph preferred the use of his middle name, Addison, so in this chapter, he will be referred to as Addison. Addison was a direct ancestor to my children. He was 15 years younger than his brother James A. Frazer, mentioned in the previous chapter. Addison was six years old when his dad, Anthony, died so his oldest brother James may have played an important father figure in his life. Addison grew up on his family's farm in rural Spotsylvania County near what is currently the Spotsylvania Courthouse area.

Sometime in the years before 1820, while a young adult, Addison moved to Greenbrier County, Virginia, which later becomes West Virginia, to work with his older brother James who was managing the White Sulphur Springs Resort. On February 24, 1820, Addison married Frances "Fannie" Renick (August 28, 1799 – April 12, 1884) in Greenbrier County.[218] Addison was 22 years old and

---

[218] Marriage of Joseph Addison Frazer and Frances "Fannie" Renick, Virginia, Compiled Marriages, 1740-1850.

Fannie was 21 years old. Earlier the same month, Addison's mother Hannah died. Addison's parents Anthony and Hannah left an estate of a sizable farm.

Fannie, Addison's new wife, was one of nine children of Robert Renick II and Letitia Wells Dalton Renick and a twin to Benjamin Franklin Renick. Her father was a large landowner. The Renick family was well-known in the area, being one of the earliest settlers in the county. At her father's death, Fannie and her twin brother Benjamin were left land to be divided. Renicks Valley, today a small unincorporated community in Greenbrier County, is located about five miles northeast of the small community of Renick, also known as Falling Spring, which is located about 16 miles from Lewisburg, West Virginia. Renicks Valley was named after Major William Renick, brother to Robert and uncle to Fannie.

Renick, West Virginia

By 1823, Addison's brother James opened a tavern and inn in Lewisburg. Working with his brother, Addison gained experience that proved beneficial to him as about 20 years later he managed a tavern and stagecoach stand of his own in Sewell Valley, which at that time was in Virginia (later became West Virginia).

Addison and Fannie made their home in Greenbrier County, and by 1822, two years after their marriage, their first son Robert was born[219] followed two years later by the birth of their daughter Sarah Renick.[220] In 1827, their third child, a daughter, Fannie, was born.[221] During these years, Addison farmed his land and helped his brother James with his tavern in Lewisburg. By 1833, Addison served as a Justice of the Peace for the Greenbrier County Court and after that he was commissioned for a year as sheriff of the county. In 1836, Addison and Fannie's fourth and youngest child, James Herndon, was born.[222]

Addison and Fannie sold their property near Renick in 1843 and purchased 350 acres in what early maps considered Sewell Valley in Greenbrier County. Today, the land would be part of Rainelle. Rainelle was not chartered as a town until 1913, so this area was undeveloped at the time with only a few farms. A gristmill was built in the area about 1790, and a sawmill was built in 1848.[223] The town and progress did not set in with a rush but was slow in developing. Even so, it had long been a passageway as the James River and Kanawha Turnpike was completed through Sewell Valley in 1826. The turnpike ran from Richmond to the Kanawha River and provided for the movement of passengers and mail. Today, U.S. Route 60, also known as the Midland Trail, is a highway swooping over the mountains and valleys through beautiful scenery that follows the historic James River and Kanawha Turnpike for most part, in some places deviating a bit. The area that bordered the turnpike in Sewell Valley is much the same as in the early days as it passes small farms and mountain trails snake its way through sweeping views.

Stagecoach service was established by Caldwell and Surbough and in operation by January 1827, making one trip a week at the cost of $7 to travel from Lewisburg to Charleston.[224] Spacious taverns and stagecoach stands sprung up and the owners of these taverns became well-known and at times

---

[219] U.S., Sons of the American Revolution Membership Applications, 1889-1970.

[220] Sarah Renick Frazer, U.S., Find A Grave Index, 1600s-Current, Memorial ID 21307820.

[221] Fannie Frazer, U.S., Find A Grave Index, 1600s-Current, Memorial ID 136496870.

[222] James Herndon Frazer, U.S., Confederate Soldiers Compiled Service Records, 1861-1865.

[223] West Virginia Department of Arts, Culture and History, Rainelle.

[224] *History of Fayette County, West Virginia,* Peters, J.T. and Carden, H.B., Chapter IX, "Stage Coaches and Stage Stands," p. 132-135.

famous men. Soon, these weekly stagecoach trips increased to three days a week, and eventually, the volume of travel increased the schedule to daily runs. By 1831, the stagecoaches carried mail as well as passengers, allowing mail delivery to remote farms. The road dropped and climbed hills and through passes and gaps and became lively with travelers from morning until late at night. Stagecoaches were painted and highly varnished with passengers' baggage carried on top of the carriage and behind on a boot. The swiftest of the coaches were called "cannonball" coaches, driven by four or six horses led by adventurous young drivers who were experts in their line of work.[225] The horses were the finest that could be obtained from Kentucky or the Valley of Virginia. These spirited horses and these young "daredevil" drivers were known to drive around mountain curves on two wheels as passengers shuddered, mountain views dazzled them, and hills and hollows greeted them.[226]

The famous line of coaches found it necessary to have roadhouses and inns to accommodate the vast hordes of people that traveled this rocky and dusty route and required accommodations for caring and feeding the horses that led them. Addison and Fannie with their new land located in the beauty of the valley and meadows joined these lists of taverns and stage stands. Addison's stagecoach tavern was in rural and picturesque Sewell Valley. *The History of Fayette County, West Virginia* lists the "proprietors of the famous stage stands" and among those proprietors was Addison "Frazier" with a stage stand in Sewell Valley.[227] Historical records such as these contribute to an understanding of the time and its people and our ancestor research. It is unknown when Addison first started the stage stand and tavern as he moved to Sewell Valley in 1843, and according to the census of 1850 and 1860, Addison was a hotel keeper.[228] Addison's tavern and inn, known as the Sewell Valley Tavern, was located at the base of the Big Sewell Mountain.[229] We were unable to locate a picture of his tavern and inn, but below is a sketch of a typical stagecoach tavern of the times and the area.

---

[225] *Midland Trail of West Virginia*, Along the Old James River and Kanawha Turnpike, Reniers, Perceval and Reniers, Ashton Woodman, Greenbrier Historical Society, Inc., 1999, p. 16.

[226] Ibid.

[227] Ibid.

[228] 1850 and 1860 United States Federal Census; District 18, Greenbrier, Virginia; Roll: 947; Page 307A.

[229] *The Renicks of Greenbrier*, Harlow, Jr., B.F., 1951,

Drawing of a typical stagecoach tavern and inn
Illustrated by John McFarland

An article printed in the *Charleston Gazette* on July 24, 1949 entitled "Taverns of Yesteryear Bring Memories of Famous Men, Low Prices, Gay Times" mentions Addison "Frazier" as follows: "Micajah Smailes was host at Mountain House, Jack Sturgeon at Big Sewell Mountain House, Addison Frazier at Sewell Valley Tavern (now Rainelle) and Harrison Hickman at Little Sewell Valley House."

By 1850, the railroad had reached as far as Jackson's River and steamboat travel on the Kanawha River was popular and cheap. Stagecoach travel began to slow, and daily trips turned back into three trips a week.[230] The 1850 census indicate that Addison's son Robert and his wife Harriet and son Richard lived with them as well as Addison's daughter Fannie and son Herndon as they continued the tavern and inn business even as it slowed.[231] Ten years later, the 1860 census indicate Addison's real estate value was $8000 and his personal assets were $4370.[232]

---

[230] *Midland Trail of West Virginia*, Along the Old James River and Kanawha Turnpike, Reniers, Perceval and Reniers, Ashton Woodman, Greenbrier Historical Society, Inc., 1999, p. 6.

[231] Year: 1850; Census Place: District 18, Greenbrier, Virginia; Roll: 947; p. 307A.

[232] Year: 1860; Census Place: District 2, Greenbrier, Virginia; Page: 443; Family History Library Film: 805348.

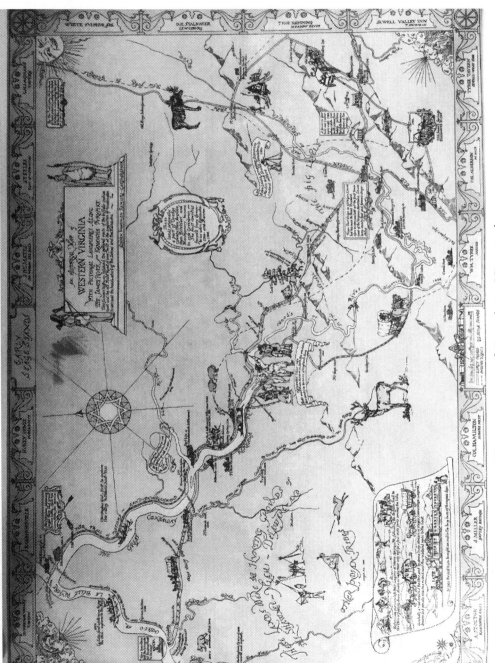

Photo courtesy of Greenbrier Historical

By spring of 1861, the Civil War erupted. The majority citizens of Greenbrier County were Southern sympathizes. As mentioned in the previous chapter, over 2000 men from Greenbrier County fought for the Confederacy.[233] Since the county was located on the James River and Kanawha Turnpike and a major stagecoach route, there were an estimated 60,000 Confederate and Union soldiers who passed through the area of Sewell Valley, often setting up encampments. The Greenbrier Valley was a strategical location for both armies.[234] These armies, Union and Confederate, most likely passed through or possibly even encamped on or near Addison's land as his tavern and inn were on the stagecoach route. Addison and Fannie left Sewell Valley and returned to Lewisburg sometime in the early years of the 1860s, the exact year is unknown. Addison would have been about 63 years old and Fannie 62 years old.

On April 17, 1861, Addison and Fannie's youngest child, James Herndon, at age 25, enlisted in the 5th Infantry as 2nd Lieutenant in the Confederate Army. James Herndon was wounded during battle on July 21, 1861 in Manassas. This was the First Battle of Bull Run also known as the Battle of Manassas. This is also the battle that General Jackson earned his nickname "Stonewall" Jackson. Before the day ended, James Herndon was wounded. He was granted leave to recover from his wound. After recovery, he returned to the Confederacy in October 1861 for duty and was promoted to Corporal. James Herndon fought in several battles and during a series of battles near Richmond, he contacted typhoid fever. James Herndon was given leave to return home to recover. He went to his sister Sarah's home in Staunton. Virginia, where his parents also lived. James Herndon did not recover. On August 23, 1862, at age 26 years old, he was one of the many soldiers who died from the disease.[235]

Also, in 1861, just a few miles beyond the base of Sewell Mountain, where Addison's inn was located, Confederate General Robert E. Lee pitched his headquarters tent on top of Sewell Mountain beneath a large Maple tree. This serene site is where Lee first viewed the beautiful light-gray-toned animal that became the famous Civil War horse. Lee acquired

---

[233] Greenbrier Historical Society, Beyond the North House Tour, More Than Meets the Eye, *The Civil War in Greenbrier County: An Overview,* July 1, 2013.
[234] Ibid.
[235] U.S., Civil War Soldier Records and Profiles, 1861-1865.

the fine-bred horse in February 1862 and changed the horse's name to Traveller for the horse's fast pace. Traveller was known for his speed, strength, and courage and Lee quickly became hooked on the horse's good looks and charm. While in Ranielle in search of Addison's tavern and inn, we rode to the top of Sewell Mountain, a trip I had done numerous times as I spent my childhood and early adult life in nearby Fayette County. This time, we visited the site of Lee's headquarters, the highest point on the Midland Trail.

Once again, I discovered that we lived near another battlefield area in Virginia without knowing that a Frazer family member fought and was wounded at the Battle of Manassas, today a peaceful and picturesque field. We pass the battlefield frequently as my thoughts go to the young men, both Union and Confederate, as they gave all they had including their lives on this field. My imagination runs wild as I resurrect the spirits of these men of long ago. Knowing the July sweltering heat and humidity in this part of Virginia, I can only imagine the heat exhaustion and weariness the combatants endured in their wool clothing, lugging their musketry while underfed and some sick and wounded. We attended a battle reenactment on one occasion, wearing our cotton summer shorts, drinking our iced drinks with camera in hand and wondered how the dedicated and authentic reenactors managed to handle an entire weekend on the open fields where the valley is dotted with ghostly scents as they battled back and forth, reminding us of our appreciation of our forefathers and the bravery held by the young as they witnessed friends killed and injured on their home front and endured the many illnesses for their beliefs.

Sometime in the early years of 1860, Addison and Fannie sold their land and moved to their daughter Sarah Summerson's home. The 1870 and 1880 census confirm they continued to live with Sarah and her husband Richard during these years. Sarah and Richard owned a farm a few miles from Staunton, which they sold and moved to the town limits of Staunton.[236] Richard Summerson, their son-in-law, died in 1880.

Addison Frazer is described in the following newspaper article published 1880 in Staunton, entitled "A Sketch of Mr. and Mrs. Addison Frazer," as stated:

---

[236] 1870 and 1880 United States Federal Census, Staunton, Augusta, Virginia; Roll M593_1634; Page 159A; Family History Library Film: 553133.

The Greenbrier (W.Va.) *Independent* copied the notice we published last week of this venerable couple, the 60th anniversary of whose marriage occurred on yesterday, March 1st, and added the following interesting sketch:

Mr. Addison Frazer was born in the county of Spotsylvania, Va., in the latter part of the last century, came to the county of Greenbrier early in the present century, was married by the Rev. John McElhenney, in the house where Mr. Joseph B. Handly now resides, on the 1st day of March, 1820, to Miss Frances Renick, daughter of the late Mr. Robert Renick and the twin sister of B.F. Renick, Esq. of Lewisburg.

Mr. Frazer was commissioned, on the recommendation of Greenbrier County Court, as a Justice of the Peace, by the Executive of Virginia, on the 15th day of March, 1833, and at the following March term of the said County Court qualified and entered upon the duties of a Justice, in which position he continued to serve his county until, on the recommendation of the Court, he was commissioned as Sheriff. He qualified at the March term, 1851, and retired from office on the 20th day of June, 1852 --- a new Constitution having been adopted by the people, all the old officers retiring and a new set of officers taking charge of State and county affairs on the 1st day of July, 1852.

It will be seen that Mr. Frazer filled office in this county for very near thirty years, and that too a trust of trouble and anxiety, with but little hope of pecuniary reward. What a commentary upon his fidelity as a public officer!

He and his wife of his youth were housekeepers in this county for over forty years, and through these years dispensed a most generous hospitality to all their friends and acquaintances. Their house was ever the retreat and welcome home of itinerant ministers of the Methodist Episcopal Church, of which society they were both honored and consistent members.

This aged and loved couple, who have been so blest of Heaven by a long life, have a large and highly respectable connection and many acquaintances and friends in the county which was so long their home, many of whom now turn to them in thought and have most pleasing recollections connected with their genial manners and unaffected goodness of heart. May these thoughts and memories incline all such to send some substantial token that may add grace and interest to title "Diamond Wedding" --- an event that happens to so few.[237]

Joseph Addison Frazer died at age 87 on March 31, 1886 in Staunton, Virginia.[238] Fannie died two years earlier on April 12, 1884 at age 84.[239] Addison and Fannie are buried at Thornrose Cemetery, 1041 West Beverley Street, Staunton, Virginia where their son James Herndon is buried.

Children of Frances "Fannie" Renick Frazer and Joseph Addison Frazer (more information on children below):

D.1.   ROBERT ADDISON FRAZER (February 11, 1822 – May 4, 1906)

D.2.   SARAH REBECCA RENICK FRAZER SUMMERSON (abt. 1824 – May 1, 1893)

D.3.   FANNIE FRAZER LINK (abt. 1827-1900)

D.4.   LIEUT. JAMES HERNDON FRAZER (abt. 1836 – August 23, 1862)

D.1.   **ROBERT ADDISON FRAZER** (1822-1906) (Son of JOSEPH ADDISON FRAZER, ANTHONY FRAZER, JAMES BENJAMIN FRAZER, WILLIAM FRAZER) Robert married

[237] *Staunton Spectator*, "A Sketch of Mr. and Mrs. Addison Frazer," March 2, 1880, p.3.

[238] Joseph Addison Frazer, U.S., Find A Grave Index, 1600s-Current, Memorial ID 21460189.

[239] Frances "Fannie" Renick Frazer, U.S., Find A Grave Index, 1600s-Current, Memorial ID 21604822.

Harriet Summerson,[240] sister to Richard Summerson who married Robert's sister Sarah. See chapter on **ROBERT ADDISON FRAZER.**

D.2. **SARAH REBECCA RENICK FRAZER SUMMERSON** (abt. 1824 – May 1, 1893) (Daughter of JOSEPH ADDISON FRAZER, ANTHONY FRAZER, JAMES BENJAMIN FRAZER, WILLIAM FRAZER) Sarah married Richard Summerson (1820 – November 20, 1880) on November 12, 1846 in Greenbrier County, West Virginia.[241] Richard was brother to Harriet Summerson who married Sarah's brother Robert. Richard was a farmer and a mail contractor. After he retired, according to a newspaper clip printed February 22, 1870, they sold their farm later known as the "Keyser Place" that was located about 2.5 miles from Staunton for $21,000[242] and moved to Staunton. Sarah's parents Addison and Fannie sold their land and home in Sewell Valley and moved in with them.

Richard died November 20, 1880. His obituary stated, "For a number of years the lower part of his body had been so badly paralyzed that it was wholly useless, but notwithstanding this severe affliction, his mind was usually active, and he was recognized as a businessman of rare shrewdness and judgment."[243]

Sarah was 56 at the time of Richard's death. Addison and Fannie continued to live with her and her children. Fannie died in 1884, and Addison died in 1886. Sarah died at age 69 after a couple of weeks illness with pneumonia on May 1, 1893 in Staunton, Virginia. Richard and Sarah are buried at Thornrose Cemetery, 1041 West Beverley Street, Staunton,

---

[240] Marriage of Robert Addison Frazer and Harriet Summerson, Virginia, Compiled Marriages, 1740-1850.

[241] Marriage of Sarah Rebecca Renick Frazer and Richard Summerson, West Virginia, Marriages Index, 1785-1971.

[242] Staunton Spectator, Staunton, Virginia, 22 February 1870, p. 3.

[243] Richard Summerson, *The Valley Virginian*, Staunton, Virginia, 25 November 1880, p. 3.

Virginia where her brother Herndon and parents are buried.[244] Known children:[245]

D.2.1. **WILLIAM FRAZER SUMMERSON** (July 21, 1847 – January 28, 1927) (Son of SARAH REBECCA RENICK FRAZER SUMMERSON, JOSEPH ADDISON FRAZER, ANTHONY FRAZER, JAMES BENJAMIN FRAZER, WILLIAM FRAZER) William married Frances Lewis "Fannie Lou" Shafer on November 18, 1873.[246] After her death, he married Cora Marshall (1865-1945) on April 17, 1906 in Washington, D.C.[247] Cora was 18 years younger than William. He and Cora lived in Washington, D.C. William worked as a dry goods merchant, farmer, and real estate developer, developing an area in Staunton known as "Summerson's Row" before he moved to Washington, D.C. He is buried at Thornrose Cemetery, 1041 West Beverley Street, Staunton, Virginia.[248]

D.2.2. **HENRY EDMUND SUMMERSON** (July 12, 1849 – July 13, 1917) (Son of SARAH REBECCA RENICK FRAZER SUMMERSON, JOSEPH ADDISON FRAZER, ANTHONY FRAZER, JAMES BENJAMIN FRAZER, WILLIAM FRAZER) Henry married Elizabeth "Bettie" Burwell Reese (1853-1929), daughter of Dr. B. P. Reese of Staunton, on October 29, 1872. He worked as a railroad clerk, and in 1881, was appointed depot agent of the C.&O. Railway.[249] Later, he worked for Andrew Bowling in his

---

[244] Sarah Rebecca Renick Frazer Summerson, U.S., Find A Grave Index, 1600s-Current, Memorial ID 21307820.

[245] *Yost's Weekly*, Staunton, Virginia, 04 May 1893.

[246] Marriage of William Frazer Summerson and Frances Lewis Shafer, Virginia Marriages, 1785-1940.

[247] Marriage of William Frazer Summerson and Cora Marshall, District of Columbia, Marriages, 1830-1921.

[248] William Frazer Summerson, U.S., Find A Grave Index, 1600s-Curretn, Memorial ID 22579530.

[249] Henry Edmund Summerson, *The Valley Virginia*, Staunton, Virginia, 02 June 1881, p. 3.

milling interests.[250] He also had an interest in a grocery firm of Wheat & Summerson located on East Main Street in Staunton, selling his interest in 1895.[251] Henry is buried at Thornrose Cemetery, 1041 West Beverley Street, Staunton, Virginia.[252]

D.2.3.   **FRANCES "FANNIE" SUMMERSON BYERS EAKLE** (May 25, 1851 – March 4, 1891) (Daughter of SARAH REBECCA RENICK FRAZER SUMMERSON, JOSEPH ADDISON FRAZER, ANTHONY FRAZER, JAMES BENJAMIN FRAZER, WILLIAM FRAZER) Fannie married James T. Byers (1848-1882)[253] on December 12, 1871.[254] James was in the grocery business, Byers and Summerson, with his brother-in-law, Henry Summerson. After James died, Fannie remarried on November 10, 1885 to Benjamin Franklin Eakle.[255] She died in 1891 at age 39 and is buried at Thornrose Cemetery, 1041 West Beverley Street, Staunton, Virginia.[256]

D.2.4.   **JUNIUS ROBERT SUMMERSON** (June 29, 1853 – December 18, 1909) (Son of SARAH REBECCA RENICK FRAZER SUMMERSON, JOSEPH ADDISON FRAZER, ANTHONY FRAZER, JAMES BENJAMIN FRAZER, WILLIAM FRAZER) Junius worked as a farmer, and in 1884, patented an invention of a pulverizing attachment

---

[250] Henry Edmund Summerson, *The News Leader*, Staunton, Virginia, 13 July 1917, p. 1.

[251] Henry Edmund Summerson, *Staunton Spectator*, Staunton, Virginia, 06 February 1895, p. 3.

[252] Henry Edmund Summerson, U.S., Find A Grave Index, 1600s-Current, Memorial ID 21307987.

[253] James T. Byers, U.S., Find A Grave Index, 1600s-Current, Memorial ID 21502081.

[254] Marriage of Frances Summerson and James T. Byers, Virginia Marriages, 1785-1940.

[255] Marriage of Frances Summerson and Benjamin Franklin Eakle, Virginia Marriages, 1785-1940.

[256] Frances Summerson Eakle, U.S., Find A Grave Index, 1600s-Current, Memorial ID 39834700.

for plows.[257] He married Mary E. Mathews Hevener (1853-1929) on January 19, 1876.[258] Junius is buried at Longwood Cemetery, Bedford, Virginia.[259]

D.2.5. **RICHARD PEYTON SUMMERSON** (abt. 1856 – March 4, 1879) (Son of SARAH REBECCA RENICK FRAZER SUMMERSON, JOSEPH ADDISON FRAZER, ANTHONY FRAZER, JAMES BENJAMIN FRAZER, WILLIAM FRAZER) Richard died of Typhoid Fever at age 23. He was a member of the West Augusta Guard, the Stonewall Brigade Band and the Staunton Artillery. Professor A. J. Turner composed a song for Richard's funeral, known as "Peyton's Funeral March."[260] Richard is buried at Thornrose Cemetery, 1041 West Beverley Street, Staunton, Virginia.[261]

D.2.6. **MARY FRAZER (FRAZIER) SUMMERSON HUNTER** (September 25, 1858 – February 7, 1931/1932)[262] (Daughter of SARAH REBECCA RENICK FRAZER SUMMERSON, JOSEPH ADDISON FRAZER, ANTHONY FRAZER, JAMES BENJAMIN FRAZER, WILLIAM FRAZER) Mary married Carter Braxton Hunter (March 6, 1861-January 11, 1947) on November 17, 1885.[263] Carter owned land in Alleghany, Virginia where he created a small summer resort. Carter was son of Dr. Henry Fielding and Mary Caroline Renick Hunter. Carter and Mary's home

---

[257] Junius Robert Summerson, *Official Gazette of the United States Patent Office*, 1318.

[258] Marriage of Junius Robert Summerson and Mary E. Mathews Hevener, Virginia, Marriages, 1785-1940.

[259] Junius Robert Summerson, U.S., Find A Grave Index, 1600s-Current, Memorial ID 95462299.

[260] Richard Peyton Summerson, *Staunton Spectator*, Staunton, Virginia, 11 March 1879.

[261] Richard Peyton Summerson, U.S. Find A Grave, 1600s-Current, Memorial ID 21307858.

[262] Mary Frazer Summerson Hunter, Virginia Department of Health; Richmond, Virginia; Virginia Deaths, 1912-2014.

[263] Marriage of Mary Frazer Summerson and Carter Braxton Hunter, Virginia, Marriages, 1785-1940.

was called "Hunterton." Death records indicate Mary died in 1931,[264] but Find A Grave indicates death was in 1932. Mary and Carter are buried at Old Stone Presbyterian Church Cemetery, Lewisburg, West Virginia.[265]

D.3.   **FANNIE FRAZER LINK** (abt. 1827-1900) (Daughter of JOSEPH ADDISON FRAZER, ANTHONY FRAZER, JAMES BENJAMIN FRAZER, WILLIAM FRAZER). Fannie married Franklin "Frank" Haskell Link (October 25, 1825 – May 22, 1889) on January 28, 1857.[266] In 1860, Fannie, Frank and their daughter Ida lived with her parents. Frank enlisted in the Confederate Army in 1863 in the Third Infantry, Local Defense.[267] By 1870, Fannie and Frank lived in Staunton.[268] Fannie (Frazier) and Frank are buried at Riverview Cemetery, Ronceverte, West Virginia.[269] Known children:

D.3.1.   **IDA FRAZER (FRAZIER) LINK HARRIS** (September 16, 1857 – February 6, 1899) (Daughter of FANNIE FRAZER LINK, JOSEPH ADDISON FRAZER, ANTHONY FRAZER, JAMES BENJAMIN FRAZER, WILLIAM FRAZER) Ida was born in Staunton, Virginia. She married Robert Windfield Harris (1849- November 23, 1902) on December 7, 1876.[270] Ida died in Salisbury, North

---

[264] Mary Frazer Summerson Hunter, Virginia, Death Records, 1912-2014.

[265] Mary Frazer Summerson, U.S. Find A Grave, 1600s-Current, Memorial ID 107158858.

[266] Marriage of Fannie Frazer and Franklin Haskell Link, West Virginia, Marriages Index, 1785-1971.

[267] Franklin Haskell Link, U.S., Confederate Soldiers Compiled Service Records, 1861-1865.

[268] Fannie Frazer Link, Year: 1870; Census Place: District 1, Augusta, Virginia; Roll: M593_1634; Page: 225A; Family History Library Film: 553133.

[269] Fannie Frazer Link, U.S. Find A Grave, 1600s-Current, Memorial ID 136496870.

[270] Marriage of Ida Frazer Link to Robert Winfield Harris, Virginia Marriages, 1785-1940.

Carolina. She and Robert are buried at Riverview Cemetery, Ronceverte, West Virginia.[271]

D.3.2. **HERNDON FRAZER LINK** (1866 – August 20, 1919) (Son of FANNIE FRAZER LINK, JOSEPH ADDISON FRAZER, ANTHONY FRAZER, JAMES BENJAMIN FRAZER, WILLIAM FRAZER) Herndon married Mary Eleanor Gee (1866-1939). Herndon is buried at Riverview Cemetery, Ronceverte, West Virginia.[272]

D.4. **LIEUT. JAMES HERNDON FRAZER** (abt. 1836 – August 23, 1862) ((Son of JOSEPH ADDISON FRAZER, ANTHONY FRAZER, JAMES BENJAMIN FRAZER, WILLIAM FRAZER) Herndon, as he was called, enlisted April 17, 1861 at Staunton, Virginia in the 5th Infantry and served as a 2nd Lieutenant[273] in the U.S. Confederate Army during the Civil War. He was wounded on July 21, 1861 in the Battle of Manassas, Virginia. After recovery, he returned to battle. He fought in several battles and during battles near Richmond, he contacted typhoid fever. He was again released to go home to recover. He went to the home of his sister Sarah where his parents also lived. Herndon did not recover. He died at age 26 on August 23, 1862 at the home of his sister and brother-in-law, Sarah and Richard Summerson, and is buried at Thornrose Cemetery, 1041 West Beverley Street, Staunton, Virginia.[274]

A touching and heartfelt obituary for James Herndon Frazer written by a friend was printed in the *Staunton Spectator*, *The Valley of the Shadow*, Civil War Era Newspapers on October 20, 1863. (Article states James died on August 28, 1863 rather than August 23, 1862 as Find A Grave indicates.) Article is as follows:

---

[271] Ida Frazer Link Harris, U.S. Find A Grave, 1600s-Current, Memorial ID 136496584.

[272] Herndon Frazer Link, U.S. Find A Grave, 1600s-Current, Memorial ID 136496872.

[273] Lieut. James Herndon Frazer, U.S., Civil War Soldier Records and Profiles, 1861-1865.

[274] Lieut. James Herndon Frazer, U.S. Find A Grave, 1600s-Current, Memorial ID 21954809.

Died, of Typhoid Fever, on the 28th day of August, 1863, at the residence of Richard Summerson, Esq., Lieutenant James Herndon Frazer, Co. L., Fifth Regiment, Va. Infantry.

At the breaking out of the present war the subject of this sketch was among the first to enter the service of his country and repaired with his Company, the West Augusta Guards, to Harper's Ferry, and under orders from Gen. Kenton Harper, assisted in the taking possession of that post. At the first battle of Manassas, he was severely wounded by a musket ball to the hip, being in close proximity to the enemy he was able to distinguish in the man who shot him and being determined he should not escape punishment, loaded his piece and supporting himself against a tree nearby, shot the Federal soldier who had wounded him. At the re-organization of the Army in April, 1862, he was elected 2nd Lieutenant, a well merited honor which his Company countered upon him. After which he fought through the battles of Winchester, Cross Keys, Port Republic, and the series of desperate fights around Richmond, where amid the fever breeding swamps at Chickahominy was contracted the disease, destined ere long to cut short the golden thread of life, and still forever the beating of a noble heart, patriotic and brave as ever beat in a bosom of man.

On the march from Richmond to camp near Gordonsville, Lieut. Frazer was sent home, suffering with Typhoid Fever. All hoped and expected that he would soon rejoin his Regiment invigorated and well, but, alas, our hopes were short lived. At home he received the attention of skillful physicians and the affectionate care of a fond mother and sister, but all efforts to arrest the disease proved unavailing and he died in the early days of his young manhood full of hope and promise to himself and friends. Young Frazer was no ordinary man. The writer knew him as a bosom friend in the happy days of peace and national tranquility. Amid the stormy scene of the death covered battlefield, on the long weary march and around the campfire, he never had a duty in life assigned him that he did not perform well. Intrepid, zealous and brave as a soldier in defense of his country's cause. With a soul full of generous and noble impulse, and a happy cheerfulness of mind amid every scene which nothing seemed to damp, he possessed indeed every quality of mind and heart that makes up the perfect man, and whom friends delight to love. He belonged to no body of professed Christians; yet he reverenced religion as a holy thing, the early teachings of a pious mother was sacredly remembered, and when the mass gathered around the bivouac fire to sing the evening's hymn of praise and send up the soldier's prayer to the soldier's God, none bowed more reverently and humbly than he.

On the battlefield, upon the rude, yet more kindly, camp cot, in the Soldier's Hospital, and amid the more favored scenes of home where fond affection kept watch and soothed the sufferings of the maimed and wounded, or the fever racked frame, have the parents and kindred of our country been called upon to offer up their loved ones as sacrifices upon the alter of liberty and their country's cause, among the fallen host is now numbered the noble gallant young man of whom we write. We mourn with them the loss of their dutiful, affectionate son and brother, for we loved him better than all our other friends, and the memory of his friendship and generous benefactions from our early boyhood, came to us and linger in the recesses of memory like some pleasant dream to come again.

Green be the turf above thee, Friend of my early days. B.P.J.[275]

---

[275] Staunton Spectator, The Valley of the Shadow, Civil War Era Newspapers, Obituary for James Herndon Frazer, October 20, 1863.

* * * * *

The Indian Attack
Family of Frances "Fannie" Renick Frazer

The Renick family of which "Fannie" was a descendant was one of the earliest families in Greenbrier County, settling fifteen miles north of Lewisburg along Route 219, The Seneca Trail. Fannie was the wife of my children's direct ancestor, Joseph Addison Frazer.

Fannie's grandfather, Robert Renick I, born about 1710 in Ireland,[276] arrived in America, fleeing from religious and political prosecution as did so many of his fellow countrymen. Robert first settled in Pennsylvania upon arrival in America and then moved to Augusta County, Virginia in about 1740.[277] Land was available for new arrivals in America and many settled in Augusta County. This land served as a buffer between the wild frontier and the native Indians and the colonies that had already been settled. The freedom and the land came with a price. The settlers were under constant Indian attacks who considered these newcomers as encroaching on their home and land.

Fannie's grandmother, Elizabeth Ann Archer Renick, was the daughter of Rebecca Thompson and Sampson Archer, who came to America from Northern Ireland in 1737. Sampson took claim of about 1000 acres of land as part of the "Borden Grant" also known as the "Irish Tract" located in what was Augusta County and in the present-day Rockbridge County. This grant was authorized by the colonial government to Benjamin Borden to recruit 100 settlers, each to receive 1000 acres. The purpose of the grant was to promote settlement. Archer's tract of land was near Natural Bridge, Virginia in what is now Rockbridge County.[278] It was stated that Sampson Archer's tract of land and home were near Gilmore's Spring, now Gilmore's Mills, near the confluence of Cedar Creek and James River, near Natural Bridge.[279]

---

[276] Harlow, Jr., B.F., *The Renicks of Greenbrier*, 1951, p. 3.

[277] Ibid.

[278] History of American Women, Colonial Women, 18th-19th Century Women, Civil War Women, Indian Captive, Elizabeth Archer Renick.

[279] "An Inquiry into the Origin of the Family of Archer in Kilkenny, with Notices of Other Families of the Name in Ireland," Lawrence-Archer, Captain, J.H., p. 41.

In 1740, Fannie's grandfather Robert Renick, who was about 30 years old, was granted a patent of 400 acres of land on the Buffalo Lick Branch in Augusta County.[280] About 1741, Elizabeth Archer married Robert Renick. It is thought that Elizabeth was about 16 years old when married, but this is not documented. Robert was in the Virginia militia and advanced quickly through the ranks. He was a captain in the cavalry, and active in warfare with the Indians. In 1757, he obtained a grant of 90 acres on Purgatory Creek, a branch of the James River in what was Augusta County. Robert and Elizabeth made their home on this land.[281] According to the following historical marker, Renick's home was a few miles north of present-day Natural Bridge, Virginia.

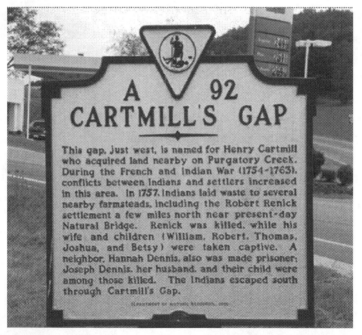

A 92
CARTMILL'S GAP

This gap, just west, is named for Henry Cartmill who acquired land nearby on Purgatory Creek. During the French and Indian War (1754-1763), conflicts between Indians and settlers increased in this area. In 1757, Indians laid waste to several nearby farmsteads, including the Robert Renick settlement a few miles north near present-day Natural Bridge. Renick was killed, while his wife and children (William, Robert, Thomas, Joshua, and Betsy) were taken captive. A neighbor, Hannah Dennis, also was made prisoner; Joseph Dennis, her husband, and their child were among those killed. The Indians escaped south through Cartmill's Gap.

The historical marker is located near Greyledge in Botetourt County on Arcadia Road (Virginia Route 614), Buchanan, Virginia

The French and Indian War, also known as The Seven Years' War, had been in progress since 1756 in the Colonies. Forts had been constructed

---

along the frontier for protection, and men were sent out from the forts daily to scout the areas, especially the mountain gaps.

On the hot summer day of July 25, 1757, a band of about 60 Shawnee warriors avoided the fort at the mouth of Looney's Creek and passed through a gap at Purgatory Mountain and ascended on Purgatory Creek where Robert and Elizabeth made their home. The Shawnee attacked the home of Joseph Dennis, killing him, his child, and Thomas Perry who was helping with chores. They took captive Joseph's wife Hannah. The warriors proceeded to the Renick home. Robert Renick was visiting a neighboring home. The Shawnee captured Robert's wife Elizabeth Renick and their seven children: William, Thomas, Joshua, Elizabeth "Betsy," Margaret, Nancy, and Robert.[282] The historical marker shown above indicates Elizabeth Renick and five children were taken captive. The Shawnee proceeded to the neighboring home of Thomas Smith where Robert Renick was visiting and shot and scalped Smith and Renick and took Mrs. Smith and a white servant girl, Sally Jew, as captives.

Audley Paul, William Maxwell, and George Matthews were on their way to Smith's home when they heard shots. Upon arriving, they saw the bodies of Smith and Renick and quickly turned their horses around to leave while bullets whizzed by them. Years later, after Elizabeth Renick returned to her family and friends, she reported that the Indians saw the men approaching the home. Some of the Shawnee hid in the home while the other warriors took the captives to the side of the home, concealing them behind fallen timber. Elizabeth stated that she sat tied between four Indians with their guns braced on a log as they shot at Matthews and the other men, wounding one.

The men escaped the Indians and alerted neighbors who gathered at Paul's stockade fort at Big Spring near Springfield. The women and children stayed within the fort guarded by six men as a party of twenty-two men, including George Matthews, who led the party, went in pursuit of the Indians.[283] George Matthews was nephew to Elizabeth and son of Captain John Matthews and Elizabeth's sister Ann Archer Matthews. George's dad, John Matthews, and Elizabeth's dad, Sampson Archer, were neighbors and fellow immigrants. Archer settled at Gilmore's Spring, east

---

[282] Harlow, Jr., B.F., *The Renicks of Greenbrier*, 1951, p. 4.
[283] Ibid.

of the Natural Bridge tavern, and Matthews settled on the Forks of the James below Natural Bridge.[284] (In 1793, George Matthews, Elizabeth's nephew, became governor of the State of Georgia.)

The Shawnee split in two groups, one took the captives and stolen horses and the other group headed to other settlements with plans of spreading further havoc. Matthews and his men caught up with one group, battling with them, but darkness settled in and rain came down and the Shawnee escaped. Nine Shawnee were dead during the battle, and the white losses were Benjamin Smith, Thomas Maury, and Mr. Jew (Sally's father).[285]

The Shawnee who escaped met up with the other group of Shawnee warriors and their captives and embarked on their journey to various Indian towns in Miami Valley in southwest Ohio. During this long journey, it was said that Elizabeth, who was pregnant, carried her son Robert, who was about 18 months and who consistently cried, irritating the Indians. Eventually, the Indians put an end to the crying infant by hitting his head against a tree, killing the young child. The horror of watching these strange men kill her helpless infant is unfathomable. What would captivity bring to her children and herself? Would they be scalped with hair hung on a pole as others had been or tortured or burned at stakes as so many stories had been told of white captives? How does one recover from living among such violent and unthinkable measures? Elizabeth's husband and young son were dead. The emotional and physical horrors would have to linger for all of them. Once the Indians reached their destination, Elizabeth and her children were separated, divided among their captors. Would she ever see her children again? Everyone and everything had been taken away except her unborn baby and her own life.

Shortly after reaching the Indian villages, Elizabeth gave birth to her child. She named this child Robert as well in honor of her dead husband and dead child. Later, Elizabeth told some of her relatives that the Indians put her in a wigwam and allowed her to attend to herself when she gave birth. Among the nourishment they gave her was fat from bear entrails.[286]

---

[284] *The Virginia Magazine of History and Biography*, Vol. 77, No. 3, "George Mathews, Frontier Patriot," Vol. 77, No. 3, Herndon, G. Melvin, P. July 1969, pp. 307-328.

[285] Ibid.

[286] Harlow, Jr., B.F., *The Renicks of Greenbrier*, 1951, p. 33.

Elizabeth's young son Joshua, who was taken from Elizabeth, was raised by an Indian family, the well-known Tecumseh's parents. Tecumseh became a Shawnee warrior and chief and one of the most celebrated Native American leaders. Joshua became companions with Tecumseh and his younger brother Tenskwatawa, a religious and political leader of the Shawnee, known as "The Prophet."[287] In the early 1800s, Tecumseh and Tenskwatawa established a village known by the Americans as Prophetstown. Today, this would be located north of Lafayette, Indiana.

About 1765, pursuant to the Bouquet peace treaty, all white captives were to be returned in exchange for a compromise not to destroy the Indian villages.[288] This was eight years after Elizabeth's capture. Elizabeth Renick and sons William and Robert II returned with her. Her daughter Elizabeth "Betsy" and the toddler Robert died during captivity and her son Joshua chose to remain with the Indian tribe. Joshua married an Indian wife and became a Miami chief. Her son Thomas returned later but then left again to settle on the Scioto River. Her daughters Margaret and Nancy returned home to Elizabeth. As Elizabeth and her children had been separated, they returned to a home after years in captivity to a family and lifestyle they no longer knew or understood.

Robert Renick II, who was born in the Indian village after his mother and siblings were captured, was the father of Frances "Fannie" Renick Frazer, the wife of Joseph Addison Frazer and a direct ancestor to my children. Robert made his home in Greenbrier County. He is buried at Jarrett Farm Cemetery, Alta, West Virginia. This is a rural cemetery with graves unmarked. There is no maintenance, and access to the cemetery is by permission of multiple property owners.

Major William Renick, older brother of Robert, became a soldier. William settled on 1000 acres he acquired in what is today Renicks Valley, West Virginia. He married Sarah Hamilton in 1768, and they made their home on this farmland.[289] Today it is known as The William Renick Farm or Renick Farm but is no longer owned by a Renick.

---

[287] History of American Women, Indian Captives, Elizabeth Archer Renick.

[288] *The Ohio Frontier: Crucible of the Old Northwest, 1720-1830*. Hurt. R. Douglas, Bloomington, IN: Indiana University Press, 1996.

[289] Greenbrier, West Virginia Pioneers and Their Homes, Dayton, Ruth Woods, West Virginia Publishing Company, 1942, pp.211-214.

Renick Farmhouse, U.S. Route 219, Built 1792
Library of Congress, Public Domain

Renicks Valley is located five miles outside the town of Renick, once known as Falling Spring, West Virginia. in 1913, the name of the town of Falling Spring was changed to Renick by the postal service to avoid the confusion of the community of Falling Spring located in Virginia. This farm owned by William Renick was passed down to other Renick generations. The historic home located on Renick Farm was listed on the *National Register of Historic Places* in 1997.[290]

During the Summer of 2020, we visited Lewisburg and Renick. Renick (also known as Falling Spring) is a small quiet rural community. The following pictures were taken of what was once William Renick's farmhouse.

---

[290] National Register Information System." *National Register of Historic Places.* National Park Service. July 9, 2010.

Photo taken by Lillian Frazer, Summer 2020

Photo taken by Lillian Frazer, Summer 2020

ROBERT ADDISON FRAZER

TAVERN KEEPER AND FARMER
SEWELL VALLEY, WEST VIRGINIA

THE FIFTH GENERATION

ROBERT ADDISON FRAZER (February 11, 1822 – May 4, 1906) (Son of JOSEPH ADDISON FRAZER, ANTHONY FRAZER, JAMES BENJAMIN FRAZER, WILLIAM FRAZER) was the oldest child of four of Joseph Addison Frazer and Frances "Fannie" Renick Frazer of the John Renick II family of Falling Spring, Greenbrier County. Robert was known as "Bob," and in written records his name was often spelled "Frazier." He was born on February 11, 1822 near Falling Spring, Greenbrier County, in what was then Virginia but later became a part of West Virginia. It is in this area that Robert grew to adulthood. Falling Spring, as mentioned in the previous chapter, is a small rural community also known as "Renick" located about 16 miles from Lewisburg, West Virginia.

In 1843, Robert's parents purchased land in Sewell Valley, Virginia in what today is known as Rainelle, West Virginia and opened a stagecoach tavern and inn at the base of Big Sewell Mountain. The tavern and inn were known as the Sewell Valley Tavern. We were unable to locate the exact location of the tavern, but the base of the mountain is a lovely area with natural scenery for the full limit of one's vision. The distant hills and valleys provide a beautiful landscape view. We once owned rental property near the base of Sewell Mountain. Each visit to the property left me in awe of the surrounding loveliness. On some mornings, the dense fog hung in folds along the tops of the surrounding hillsides. In the fall, the splendor of the blue sky riding the horizon of the golds, oranges, and yellows that burst from the trees was a sight to behold. The magnificence of it all seemed to cast a spell of peace and tranquility upon me. And, yet, in the years of the Civil War, the area was far from peaceful.

During the mid-1800s, only a few people inhabited Sewell Valley and the surrounding mountain slopes with just a few farms that dotted the valley. Robert lived with his parents, farmed the land, and assisted with the tavern and inn. He married Harriet E. Summerson (1830-1906) on March 6, 1849 in Greenbrier County.[291] Robert was about 27 years old and Harriet 19. Harriet was born in 1830 in Charlottesville, Albemarle County, Virginia and was sister to Richard Summerson, who married Robert's sister Sarah a few years earlier in 1846.

Robert and Harriet had their first child, Richard "Dick" in December 1849.[292] The 1850 census indicates that Robert, Harriet, and Richard lived with Robert's parents Addison and Fannie at Sewell Valley, and Robert worked with his dad in the inn and tavern.[293] Business was good. The road had been lively as the stagecoach movement kept them busy and added to the excitement of their lives. Now, clouds started appearing as railroad lines and trains began replacing the need of stagecoach stands. Coach line schedules dwindled down. The Frazer family continued living in Sewell Valley even as business and travel slowly stilled. The magic of the railroad was striking slow deathblows to the stagecoach lines and Robert's life. Then the Civil War approached in the spring of 1861, leaving nothing much to travel the roads other than soldiers and cannons. Robert's dad, Addison, was now 62 years old and Robert about 39.

Greenbrier County was located on the James River and Kanawha Turnpike as well as Frazer's land and tavern. In addition to the Union and Confederate troops, Guerrilla conflict was strong in the mountains. Not only did the Guerilla warfare contribute to war efforts close to home, but it also opened a door to violence and lawlessness among some of the men. The war unleashed chaos in the sparsely populated mountains and the valley settlers felt that turmoil and feared the unruliness it brought. As

---

[291] Marriage of Robert Addison Frazer and Harriet E. Summerson, Virginia, Compiled Marriages, 1740-1850.

[292] Richard Summerson Frazer, U.S., Find A Grave Index, 1600s-Current.

[293] Year: 1850; Census Place: District 18, Greenbrier, Virginia; Roll: 31774_4206369.

mentioned in the previous chapter, just a few miles from the Frazer's tavern and home, upon the summit at the top of the mountain, among the giant trees of Big Sewell, General Lee set up headquarters in the Fall of 1861.[294] The Federals faced the Confederates from the opposite hill, sparring back and forth as canons exploded. It was said about 17,000 of these troops operated near Sewell Mountain area.[295]

Robert and Harriet now had a large family of six children: Richard, William, Charles, Sarah "Sallie," Benjamin Franklin, Hannah, and their seventh child Rosabel was born in 1861. The home and inn were unsafe for 7 young children, and business had ceased along with the stagecoaches.

---

[294] The Greenbrier Historical Society, *Beyond the North House Tour*, "The Civil War in Greenbrier County: An Overview," July 1, 2013.
[295] W.V. Roadsides and History, 2015, Sewell Mountain Campaign.

The following was written for the *Richmond Daily Dispatch*, "Top of the Big Sewell Mountain, September 16, 1861" and described life in the Sewell Valley and Sewell Mountain for families during the war.

> For the short time I have been in the service I have seen much of the article we call war, in all its degrees of sunshine and of shadow. I have seen the sick and the wounded, the dead and the dying. I have seen our brave men marching along almost impassable roads and soaked by the most drenching rains. I have seen them sometimes hungry, and thirsty, and compelled to lie down at night upon the naked earth for their beds and a single blanket for their covering. All these things and more are the necessary concomitants of war, and never fail to touch the sympathies of the human heart. But that sight which has touched me most, and which makes the blood of our soldiers burn hottest, is that of the helpless families of women and children who have been compelled to flee past us to escape the vandalism of the scoundrels who are so wickedly invading our soil. These helpless people are compelled to bundle up what little of their chattels they can carry with them, on horses and in their hands and, leaving their comfortable homes and property to the savage depredations of the enemy, flee to the rear of our lines for safety. R.H.G.[296]

---

[296] West Virginia Archives and History, "Timeline of West Virginia: Civil War and Statehood, September 23, 1861," West Virginia Department of Arts, Culture and History.

No records indicate that Robert fought in the war. According to a family member as stated in his writings, Robert was a "self-taught medical doctor," treating man and beast. He supposedly unofficially treated men from both the Union and Confederate Armies during the Civil War.[297]

Sometime in the early years of 1860s, Robert's dad Addison sold his land and moved into the home of their daughter Sarah Frazer Summerson and Richard Summerson in Staunton, Virginia. Robert and Harriet also moved. In Robert's obituary posted by "A Friend" in the *Nicholas Chronicle* as printed below states that Robert Frazer was a prosperous businessman before the Civil War and *"lost everything during that troublous period"* and *"he was never able to recover from the effects of his loss."* By the 1870 census, Robert was living in Cabin Creek in Kanawha County, West

---

[297] Frazer, Lyle and Loretta, *The Frazer Family from Scotland to America*, 2015, p. 71.

Virginia[298] and farming the land. By 1880, Robert lived in Hamilton, Nicholas County, West Virginia and continued farming. By 1900, he lived in Summersville with his son Richard and family.

According to William Sydney Laidley in his book of Charleston and Kanawha County, he writes the following:

> Robert A. Frazer was born February 11, 1822, near Falling Spring, Greenbrier County, Virginia. now West Virginia, where he followed farming at the foot of the Big Sewell Mountain, and, in earlier days, with his father, conducted a tavern there on a stagecoach line. Mr. Frazer was descended from Scottish ancestry. The Frazers were among the most prominent families of Scotland and came to Virginia at an early day. Addison Frazer, the father of Robert A. Frazer, came to Greenbrier County from Spotsylvania County, Virginia. His mother was a Miss Renick of Falling Springs, Greenbrier County. The Renicks were also Scotch. Both Robert A. Frazer and wife died in Nicholas County. They had seven children, namely: Richard S., William A., Charles Herndon, Benjamin F. R. F., Sallie, Hannah T. and Rose. Robert A. Frazer died May 4, 1906. His wife was Harriet E. Summerson, of Charlottesville, Virginia, sister of Richard Summerson, of Augusta County, Virginia.[299]

Robert died on May 4, 1906 in Nicholas County, West Virginia at age 84.[300] According to Frazer family descendants, Robert and Harriet are buried at Pettigrew Cemetery in Enon, Virginia.[301] This cemetery does not list all names of those buried there, so we were unable to verify these

---

[298] Year: 1870; Census Place: Cabin Creek, Kanawha, West Virginia: Roll: M593_ 1690; Page: 30A; Family History Library Film: 553189.

[299] *History of Charleston and Kanawha County, West Virginia, and Representative Citizens,* by Laidley, W.S. (William Sydney), 1839-1917, p. 485.

[300] Robert Addison Frazer, West Virginia, Deaths Index, 1853-1973.

[301] Frazer, Lyle and Loretta, *The Frazer Family from Scotland to America,* 2015, p.72.

burial grounds for Robert and Harriet. An obituary of Robert as printed in the *Nicholas Chronicle* states:

> Robert A. Frazer was born Feb. 11, 1822, near Falling Spring, Greenbrier County, Virginia (now W.Va.), and died May 4, 1906, at the home of his son, Richard S. Frazer, near Summersville, Nicholas County, West Virginia, aged 84 years, 2 months, and 23 days.
>
> Mr. Frazer was descended from Scottish ancestry. The Frazer's were among the most prominent families of Scotland and came to Virginia at an early day. His father, Addison Frazer came to Greenbrier County, from Spotsylvania County, Virginia. His mother was a Miss Renick, a sister of the late B.F. Renick, of Falling Spring, Greenbrier County. The Renicks were also Scotch. Addison Frazer, after his marriage, settled in the Sewell Valley, where he kept a stage stand to the beginning of the Civil War.
>
> Robert A. Frazer married a Miss Summerson, sister of Richard Summerson of Augusta County, Virginia. Mrs. Frazer died several years since.
>
> In 1865 Mr. Frazer, having lost everything during the war, moved to Kanawha County, where he lived till 1873 when he came to Nicholas County and for a time lived in Beaver District. Before the death of Mrs. Frazer he and she made their home with their son Richard S.
>
> At the beginning of the Civil War he was a prosperous businessman but, as we have said, lost everything during that troublous period, and being well advanced in age, and somewhat disheartened by his financial troubles, he was never able to recover from the effects of his loss. He was a big hearted, open handed man and one cause of his failure in business was his inability to refuse to "go security" for some friend.
>
> Mr. Frazer was, intellectually, a strong man. His mind was a retentive one and he had read and studied

until he was well posted on the current topics of the day. Intelligent, with a fine conversational talent, it was a pleasure to converse with him. One could always feel assured of learning from him. No man was more genial, pleasant and interesting, in social life, than R.A. Frazer. He numbered his friends by the hundred; was always ready and willing to assist any one in trouble; faithful in his friendships; forgiving his enemies, if any he had; law abiding; a good neighbor, a tender loving husband and an indulgent father. His life had been such toward his fellow men, that when other blessings were taken away, he realized that he had acquired a good friend, he had a blessing which improved in value when the others failed.

Four sons, Richard S., William A., B.F., who reside in Nicholas County, and Charles, who lives in Kanawha County, one daughter, Miss Hannah Frazer of New York, 23 grandchildren and 14 great-grandchildren survive him.

Of the inner life, his religious convictions, one may judge when he considers that Mr. Frazer's ancestry was Scotch. His people were members of the different protestant denominations and his early training had formed his mind so that it received the truth as taught by Christianity. Quiet, undemonstrative, he rarely spoke of his views concerning the higher life yet we are assured that he was a believer. His life was pure, upright and clean and those who knew him best can say that he was a good and true man.

He lived to an old age, with mind and senses unimpaired. He knew that most difficult chapter in the great art of living, how to grow old. Surrounded by those he loved he passed into the valley. A Friend[302]

Known children of Robert and Frances "Fannie" Renick Frazer were (more information on children below):

---

[302] As posted in the *Nicholas Chronicle taken from The Frazer Family from Scotland to America*, Frazer, Lyle and Loretta, 2015, p.72.

E.1.   RICHARD SUMMERSON FRAZER (December 25, 1849 –
        July 7, 1938)

E.2.   WILLIAM ADDISON FRAZER (1851- July 7, 1940)

E.3.   CHARLES HERNDON FRAZER (May 5, 1853 – January
        19, 1922)

E.4.   SARAH "SALLIE" FRAZER (abt. 1856 - Unknown)

E.5.   BENJAMIN FRANKLIN RENICK FRAZER (January 19,
        1858 – September 25, 1934)

E.6.   HANNAH FRAZER (June 22, 1859 - Unknown)

E.7.   ROSABEL FRAZER REYNOLDS (August 31, 1861 - Unknown)

E.1.   **RICHARD SUMMERSON FRAZER** (December 25, 1849 –
        July 7, 1938) (Son of ROBERT ADDISON FRAZER, JOSEPH
        ADDISON FRAZER, ANTHONY FRAZER, JAMES
        BENJAMIN FRAZER, WILLIAM FRAZER) Richard was born
        on December 25, 1849 in what was Sewell Valley and later known
        as Rainelle, West Virginia. In 1870, he worked as a coal miner
        and lived with his parents at Cabin Creek in Kanawha County,
        West Virginia.[303] Also in 1870, he married Hannora "Nora"
        O'Meara (January 14, 1853 – December 4, 1920), daughter of
        Daniel O'Meara.[304] In 1880, Richard, at age 31, lived in Cabin
        Creek, West Virginia and continued working as a coal miner.[305]
        Before 1900, Richard and Hanora lived in Summersville, West
        Virginia and worked as a farmer, and by 1910, he was living in
        Beaver working as a farmer. In 1920, by age 70, Richard lived in
        Richwood and worked as an upholsterer[306] and repaired furniture.
        Richard died on July 7, 1938 at age 88. Hannora died at age 67 on
        December 4, 1920. Richard and Hannora are buried at Saint John's
        Catholic Church Cemetery, Summersville, Nicholas County, West

---

[303] Richard Summerson Frazer, 1870 United States Federal Census.

[304] Marriage of Richard Summerson Frazer and Hannora "Nora" O'Meara, West
Virginia, Marriages Index, 1785-1971.

[305] Year: 1880; Census Place: Cabin Creek, Kanawha, West Virginia; Roll: 1405;
Page 172D; Enumeration District: 047.

[306] Year: 1920; Census Place: Richwood, Nicholas, West Virginia; Roll: T625-1965;
Page: 3B; Enumeration District: 100.

Virginia.[307] Among their children are (names of children taken from 1880 and 1900 census and verified with Find A Grave):

E.1.1. **MARY JOSPHINE FRAZER TRENT** (April 27, 1871 – July 28, 1953) (Daughter of RICHARD SUMMERSON FRAZER, ROBERT ADDISON FRAZER, JOSEPH ADDISON FRAZER, ANTHONY FRAZER, JAMES BENJAMIN FRAZER, WILLIAM FRAZER) Mary married Andrew J. Trent in 1894.[308]

E.1.2. **ROBERT FRAZER** (abt. 1872 - Unknown) (Son of RICHARD SUMMERSON FRAZER, ROBERT ADDISON FRAZER, JOSEPH ADDISON FRAZER, ANTHONY FRAZER, JAMES BENJAMIN FRAZER, WILLIAM FRAZER)

E.1.3. **HARRIET T. FRAZER** (July 23, 1874 – February 12, 1894) (Daughter of RICHARD SUMMERSON FRAZER, ROBERT ADDISON FRAZER, JOSEPH ADDISON FRAZER, ANTHONY FRAZER, JAMES BENJAMIN FRAZER, WILLIAM FRAZER) Harriet died at age 19. She is buried at Saint John's Catholic Church Cemetery, Summersville, West Virginia.[309]

E.1.4. **WILLIAM D. FRAZER** (July 8, 1876 – March 5, 1928) (Son of RICHARD SUMMERSON FRAZER, ROBERT ADDISON FRAZER, JOSEPH ADDISON FRAZER, ANTHONY FRAZER, JAMES BENJAMIN FRAZER, WILLIAM FRAZER) William married Lula Edna Neil in 1902.[310]

E.1.5. **HANORA ELLEN FRAZER** (March 2, 1879 – January 8, 1957) (Daughter of RICHARD SUMMERSON FRAZER,

---

[307] Richard Summerson Frazer, U.S., Find A Grave Index, 1600s-Current, Memorial ID 122588208.

[308] Marriage of Mary Josphine Frazer and Andrew J. Trent, West Virginia, Marriages Index, 1785-1971.

[309] Harriet T. Frazer, U.S., Find A Grave Index, 1600s-Current, Memorial ID 122588163.

[310] Marriage of William D. Frazer and Lula Edna Neil, West Virginia Marriages, 1853-1970.

ROBERT ADDISON FRAZER, JOSEPH ADDISON FRAZER, ANTHONY FRAZER, JAMES BENJAMIN FRAZER, WILLIAM FRAZER) Hanora was single. She is buried at Saint John's Catholic Church Cemetery, Summersville, West Virginia.[311]

E.1.6.   **GERTRUDE FRAZER** (February 11, 1881 – November 29, 1962) (Daughter of RICHARD SUMMERSON FRAZER, ROBERT ADDISON FRAZER, JOSEPH ADDISON FRAZER, ANTHONY FRAZER, JAMES BENJAMIN FRAZER, WILLIAM FRAZER) Gertrude is buried at Saint John's Catholic Church Cemetery, Summersville, West Virginia.[312]

E.1.7.   **RICHARD PEYTON (PAYTON) FRAZER** (November 15, 1882 - Unknown) (Son of RICHARD SUMMERSON FRAZER, ROBERT ADDISON FRAZER, JOSEPH ADDISON FRAZER, ANTHONY FRAZER, JAMES BENJAMIN FRAZER, WILLIAM FRAZER)

E.1.8.   **BENJAMIN F. FRAZER** (August 10, 1883 - Unknown) (Son of RICHARD SUMMERSON FRAZER, ROBERT ADDISON FRAZER, JOSEPH ADDISON FRAZER, ANTHONY FRAZER, JAMES BENJAMIN FRAZER, WILLIAM FRAZER)

E.1.9.   **FLORENCE ROSELLA FRAZER** (August 1885 – October 27, 1967) (Daughter of RICHARD SUMMERSON FRAZER, ROBERT ADDISON FRAZER, JOSEPH ADDISON FRAZER, ANTHONY FRAZER, JAMES BENJAMIN FRAZER, WILLIAM FRAZER) Florence is buried at Saint John's Catholic Church Cemetery, Summersville, West Virginia.[313]

---

[311] Hanora Ellen Frazer, U.S., Find A Grave Index, 1600s-Current, Memorial ID 122587866.

[312] Gertrude Frazer, U.S., Find A Grave Index, 1600s-Current, Memorial ID 122587845.

[313] U.S., Find A Grave Index, 1600s-Current, Memorial ID 122587827.

E.2.   **WILLIAM ADDISON FRAZER** (1851- July 7, 1940) (Son of ROBERT ADDISON FRAZER, JOSEPH ADDISON FRAZER, ANTHONY FRAZER, JAMES BENJAMIN FRAZER, WILLIAM FRAZER) William was born in 1851 in Greenbrier County. The family lived in Rainelle, West Virginia. In 1870, he lived with his family in Cabin Creek. William married Emily Frances Baber (October 14, 1857 – January 7, 1948) on November 21, 1878 in Nicholas County.[314] In 1880, he and "Fanny" lived with his parents in Hamilton in Nicholas County. By 1900, and perhaps earlier, William lived in Beaver, West Virginia. He worked as a farmer. He continued living in Beaver until his death on July 7, 1940[315] at age 88. He and Emily were buried at the Frazer Cemetery, Tioga, Nicholas County, West Virginia.[316] The family cemetery is located off Route 55 at Beaver, off Tioga Road to Lick Ford Road. The cemetery is on a ridge behind a farmhouse. The 1900 census lists the following as children of William and Emily Frazer and verified by Find A Grave:

E.2.1.   **WILLIE BELLE FRAZER** (January 24, 1880 – October 22, 1883) (Son of WILLIAM ADDISON FRAZER, ROBERT ADDISON FRAZER, JOSEPH ADDISON FRAZER, ANTHONY FRAZER, JAMES BENJAMIN FRAZER, WILLIAM FRAZER) Willie died at age two or three and is buried at the Frazer Cemetery, Tioga, Nicholas County, West Virginia.

E.2.2.   **JAMES HERNDON FRAZER** (October 29, 1881 – May 14, 1944) (Son of WILLIAM ADDISON FRAZER, ROBERT ADDISON FRAZER, JOSEPH ADDISON FRAZER, ANTHONY FRAZER, JAMES BENJAMIN FRAZER, WILLIAM FRAZER) James married Loretta Philena Cummins (October 30, 1879 – October 27, 1965)

---

[314] Marriage of William Addison Frazer and Emily Frances Baber, West Virginia, Compiled Marriage Records, 1863-1900.

[315] William Addison Frazer, West Virginia Deaths, 1853-1970.

[316] William Addison Frazer, U.S., Find A Grave, 1600s-Current, Memorial ID 203412391.

in 1903.[317] James and Loretta are buried at Fairview-Curry Cemetery, Nicholas County, West Virginia.

E.2.3. **CHARLES EDWARD FRAZER** (1883-1968) (Son of WILLIAM ADDISON FRAZER, ROBERT ADDISON FRAZER, JOSEPH ADDISON FRAZER, ANTHONY FRAZER, JAMES BENJAMIN FRAZER, WILLIAM FRAZER) Charles married Clara Rachel Forinash (September 17, 1882 – May 27, 1967).[318] Charles is buried at Fairview-Curry Cemetery, Nicholas County, West Virginia.[319]

E.2.4. **LESLIE BROOKE FRAZER** (May 12, 1885 – March 13, 1968) (Son of WILLIAM ADDISON FRAZER, ROBERT ADDISON FRAZER, JOSEPH ADDISON FRAZER, ANTHONY FRAZER, JAMES BENJAMIN FRAZER, WILLIAM FRAZER) Leslie is buried at Fairview-Curry Cemetery, Nicholas County, West Virginia.

E.2.5. **ELLA D. FRAZER FISHER** (1887-1979) (Daughter of WILLIAM ADDISON FRAZER, ROBERT ADDISON FRAZER, JOSEPH ADDISON FRAZER, ANTHONY FRAZER, JAMES BENJAMIN FRAZER, WILLIAM FRAZER) Ella married J. Harry Fisher.[320]

E.2.6. **LULA E. FRAZER RADER** (October 19, 1889 – August 20, 1928) (Daughter of WILLIAM ADDISON FRAZER, ROBERT ADDISON FRAZER, JOSEPH ADDISON FRAZER, ANTHONY FRAZER, JAMES BENJAMIN FRAZER, WILLIAM FRAZER) Lula married Leland S. Rader.[321]

E.2.7. **STANLEY CLYDE FRAZER** (May 10, 1892 – May 9, 1958) (Son of WILLIAM ADDISON FRAZER, ROBERT

[317] Marriage of James Herndon Frazer and Loretta Philena Cummins, West Virginia Marriages, 1853-1970.
[318] Marriage of Charles Edward Frazer and Clara Rachel Forinash, West Virginia Marriages, 1853-1970.
[319] Charles Edward Frazer, U.S., Find A Grave, 1600s-Current, Memorial ID 110848527.
[320] Marriage of Ella D. Frazer and J. Harry Fisher, Summit County, Ohio, U.S., Marriage Records, 1840-1980.
[321] Social Security Applications and Claims, 1936-2007.

ADDISON FRAZER, JOSEPH ADDISON FRAZER, ANTHONY FRAZER, JAMES BENJAMIN FRAZER, WILLIAM FRAZER) Stanley married Dessie Underwood (December 27, 1892 – April 28, 1956).[322] He is buried at Fairview-Curry Cemetery, Nicholas County, West Virginia.

E.2.8. **WILBUR WATSON FRAZER** (November 3, 1895 – February 23, 1963) (Son of WILLIAM ADDISON FRAZER, ROBERT ADDISON FRAZER, JOSEPH ADDISON FRAZER, ANTHONY FRAZER, JAMES BENJAMIN FRAZER, WILLIAM FRAZER) Wilber is buried at Fairview-Curry Cemetery, Nicholas County, West Virginia.

E.2.9. **HOWARD VIRGIL FRAZER** (January 11, 1903 – February 20, 1999) (Son of WILLIAM ADDISON FRAZER, ROBERT ADDISON FRAZER, JOSEPH ADDISON FRAZER, ANTHONY FRAZER, JAMES BENJAMIN FRAZER, WILLIAM FRAZER) Howard married Minnie G. Starcher (September 27, 1908 – September 29, 1991). He is buried at Fairview-Curry Cemetery, Nicholas County, West Virginia.

E.3. **CHARLES HERNDON FRAZER** (May 5, 1853 – January 19, 1922) (Son of ROBERT ADDISON FRAZER, JOSEPH ADDISON FRAZER, ANTHONY FRAZER, JAMES BENJAMIN FRAZER, WILLIAM FRAZER) Charles was born on May 5, 1853 in Greenbrier County, West Virginia. He married Carrie Vincent Smith (1859-November 16, 1940). Charles died on January 19, 1922 in Hansford, Kanawha County.[323] See Chapter on **CHARLES HERNDON FRAZER**.

E.4. **SARAH "SALLIE" FRAZER** (abt. 1856-Unknown) (Daughter of ROBERT ADDISON FRAZER, JOSEPH ADDISON FRAZER, ANTHONY FRAZER, JAMES BENJAMIN FRAZER, WILIAM FRAZER) Sallie's early life was in Greenbrier County, Virginia.

---

[322] Marriage of Stanley Clyde Frazer and Dessie Underwood, Virginia Marriages, 1936-2014.

[323] Charles Herndon Frazer, U.S., Find A Grave, 1600s-Current, Memorial ID 146800490.

At 22 years old, she lived in Hamilton, West Virginia with her parents.[324]

E.5. **BENJAMIN FRANKLIN RENICK FRAZER** (January 19, 1858 – September 25, 1934) (Son of ROBERT ADDISON FRAZER, JOSEPH ADDISON FRAZER, ANTHONY FRAZER, JAMES BENJAMIN FRAZER, WILLIAM FRAZER) Benjamin was born on January 19, 1858 in Greenbrier County, West Virginia. Benjamin married Laura Hortense Williams. After they divorced, he married Margaret Mary Spencer in 1902 in Nicholas County.[325] Benjamin is the direct ancestor to my children. See Chapter on **BENJAMIN FRANKLIN RENICK FRAZER**.

E.6. **HANNAH FRAZER** (June 22, 1859 - Unknown) (Daughter of ROBERT ADDISON FRAZER, JOSEPH ADDISON FRAZER, ANTHONY FRAZER, JAMES BENJAMIN FRAZER, WILLIAM FRAZER) Hannah was born on June 22, 1859 in Greenbrier County, West Virginia.[326] By 1865, Hannah's family moved to Cabin Creek in Kanawha County. By 1880, Hannah was 20 years old and lived with her family in Hamilton, Nicholas County, West Virginia.

E.7. **ROSABEL FRAZER REYNOLDS** (August 31, 1861 - Unknown) (Daughter of ROBERT A. FRAZER, JOSEPH ADDISON FRAZER, ANTHONY FRAZER, JAMES BENJAMIN FRAZER, WILLIAM FRAZER) Rosabel was born on August 31, 1861 in Greenbrier County, West Virginia.[327] As a young child, she lived with her family on Cabin Creek. On March 16, 1876, Rosabel married Thomas Phillip Reynolds in Nicholas County, West Virginia.[328]

---

[324] Year; 1880; Census Place: Hamilton, Nicholas, West Virginia; Roll: 1410; Page: 88B; Enumeration District: 104.

[325] Marriage of Benjamin Franklin Renick Frazer and Margaret Mary Spencer, West Virginia, Marriages Index, 1785-1971.

[326] Hannah Frazer, West Virginia, Births Index, 1804-1938.

[327] Rosabel Frazer, West Virginia, Births Index, 1804-1938.

[328] Marriage of Rosabel Frazer and Thomas Phillip Reynolds, West Virginia, Compiled Marriage Records, 1863-1900.

* * * * *

"Surprise Ending to the Surprise Ending"
"She Couldn't Die Till She Confessed"

A Story of The Death of Harriet Frazer

Harriet Frazer was the daughter and third child of Richard Summerson Frazer and Hannora "Nora" O'Meara and granddaughter of Robert Addison Frazer. Harriet's young life was tragically taken from her and her family and friends on February 12, 1894. A loss of a child is devastating and beyond what this writer can express.

An "attorney and fisherman," W.E.R. Byrne, tells the story of Harriet's death in his book, *Tale of the Elk*. Harriet, a young and pretty 19-year-old, was visiting her friend, 18-year-old Abbie Thompson, who lived on a small tributary of Muddlety, an unincorporated community in Nicholas County, West Virginia. The Thompson's home was located about four to seven miles from Summersville, West Virginia. Living in the home was Abbie's father, Bob Thompson; Abbie's brother Stonewall, who was about 15 or 16; and two younger brothers about five and seven. Abbie's mother had recently died. Also living in the Thompson's home was Abbie's unmarried aunt, Margaret Havens, who was sister to Abbie's deceased mother. Margaret had been living with the Thompsons for several years before the death of her sister. After her sister's death, she remained living in the home.

Harriet Frazer and Abbie Thompson were good friends and frequently visited each other. The Thompson home was a one-story, "Jenny Lind" structure, consisting of three rooms. A "Jenny Lind" home refers to the type of construction, not the style, and in West Virginia it is often a generic term for a home of simple and inexpensive construction. The main or front room was the largest with two small rooms in the rear with doors leading to each room. One of the rooms in the rear was used as a kitchen.

Supposedly, Margaret thought her widowed brother-in-law, Bob Thompson, was paying too much attention to the pretty Harriet. It was said Margaret had hopes of being the next Mrs. Bob Thompson. That night, the father, Bob Thompson, was not at home. Margaret Havens often told fortunes, both at home and on occasional gatherings in the neighborhood. Her method of fortune telling was by both cards and coffee grounds. On the fatal night, Margaret used both methods to tell Abbie, Harriet, and Stonewall's fortunes. She told Harriet to beware of "a dark man" as she had told Harriet on several previous fortune telling occasions.

Upon retiring the night in question, Abbie and Harriet slept in the main room in the large bed usually occupied by Mr. Thompson, who was not at home. Abbie slept next to the wall and Harriet in front. The three boys slept in the same main room in a trundle bed, which pulled out from under the big bed. Margaret slept alone that night in one of the small back rooms. Lodged on two pegs above the small room where Margaret slept was a loaded double-barreled shotgun.

There was a rainstorm that night with heavy rain and wind. Sometime during the night, the household was awakened by the sound of a gunshot. The shotgun that was hung on the pegs over the door had supposedly fallen on the trundle bed, hitting Stonewall in the head, leaving a knot. Stonewall lit a lamp as Abbie and Margaret joined him. They found *"Harriet Frazier, lying there in bed with the top of her head shot off---the blood and brains oozing out on the pillow."*[329]

An investigation was conducted, and Margaret, a 45-year-old "spinster," was arrested for the murder of Harriet Frazier (Frazer). "The theory of the state as developed at the trial, which began on April 10, and was concluded April 18, 1895, was that Margaret Havens was desperately in love with her brother-in-law Bob Thompson, and likewise, insanely jealous of Harriett Frazier, who was quite a pretty and attractive young woman, who Margaret feared was trying to 'cut her out,' and whose frequent visits to the Thompson home were calculated to ingratiate her with the Thompson family and pave the way to the desired end."[330] Margaret denied the accusation, and Bob Thompson stood loyally by Margaret's side assuring all that the jealousy proposition was fabricated and groundless.

In the trial, State vs. Havens, attorneys John D. Alderson, Andrew J. Horan, Ed Andrews (lead attorney) and W.E.R. Byrne were employed on behalf of the accused. Theodore B. Horan, prosecuting attorney of Nicholas County and George H. Morrison, represented the State.[331] During the trial, the defendant's attorneys convinced the court that a visit

---

[329] W.E.R. Byrne, *Tale of the Elk*, Quarrier Press, Charleston, WV, p. 347-354.
[330] Ibid.
[331] Ibid.

to the home where the death occurred was necessary. The attorneys for the accused demonstrated by a reenactment while visiting the crime scene that a violent rainstorm, as they supposedly had the night of Harriet's death, could cause the loaded shotgun, which was thought to have been left half-cocked (although this was not proven) to fall off its pegs and discharge, killing Harriet. To demonstrate the effects of a heavy rainstorm, the attorneys "had three or four men stationed on the outside, who applied to the building sufficient force to cause it to sway back and forth as from the effects of a windstorm."[332]

Margaret received a verdict of not guilty. The death of the young and vibrant 19-year-old Harriet was ruled accidental. The attorneys were complimented with high respects for a "remarkable representation." Bob Thompson and family moved from the home. Harriet's family sadly and unexpectedly lost a daughter and sister. Was this the end of a sorrowful and heartbreaking story? According to a newspaper article printed many years later, there was a surprise ending to the story as the article resurrected people from long ago. You may come to your own conclusion. The *Nicholas County News Leader*, January 1957 edition, shares this story in an article, "She Couldn't Die Till She Confessed" as follows:

> You have all been on pins and needles since last week, waiting breathlessly for the surprise ending to the surprise ending to the story that W.F. Byrne, the all-around lawyer, told in his book *Tale of the Elk*, and which this paper reprinted in the last two issues.
>
> Briefly, to rehash, a young girl is found dead in a rickety house in the Muddlety section of Nicholas County. Margaret Havens, a spinster of about 45, is held for "the murder."
>
> Smart lawyers saved Margaret by proving that Harriet Frazier was killed by the explosion of a gun, discharged when a storm shook the house, and the wall on which the gun reposed on pegs. The lawyers simply did it by reloading the gun, placing it on its pegs, while persons hired for the purpose shook the house to simulate the fury

---

[332] Ibid.

of a storm. The gun exploded right into the dummy in the bed where Harriet Frazier lay sleeping and where she died.

Margaret Havens went free.

Now the story passes to Jim Comstock who got it from the late Annie White. He had the best intentions of getting more details to the brief story that Annie White told him years ago. But, he kept putting it off, and now there's nobody in the world to ask because Annie was the last survivor of a bunch of Nicholas County people who were invited to come to Fayette County years ago and pray for an old woman who was on her death bed but would not die until she had been shrieved of a great sin, a wrong she had done.

Mrs. White told Jim Comstock that when she entered the house with the rest of the folks, that she recognized the dying old woman as Margaret Havens, the woman who had gone scott (sic) free of the Muddlety murder back so many years ago. Annie said the party knelt and prayed, and prayed long and hard, but Margaret Havens could not die.

At last she told them that she would have to unburden her soul to them, that God was punishing her for a great wrong she had committed and made her endure the agony of living beyond her time. She told them that she had deliberately and willfully killed Harriet Frazier. She had got up during the night when the household slept and removed the gun from its pegs on the wall and shot the sleeping girl dead.

That is the surprise ending to the surprise, and some young man with a writing skill could use that brief framework to create a story equal to, if not better than, Melville Davisson Post's "Doomdorf Mystery".

And that story is indeed a corker.[333]

---

[333] *Nicholas County News Leader,* "She Couldn't Die Till She Confessed," January 1957 edition.

CHARLES HERNDON FRAZER

COAL OPERATOR AND DEVELOPER AND RAILROAD SUPERINTENDENT PRATT, WEST VIRGINIA

THE SIXTH GENERATION

CHARLES HERNDON FRAZER (May 5, 1853 – January 19, 1922) (Son of ROBERT A. FRAZER, JOSEPH ADDISON FRAZER, ANTHONY FRAZER, JAMES BENJAMIN FRAZER, WILLIAM FRAZER) was the third son of Robert Addison Frazer and Harriet E. Summerson Frazer, born on May 5, 1853 in Greenbrier County, West Virginia. He was a fourth-generation uncle to my children and an older brother to my children's direct ancestor Benjamin Franklin Renick Frazer.

In 1865 or earlier, during Charles' youth, his parents, Robert and Harriet, moved to Cabin Creek, Kanawha County, West Virginia. Charles began working young in life. In 1870, at age 17, he was already working on the railroad and continued living in Cabin Creek.[334]

Charles, at age 26, married Carrie Vincent Hansford Smith (1859 - November 16, 1940) on June 24, 1879. In 1880, Charles and Carrie lived with Carrie's parents in Cabin Creek.[335] Carrie was daughter to Martha Jane Hansford of Kanawha County and John Samuel Smith of South Carolina and granddaughter of Felix Gilbert Hansford, Sr., son of Major

---

[334] Year: 1870; Census Place: Cabin Creek, Kanawha, West Virginia; Roll: M593_1690; Page 30B; Family History Library Film: 553189.

[335] Year: 1880; Census Place: Cabin Creek, Kanawha, West Virginia; Roll: 1405; Page 207D; Enumeration District: 048.

John Hansford and Jane Morris Hansford, descendent of William Morris. Carrie's great grandmother, Jane Morris Hansford, wife of Major John Hansford, was the oldest child of William Morris, the first permanent settler in Kanawha Valley in 1774, establishing homestead at the mouth of Kelly's Creek, which became the present Town of Cedar Grove.[336] This land was part of the sacred hunting grounds for the Shawnee and Cherokee nations. Prior to Morris, Walter Kelly settled there in 1773 for a short time but was killed by Indians. For years, the Morris family stood alone against the many raids by the Indians who continued to attack. William Morris not only established a homestead for his family but also built a fort, a boatyard, a church, and a school.

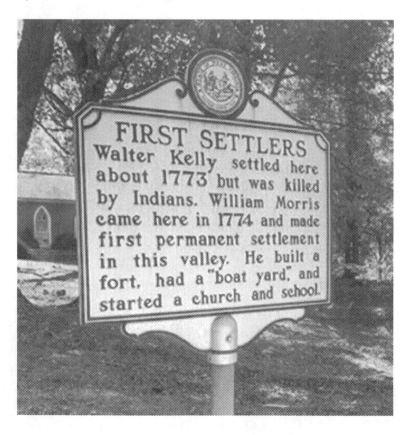

---

[336] *Beckley Post-Herald*, Beckley, West Virginia, "Hansford on Kanawha Is Old Community," by Donnelly, Shirley, June 26, 1958, p.4.

A newspaper article recalling incidents of William Morris' life posted in *The Charleston Daily Mail* in 1922 stated in part:

> William Morris was a frontiersman. He fought through the Indian wars and the Revolutionary war, and lived to see his tiny, fortified home become the center of a backwoods settlement. It was in commemoration of his sterling qualities that the Pratt Chapter of the D.A.R. was named.[337]

The William Morris Chapter of the D.A.R. was organized and named in honor of William Morris on February 27, 1922 in Pratt and confirmed by the NSDAR on March 27, 1922. On November 5, 1927, the Chapter unveiled a marker at Virginia's Chapel in Cedar Grove in memory of William Morris. Since then, this Chapter has merged with the Fort Lee Chapter and the Charleston Chapter.[338]

---

[337] *The Charleston Daily Mail*, Charleston, West Virginia, March 19, 1922, "History of First Settler to Locate in Valley of Kanawha," p. 30.
[338] William Morris Chapter, Daughters of the American Revolution, Pratt, Kanawha County, West Virginia.

Carrie's great-granddad, Major John Hansford (1765-1850), was described as a handsome man. He represented Kanawha in the Virginia Assembly from 1811 to 1818 and served as a magistrate and captain of the County Militia.[339] He was known to be a religious man.[340] John Hansford and wife Jane Morris Hansford built their house in 1798 below Paint Creek on land that his father-in-law William Morris had given them. Their house was supposedly the finest house in the valley, a two-story, six-room home that has long since been gone. The inside was finish of cherry and walnut. [341] Known children of Major John Hansford, Sr. (1765-1850)[342] and Jane Morris Hansford (1770-1854) were: Herman Hansford, William Hansford, Sarah Hansford Morris, Morris Hansford, Felix Gilbert Hansford Sr., Dr. John Hansford Jr., Carrol Hansford, Charles Hansford, Dr. Marshall Hansford, Alvah Hansford, Gallaton (Gallatin) Hansford, and Milton Hansford. [343] The Hansford and the Morris families played significant roles in the settlement of the Kanawha Valley and the area of what would become towns of Hansford and Pratt.

Felix G. Hansford (December 12, 1795 – May 27, 1867), Carrie's grandfather, was President of the Giles, Fayette & Kanawha Turnpike Company.

---

[339] *National Register of Historic Places* Inventory Nomination Form, Hansford, Felix G. House, Kanawha County, West Virginia.

[340] *Three Homes of the Hansfords*, p. 86–89.

[341] Genealogies of West Virginia Families, The West Virginia Historical Magazine Quarterly, Major John Hansford, West Virginia Historical Society, June 1, 2009, p. 43.

[342] U.S., Sons of the American Revolution Membership Applications, 1889-1970.

[343] Genealogies of West Virginia Families, The West Virginia Historical Magazine Quarterly, Major John Hansford, West Virginia Historical Society, June 1, 2009, pp. 46-47.

Felix Hansford was as prominent as his father. He married Sarah "Sallie" Kenyon Frazer (February 10, 1792 – September 3, 1888), daughter of James Frazer II of Greenbrier County. His company was formed on March 1, 1837, when the Virginia General Assembly passed legislation for the formation of the Giles, Fayette & Kanawha Turnpike Company to build a turnpike. The turnpike was a 15-foot roadway "suitable for the passage of wagons and other wheeled carriages" from Pearisburg, Virginia to Gauley Bridge.[344] As well as his involvement in the Giles, Fayette & Kanawha Turnpike Company, Felix had a large farm.

The Town of Hansford is named for the Hansford family. Felix Hansford's house, built in 1824, is the oldest building in the Town of Hansford and one of the oldest buildings in the Kanawha Valley. The building is located on Centre and 14th Streets and is listed on the *National*

---

[344] *Acts of the General Assembly of Virginia*, Richmond, Thomas Ritchie, Printer to the Commonwealth, 1837.

Register of Historic Places. It is a three-bay Federal style L-shaped house, two stories and brick construction.

Known children of Felix Gilbert Hansford, Sr. and Sarah "Sally" Kenyon Frazer (Frazier) Hansford (1792-1888) were: James Frazier Hansford, Martha Jane Hansford Smith (mother of Carrie Hansford Smith Frazer), Sallie Hansford Doddridge, Felix Gilbert Hansford Jr., Bettie (Betty) Hansford Middleton and Philadelphia Hansford Howell. Felix and Sarah Hansford are buried at the family cemetery, Hansford Cemetery, Hansford, West Virginia.

Home of Felix Gilbert Hansford, Sr. in Hansford

Charles Herndon Frazer, the subject of this chapter, was instrumental in the development of coal mining in West Virginia. He was a coal operator and identified as a prominent coal developer in Kanawha Valley. For 26 years, he had an active role in developing the lands of the Paint Creek Coal Company. *"He was superintendent of a narrow-gauge railroad in Paint Creek"* and lived in Cabin Creek.[345] It is said that Paint Creek received its name from the fact that the Indians peeled off the bark from large trees along the creek, painting the bark red to indicate their route while traveling through the country.[346]

Since "Coal was King" for those of us who grew up in coal country and I was a daughter of the mountains and a coal miner, my interest in Charles Frazer's life piqued. His energy and efforts involved the management of railroad and coal companies. A generation later, my granddads and dad

---

[345] Year: 1910. Census Place: Cabin Creek, Kanawha, West Virginia; Roll: T624_ 1684; Page 26B; Enumeration District: 0048; FHL microfilm: 1375697.
[346] West Virginia Historical Magazine Quarterly, Volumes 4-5, Laidley, W.S., Jan. 1904, p. 56.

were union miners, which meant at times they stood on opposing sides of what Charles represented.

The Town of Pratt was home to Charles and his family for many years. This small town, which today is a Historic District, was significant to Kanawha Valley and was *"the scene of events pivotal to the history of West Virginia."*[347] Pratt was settled about 1781, but it was not incorporated as the Town of Pratt until 1905. During the Civil War, the town was called Clifton. About 1873, the town took the name of "Dego" and maintained that name until 1899.[348]

Charles Frazer made his home at what is known on the *National Register of Historic Places* as the Frazer-Thompson House (ca. 1879), being the original owner of that home. This is a three-bay, two-story, L-shaped frame house with a porch across the west façade facing Charles Street and a bay window facing Pratt Avenue. Charles sold this home to the William Thompson family and moved to the house known as "Harmony Hill." Harmony Hill was built by Dickinson Morris in 1842. The house is a five-bay colonial building, brick walls and a stone foundation. Dickinson, who laid out the town in 1851, called the town Clifton.

Coal mining became the most important economic activity in the Kanawha Valley, and in 1889, the Charles Pratt Coal Company made this area their headquarters. Charles Frazer was the superintendent for the company and responsible for opening this territory for the Charles Pratt Coal Company. The Pratt Coal Company Clubhouse was built for the miners and numerous company houses were built to home the miners and their families. By 1905, the town took the name Pratt.[349]

---

[347] Pratt Historic District, LivingPlaces.com, 1997-2020.
[348] "A Brief History of Pratt, WV, 1781-1913," What is Old is New Again.
[349] "Pratt's Bicentennial Book," Compiled by Opal Norton, Patty Nugent, Min Powell, Sally Jacobs, Virginia Johnson, Cebert Elkins, 1976.

"Harmony Hill," located in Pratt, was home to Charles Herndon Frazer

William Sydney Laidley wrote the following about Charles in his writings, *History of Charleston and Kanawha County, West Virginia and Representative Citizens,"*

> Charles H. Frazer who is superintendent and field manager for Charles Pratt & Company and the Paint Creek Coal & Land Company, owners of about 22,000 acres of coal land, including 25 leases, on Paint Creek, Kanawha County, West Virginia, is a resident of Pratt, W.Va., and was born in Greenbrier County, Virginia (now West Virginia), May 5, 1853, being a son of Robert A. and Harriet E. (Summerson) Frazer. . .
>
> Charles H. Frazer spent his boyhood on the farm and obtained his education in the subscription schools. He was eight years of age when he came to Kanawha County in 1865, and he was afterwards a member of an engineering corps engaged in construction work for the C & O Railroad Company. After the close of the Civil War when the mines were opened in this county, Mr. Frazer became

a coal prospector, first as an expert for individual investors and later for Charles Pratt & Company of New York, large landowners. He opened up the territory they own on Paint Creek in this section, interested outside capital in the same and later superintended the construction of the Kanawha & Pocahontas Railroad, now known as the Paint Creek Branch of the Chesapeake & Ohio Railway, for a distance of twenty miles between Pratt and Millburn Creek. Mr. Frazer has been general superintendent for Charles Pratt & Company and the Paint Creek Coal & Land Company since 1896. He has had many interesting experiences and perhaps no one in this section is better qualified to pass judgment on coal properties and their possible means of development. In 1882 Mr. Frazer was superintendent of the laying of the track of the Paint Creek Railroad, a narrow-gauge line up Paint Creek for a distance of five miles to the noted Wacomah Mine, which was set on fire accidentally or otherwise during the Civil War and is still aflame. He worked there for two years as foreman, and afterward was superintendent of the road for five years, when he entered the employ of Charles Pratt & Company, and examined for them 32,000 acres of coal and timber land in Webster County, West Virginia, on the headwaters of Gauley and Elk Rivers. Since then 22,000 acres of coal land have been developed under his superintendence on Paint Creek. Mr. Frazer is a stockholder in the Sullivan Coal & Coke Company and in the Wood Peck Coal Company on New River.[350]

By 1912-1913, the upheaval between coal company management and the miners became paramount with the outbreak of the "Mine Wars." The Town of Pratt and the Mine Wars gained national notoriety. Charles Frazer would be about 59 to 60 years old. Pratt was located where the Paint Creek flows into Kanawha and the Paint Creek railroad joined the

---

[350] *History of Charleston and Kanawha County, West Virginia, and Representative Citizens,* by Laidley, W.S. (William Sydney), 1839-1917, p. 485.

main railroad line. The coal company management hired guards, or better known by the miners as "thugs," and Pratt became the headquarters for the mine guards. These Baldwin-Felt guards were numerous, treacherous, and heavily armed.

Should you arrive to the town of Pratt by train during these years, you looked out the dirty, grimy train windows upon the Baldwin-Felt guards walking the streets with a rifle over their shoulders. As with other coal company towns or camps, as they were often called, the coal operators and companies owned the land and the homes as well as the company store. These homes were rented to the miners. Once a miner was fired or during the strike when the miners refused to work, the coal operators instructed the mine guards to evict the miners and the families from the company homes. If the miners refused to leave, they were considered trespassers. The miners who participated in the strike were not allowed to step on any coal company property, including land. If the striking miners and families did not leave the home voluntarily, the guards would place the family's belongings out of the home onto land that did not belong to the company. The guards were to make the lives of the miners as uncomfortable as possible.[351] These families had no place to go, so they moved to tent camps outside of town provided by the United Mine Workers Association (UMWA). Striking miners who were arrested were imprisoned in Pratt by the mine guards in areas known as "bullpens." Paint Creek and other areas around Pratt were declared to be a "state of lawlessness and insurrection." The National Guard was called in for martial law on three occasions.

Charles not only lived through these years, but he was actively involved with the management as Superintendent of the Charles Pratt & Company and the Paint Creek Coal & Land Company.

---

[351] West Virginia Department of Arts, Culture and History, West Virginia Archives and History, "West Virginia's Mine Wars.

The most famous imprisonment in Pratt was that of the union organizer Mother Mary Jones. The white-haired motherly figure with rimless glasses was a labor activist who came to the area to support the striking miners and the labor movement, a cause she had dedicated her life to after the death of her husband and children from yellow fever decades before. Mary Harris "Mother" Jones (circa 1837 – 1930) was born in Ireland and moved to the United States at an early age. She was a flamboyant and dynamic speaker, union organizer, and agitator.

It was said that Mother Jones appeared as "meek and mild," dressed in her black silk and white lace, but she was far from that description. Numerous portrayals of Mother Jones state she "cursed like a sailor" and was totally devoted to her cause of helping the miners. She delighted in her "hell-cat" image to protect her children as she considered them. The coal fields of West Virginia aroused Mother Jones' need to speak out against the mine operators use of armed guards, denying miners the freedom of speech and assembly on public roads. Their treatment brought out the righteous fury in her need to protect them from the danger.

Mother Jones' motto: "Pray for the dead and fight like hell for the living."[352]

Mother Jones delivered a speech on the courthouse square of Charleston, West Virginia in 1912 in support of the striking miner. The speech would later be used against her in a conviction of inciting violence in the West Virginia coal fields and of conspiracy to commit murder. Mother Jones began her speech as follows:

> This great gathering that is here tonight signals there is a disease in the State that must be wiped out. The people have suffered from that disease patiently; they have borne insults, oppression, outrages; they appealed to their chief executive, they appealed to the courts, they appealed to the attorney general, and in every case they were turned down. They were ignored. The people must not be listened to, the corporations must get a hearing.
>
> When we were on the Capitol grounds the last time you came here, you had a petition to the Governor for a peaceful remedy and solution of this condition. The mine owners, the bankers, the plunderers of the State went in on the side door and got a hearing, and you didn't.
>
> Now, then, they offer to get a commission, suggested by the mine owners. The miners submitted a list of names to be selected from, and the mine owners said, "We will have no commission." Then when they found out that Congress, the Federal Government was going to come down and examine your damnable peonage system, then they were ready for the commission.
>
> Then they got together—the cunning brains of the operators got together. What kind of a commission have they got? A bishop, a sky pilot working for Jesus; a lawyer, and a member of the State Militia, from Fayette City.

---

[352] West Virginia History, *The Old Mother and Her Army: The Agitative Strategies of Mary Harris Jones, Scholten, Pat Creech Volume XL, No. 4, Summer 1979*, p. 366.

In the name of God, what do any of those men know about your troubles up on Cabin Creek, and Paint Creek? Do you see the direct insult offered by your officials to your intelligence? They look upon you as a lot of enemies instead of those who do the work. If they wanted to be fair they would have selected three miners, three operators and two citizens. And would have said, "Now, go to work and bring in an impartial decision." But they went up on Cabin Creek—I wouldn't have made those fellows walk in the water, but they make me. Because they knew I have something to tell you, and all Hell and all the governors on the earth couldn't keep me from telling it. . . [353]

Mother Jones' speech was long, and she received support from the striking miners as they cheered her on as she created a sensation. She ended her speech as follows:

. . .The whole machinery of capitalism is rotten to the core. This meeting tonight indicates a milestone of progress of the miners and workers of the State of West Virginia. I will be with you, and the Baldwin guards will go. You will not be serfs, you will march, march, march on from milestone to milestone of human freedom, you will rise like men in the new day and slavery will get its death blow. It has got to die. Good night.[354]

Mother Jones continued her support of the miner's cause as a forceful figure and a heroine to the miners and their families. Eventually, she was arrested and convicted and sentenced to twenty years in prison. The sentence was later commuted. On February 13, 1913, Mother Jones was arrested in Charleston as she accompanied miners on their way to the Capitol Building. She and four other organizers were taken by taxis and driven to the C&O Railroad, awaiting the train to Pratt. Upon arrival

[353] History Is a Weapon, *Speech to Striking Coal Miners,* By Mother Jones, *The Radical Reader*, Edited by McCarthy, Timothy Patrick and McMillian, John, 1912.
[354] Ibid.

at Pratt, the marital law zone, they were turned over to the military authorities. News of the arrest of Mother Jones traveled not only across the state but also the nation.[355]

Mother Jones was kept prisoner in Pratt at Mrs. Carney's Boarding House located on Center Street, awaiting her trial. It was said that Mother Jones and Mrs. Carney became friends. The house was a large two-story structure used much of the time as a boarding house. The Carney family supposedly received $1.50 per day to house Mother Jones. Mother Jones, in a letter, described them as being "poor, very poor." The boarding house, or cottage as it was called, was about two blocks from the "Bull Pen" where the other prisoners were held. Mother Jones stated the house was "surrounded by militiamen who . . . marched around that house day and night. . . "[356] Dr. John Hansford, (a relative to Charles Frazer's wife Carrie) a physician in town, attended Mother Jones when she was first detained by the authorities.[357] The boarding house was listed in 1992 on the *National Register of Historic Places* along with the Pratt Historic District. The boarding house was removed from the Register in 1997 after demolition of the building.

As the number of prisoners continued to grow, they were held under guard at Camp Pratt, as it was called, in boxcars and empty houses. The freight room at the C&O station at Paint Creek Junction was the largest enclosed space. The prisoners were taken to this dirty, dingy building and it soon became known as the "Bull Pen."

On Friday, March 7, 1913, in the town of Pratt, the trial of Mother Jones and her compatriots was conducted. An article from the *San Francisco Bulletin* on March 21, 1913 by Mrs. Fremont Older states that Mother Jones and forty-eight strikers and sympathizers were being tried as she continued to describe her visit there as they "passed monotonous rows of weather-beaten, unpainted houses – miners' shacks; there are no miners'

---

[355] Never Justice, Never Peace: Mother Jones and the Miner Rebellion at Paint and Cabin Creeks, Savage, Lon Kelly and Ayers Savage, Ginny, WV University Press, 2018, 185-186.

[356] Ibid.

[357] *U.S. National Register of Historic Places Inventory* – Nomination Form, Pratt Historic District, Kanawha County, West Virginia, 36. Dr. John Hansford House, p. 19.

homes in West Virginia. As we whirled through the mountains, beauty seemed lost." The trial was held at the Odd Fellows Hall, which occupied the second floor above the general merchandise store. The trial was open to the press.

On March 4, 1913, Henry D. Hatfield was sworn in as the new governor. The incoming Governor Hatfield visited Mother Jones in Pratt and shortly afterward was able to bring a compromise settlement between the operators and the miners for a temporary end of the conflict. [358]

Charles and Carrie lived in Cabin Creek and Pratt during these years of the Mine Wars and worked for the Charles Pratt Coal Company. There are writings, books, documentaries, and movies telling of the Mine Wars. I was unsuccessful in my research to locate any direct involvement Charles Herndon Frazer may have had in these conflicts. Any resident of the Town of Pratt during these trying times would have had some participation. There would be no escaping the chaotic activity in a town where private guards walked the streets with guns and rifles over their shoulders and where town people feared for their livelihood and their lives. A war raged in these surrounding hills and the effect would have tumbled down on all. Charles would have known those involved on both sides. Working for Charles Pratt and Company, his stand would have been for the coal operator. He would have known Mother Jones and the union supporters as well as representing the coal company and the Baldwin-Felt guards. He was a Frazer family ancestor; and, yet, my grandfathers, both paternal and maternal, worked as miners in a nearby county just short years later, in support of the union. Had they worked during the coal mining wars, they would have stood with the striking miners.

Generations after the Mine Wars, families felt the effects of mine shutdowns while living in coal company homes and the shuttering of company stores. Those feelings of fear and helplessness stayed strong in their minds. How much more devastating it would be with armed guards walking the streets, the fear of retribution and the loss of lives. It would take courage to face the fears.

Today, the Town of Pratt is a quiet and small town with its historical

---

[358] Laidley, W. S., *History of Charleston and Kanawha County, West Virginia and Representative Citizens*, Richmond-Arnold Publishing Company, Chicago, Illinois, 1911.

buildings and proud heritage. I enjoyed our recent visit, walking the peaceful rural streets, amazed that so much activity and history for the coal mining families occurred in bygone days in such a small-scale area surrounded by the strong, peaceful mountains that always brought feelings of serenity. Our visit was on a rainy day, clouds shifted over the sky, blocking the sun as we visited peaks and hollers. The rain turned into a smokey fog low to the ground as it crawled its way to us. It was fascinating that these green hills running up and down that represented peace to me held emotional weights for others only generations before in the threshold of their lives.

Photo taken at the river in Town of Pratt on a rainy day in July 2020. The streets in town run nearly to the river.

Marshall Hansford House in Pratt
Headquarters of Union Colonel Edward Siber during the Civil War
Photo taken by Lillian Frazer, July 2020

Charles died on January 19, 1922 at age 69 in the Sheltering Arms Hospital at Hansford, the town that took the name of his wife's family name. His funeral was held in Pratt, West Virginia, and he is buried at the family cemetery at Hansford Cemetery, Hansford, Kanawha County, West Virginia.[359] An obituary states that he had been ill during the last eight months of his life and was confined to bed. It also stated that he was a member of the First Baptist Church of Pratt and served as a deacon of the church. Carrie Smith Frazer died November 16, 1940 and is also buried at Hansford Cemetery. Known children of Charles Herndon Frazer and Carrie Hansford Smith Frazer (more information on children below):

E.3.1.   HERNDON VEAZEY FRAZER (August 24, 1880 – July 7, 1957)

---

[359] Charles Herndon Frazer, U.S., Find A Grave Index, 1600s-Current, Memorial ID 146800490.

E.3.2. MARGARET FRAZER COLEMAN (May 15, 1882 – April 8, 1935)

E.3.3. FELIX ADISON FRAZER (November 19, 1895 – April 26, 1897)

E.3.4. ROLAND CARTER FRAZER (March 14, 1899 – September 26, 1972)

E.3.1. **HERNDON VEAZEY FRAZER** (August 24, 1880 – July 7, 1957) (Son of CHARLES HERNDON FRAZER, ROBERT ADDISON FRAZER, JOSEPH ADDISON FRAZER, ANTHONY FRAZER, JAMES BENJAMIN FRAZER, WILLIAM FRAZER) Herndon was born on August 24, 1880 in Pratt, West Virginia.[360] He married Nan Gilkeson (December 16, 1886 – November 2, 1982). On November 29, 1911, Herndon and Nan lived with his parents in Pratt, and he worked as a salesman.[361] The 1930 and 1940 census indicate Herndon completed high school and owned a home in Jefferson in Kanawha County. Herndon died on July 7, 1957 at age 76 in Saint Albans. Herndon and Nan are buried at Cunningham Memorial Park, 815 Cunningham Lane, Saint Albans, Kanawha County, West Virginia.[362]

E.3.2. **MARGARET FRAZER COLEMAN** (May 15, 1882 – April 8, 1935) (Daughter of CHARLES HERNDON FRAZER, ROBERT ADDISON FRAZER, JOSEPH ADDISON FRAZER, ANTHONY FRAZER, JAMES BENJAMIN FRAZER, WILLIAM FRAZER) Margaret was born on May 15, 1882 in Pratt, West Virginia. She married Charles Bradford Coleman (March 13, 1880 – June 13, 1958) in 1904.[363] By 1910, Charles was a cashier for the Charles Pratt & Company and later

---

[360] Herndon Veazey Frazer, West Virginia, Deaths Index, 1853-1973.

[361] Marriage of Herndon Veazey Frazer and Nan Gilkeson, Newspapers.com Marriage Index, 1800s-1999.

[362] Herndon Veazey Frazer, U.S., Find A Grave Index, 1600s-Current, Memorial ID 146800575.

[363] Marriage of Margaret Frazer Coleman and Charles Bradford Coleman, West Virginia Marriages, 1853-1970.

became a manager for the company. Margaret died unexpectedly of heart disease on April 8, 1935 at age 52. She is buried at the family cemetery at Hansford Cemetery, Hansford, Kanawha County, West Virginia.[364] Her husband, Charles Bradford Coleman, Sr., is buried at Montgomery Memorial Park, 9619 Dupont Avenue, London, Kanawha County, West Virginia.[365] She had two known children:

E.3.2.1.   **CHARLES BRADFORD COLEMAN, JR.** (August 14, 1905 - June 29, 1983) (Son of MARGARET FRAZER COLEMAN, CHARLES HERNDON FRAZER, ROBERT ADDISON FRAZER, JOSEPH ADDISON FRAZER, ANTHONY FRAZER, JAMES BENJAMIN FRAZER, WILLIAM FRAZER) Charles was born in the town of Pratt, West Virginia. He became an actor and known by the screen name of John Bradford. He was known for his acting parts in *365 Nights in Hollywood (1934 – he played the part of Adrian Almont)*, *Undersea Kingdom* (1936 – played the part of Joe) and *Life Begins at 40* (1935 – he played the part of Wally Stevens). Bradford also played a gangster in *Old Corral*, starring Gene Autry and Roy Rogers. Gene, who plays the sheriff, eventually arrests Bradford who plays the part of the gangster Mike Scarlotti. In addition, he played an uncredited part of Joe in *Dick Tracy (1937)* and an uncredited part in *The King Steps Out* (1936).

On September 11, 1929, Charles married Mary Josephine Matthews in Mannington, West Virginia.[366] In 1930, Charles and Mary lived in Chicago, Illinois. On April 19, 1943, Charles was separated, without children, and

---

[364] Margaret Frazer Coleman, U.S., Find A Grave Index, 1600s-Current, Memorial ID 176257500.

[365] Charles Bradford Coleman, Sr., U.S., Find A Grave Index, 1600s-Current, Memorial ID 176258944.

[366] Marriage of Charles Bradford Coleman, Jr. and Mary Josephine Matthews, *The News Leader*; Publication Date: 7 September 1929; Publication Place: Staunton, Virginia.

enlisted as a Private in the Army during World War II. The records indicate he had four years of college.[367] In 1947, Charles married Geneva Mae Harrah in Kanawha County.[368] Charles and Geneva divorced. Charles died in 1983 in Charleston, West Virginia. Known children of Charles Bradford Coleman, Jr. and Geneva Mae Harrah:

Charles Coleman (actor screenname: John Bradford)
Son of Margaret Frazer Coleman

CHARLES BRADFORD COLEMAN III (March 20, 1948 – May 2, 2015) (Son of CHARLES BRADFORD COLEMAN, JR., MARGARET FRAZER COLEMAN, CHARLES HERNDON FRAZER, ROBERT ADDISON FRAZER, JOSEPH ADDISON FRAZER, ANTHONY FRAZER, JAMES BENJAMIN FRAZER, WILLIAM FRAZER)

---

[367] National Archives at College Park; College Park, Maryland, USA; Electronic Army Serial Number Merged File, 1938-1946.
[368] Marriage of Charles Bradford Coleman, Jr. and Geneva Mae Harrah, West Virginia Marriages, 1853-1970.

E.3.2.2. **CAROLINE CAPERTON COLEMAN MYERS HICKS** (March 27, 1910 – July 14, 1983) (Daughter of MARGARET FRAZER COLEMAN, CHARLES HERNDON FRAZER, ROBERT ADDISON FRAZER, JOSEPH ADDISON FRAZER, ANTHONY FRAZER, JAMES BENJAMIN FRAZER, WILLIAM FRAZER) On May 18, 1928, Caroline married Ralph Coleman Myers in Indiana.[369] The 1930 Census indicated Caroline lived with her parents in Pratt, was divorced, and worked as a clerk. A newspaper article in the *Charleston Gazette* on November 16, 1942, announced Caroline's marriage to Sgt. Robert "Bob" Lee Hicks. They married at the Army Lounge in Nashville, Tennessee. According to the newspaper article, Caroline had attended "Miss Scarrett's School" in Chicago and was a student at the "District Theological School" in Michigan. Caroline died in 1983 and is buried at Forest Lawn Memorial Park, 6300 Forest Lawn Drive, Los Angeles, California.[370]

E.3.3. **FELIX ADISON FRAZER** (November 19, 1895 – April 26, 1897) (Son of CHARLES HERNDON FRAZER, ROBERT ADDISON FRAZER, JOSEPH ADDISON FRAZER, ANTHONY FRAZER, JAMES BENJAMIN FRAZER, WILLIAM FRAZER) Felix died at age 1. Felix is buried in the family cemetery at Hansford Cemetery, Hansford, Kanawha County, West Virginia.[371]

E.3.4. **ROLAND CARTER FRAZER** (March 14, 1899 – September 26, 1972) (Son of CHARLES HERNDON FRAZER, ROBERT ADDISON FRAZER, JOSEPH ADDISON FRAZER, ANTHONY FRAZER, JAMES BENJAMIN FRAZER, WILLIAM FRAZER) Roland was born in Pratt,

---

[369] Marriage of Caroline Caperton Coleman and Ralph Coleman Myers, Indiana, U.S., Marriages, 1810-2001.

[370] Caroline Caperton Coleman Myers Hicks, U.S., Find A Grave, 1600s-Current, Memorial ID 85890732.

[371] Felix A. Frazer, U.S., Find A Grave, 1600s-Current, Memorial ID 176469703.

West Virginia on March 14, 1899. He married Kathleen Ford (April 25, 1915 – March 19, 1957) in 1947.[372] In 1960, he married Charlotte Stricklen Peck in Kanawha County.[373] He died at age 73 on September 26, 1972. Roland and Kathleen are buried at Cunningham Memorial Park, 815 Cunningham Lane, Saint Albans, Kanawha County, West Virginia.[374]

---

[372] Marriage of Roland Carter Frazer and Kathleen Ford, West Virginia, Marriages Index, 1785-1971.

[373] Marriage of Roland Carter Frazer and Charlotte Stricklen Peck, West Virginia, Marriages Index, 1853-1970.

[374] Roland Carter Frazer, U.S., Find A Grave, 1600s-Current, Memorial ID 176261139.

BENJAMIN FRANKLIN RENICK FRAZER

YOUNGER BROTHER TO CHARLES HERNDON FRAZER
FARMER IN NICHOLAS COUNTY, WEST VIRGINIA

THE SIXTH GENERATION

BENJAMIN FRANKLIN RENICK FRAZER (January 19, 1858 – September 25, 1934) (Son of ROBERT ADDISON FRAZER, JOSEPH ADDISON FRAZER, ANTHONY FRAZER, JAMES BENJAMIN FRAZER, WILLIAM FRAZER) was born on January 19, 1858, one of the seven children of Harriet Summerson Frazer (1830-1906) and Robert Addison Frazer (1822-1906) in Greenbrier County, in what was at the time Virginia and later became West Virginia. Benjamin was the youngest son. According to census records, Benjamin preferred his middle name "Frank."

His dad and granddad owned and operated a stagecoach tavern and inn in Sewell Valley. Progress was in full swing as the railroad and train slowly crept in, replacing the long and dusty stagecoach travel, which in return resulted in death to many of the taverns and inns as business came to a sudden halt. Frazer's Sewell Valley Tavern was one of those stagecoach stands that felt the death blow. Then, the Civil War erupted while Benjamin was just a toddler. The land where the tavern and inn once stood was on the traveled road where both Union and Confederate soldiers marched and at times set up encampments along this road. Addison Frazer,

Benjamin's granddad, now aged, sold the land and both grandparents and parents moved from the area.

Benjamin's parents, by 1870 and perhaps much earlier, were living in Cabin Creek, West Virginia. Cabin Creek is an unincorporated community in Kanawha County located about 18 miles from Charleston, West Virginia. The creek is a tributary to the Kanawha River. Benjamin's dad Robert worked as a farmer[375] and it was said that his dad had lost most of what he owned during the tavern closure and the Civil War. Benjamin's older brothers worked early in life as coal miners or on the railroad in the Cabin Creek area. Paint Creek and Cabin Creek are known for the 1913 coal mine strike and the bloody coal wars over the living and working conditions of miners and violating miners' constitutional rights. Unlike his brothers, Benjamin appeared to enjoy working with the land, farming as had his dad.

Sometime before 1880, Benjamin married Laura Hortense Williams (b. 1864).[376] The census for 1880 indicates that Benjamin and Laura lived in Hamilton, West Virginia. Laura was 16 years old when they had their first child, Oscar Wallace, in 1880. [377] A couple years later in 1882, they had their second son, Arthur Watson.[378] Laura and Benjamin divorced by 1900 and perhaps earlier.

In 1902, Benjamin married Margaret (Martha) Mary Spencer in Nicholas County, West Virginia.[379] By 1910, Benjamin and Martha lived in Beaver and Benjamin worked as a butcher.[380] Little information was located on Benjamin and Martha. By 1920, the census indicates that they lived in Vernon, Missouri and Benjamin worked as a farmer on his own farm.[381] The 1930 census indicate Benjamin owned a farm and lived in Springdale, Arkansas.

---

[375] Year: 1870; Census Place: Cabin Creek, Kanawha, West Virginia; Roll: M593_1690; Page: 30A; Family History Library Film: 553189.

[376] West Virginia, Births Index, 1804-1938.

[377] Oscar Wallace Frazer, West Virginia, Births Index, 1804-1938.

[378] Arthur Watson Frazer, West Virginia, Births Index, 1804-1938.

[379] Marriage of Benjamin Franklin Renick Frazer and Margaret Mary Spencer, West Virginia, Marriages Index, 1785-1971.

[380] 1910 United States Federal Census.

[381] Year: 1920; Census Place: Nevada Ward 4, Vernon, Missouri; Roll: T625_965; Page: 10B; Enumeration District: 164.

Benjamin died on September 25, 1934 at age 76 and is buried at Friendship Cemetery, Springdale, Washington County, Arkansas.[382] Martha died on December 17, 1938 in Washington County, Arkansas and is also buried at Friendship Cemetery.

Known children of Benjamin Franklin Renick Frazer and Laura Williams are:

F.1. OSCAR W. FRAZER, SR. (September 17, 1880 – February 20, 1931)

F.2. ARTHUR WATSON FRAZER, SR. (September 2. 1882 - May 1947)

F.1. **OSCAR W. FRAZER, SR.** (September 17, 1880 – February 20, 1931) (Son of BENJAMIN FRANKLIN RENICK FRAZER, ROBERT ADDISON FRAZER, JOSEPH ADDISON FRAZER, ANTHONY FRAZER, JAMES BENJAMIN FRAZER, WILLIAM FRAZER) Oscar was the oldest son born in 1880. He married Laura Belle Dyer in 1907. See chapter on **OSCAR W. FRAZER, SR.**

F.2. **ARTHUR WATSON FRAZER, SR.** (September 2. 1882 - May 1947) (Son of BENJAMIN FRANKLIN RENICK FRAZER, ROBERT ADDISON FRAZER, JOSEPH ADDISON FRAZER, ANTHONY FRAZER, JAMES BENJAMIN FRAZER, WILLIAM FRAZER) Arthur was born on September 2, 1882 in Nicholas County, West Virginia, the second child of Benjamin and Laura Williams Frazer.[383] In 1900, Arthur, along with his brother Oscar, lived with the Cogar family in Glade while Arthur was a student telegram operator for the railroad. Arthur may have become a minister at some point as he was referred to as Reverend. In 1912, Arthur married Evalyn L. Myers (1889-1959), daughter of Margaret and Henry Myers.[384] According to the 1920 and 1930 census, Arthur and Evelyn lived in Ohio. Arthur died on May

---

[382] Benjamin Franklin Renick Frazer, U.S., Find A Grave Index, 1600s-Current, Memorial ID 31140612.

[383] U.S., Social Security Applications and Claims Index, 1936-2007.

[384] West Virginia, Marriages Index, 1785-1971.

29, 1947 and is buried at Broadfording Church of God Cemetery, 16109 Broadfording Road, Broadfording, Washington County, Maryland.[385] Evalyn died in 1959 and is also buried at Broadfording Church of God Cemetery. Known children of Arthur and Evalyn:

F.2.1.　**ARTHUR WATSON FRAZER, JR.** (May 24, 1913 – April 28, 1990) (Son of ARTHUR WATSON FRAZER, SR., BENJAMIN FRANKLIN RENICK FRAZER, ROBERT ADDISON FRAZER, JOSEPH ADDISON FRAZER, ANTHONY FRAZER, JAMES BENJAMIN FRAZER, WILLIAM FRAZER) Arthur was born on May 28, 1913 in Wheeling, West Virginia. Arthur married Beulah L. Edmond on August 20, 1933 in West Virginia when she was 17 and he was 21.[386] They lived in Washington, D.C., and Arthur worked as a field representative with a government agency. They divorced, and Arthur married Virginia G. Gayle on September 21, 1946 in Alexandria, Virginia.[387] They were divorced in 1948. Arthur married Elizabeth Irene Hostetler on July 23, 1948 in Alexandria, Virginia.[388] They divorced, and he married Anita a De La Fuente in 1961 in Jefferson County, West Virginia.[389] Arthur died April 28, 1990 at age 76 at which time he lived in Alexandria, Virginia. Arthur is buried at Germantown Bethel Cemetery, 16924 Raven Rock Road, Cascade, Frederick County, Maryland.[390]

F.2.2.　**DOROTHY EVALYN FRAZER MCCLEAF** (December

---

[385] Arthur Watson Frazer, Sr., U.S., Find A Grave Index, 1600s-Current, Memorial ID 54174153.

[386] Marriage of Arthur Watson Frazer, Jr. and Beulah L. Edmond, West Virginia, Marriage Index, 1931-1970.

[387] Marriage of Arthur Watson Frazer, Jr. and Virginia G. Gayle, Virginia, Marriage Records, 1936-2014.

[388] Marriage of Arthur Watson Frazer, Jr. and Elizabeth Irene Hostetler, Virginia, Marriage Records, 1936-2014.

[389] Marriage of Arthur Watson Frazer, Jr. and Anita a De La Fuente, West Virginia, Marriages Index, 1785-1971.

[390] Arthur Watson Frazer, Sr., U.S., Find A Grave, 1600s-Current, Memorial ID 54668747.

5, 1915 – June 26, 2002) (Daughter of ARTHUR WATSON FRAZER, SR., BENJAMIN FRANKLIN RENICK FRAZER, ROBERT A. FRAZER, JOSEPH ADDISON FRAZER, ANTHONY FRAZER, JAMES BENJAMIN FRAZER, WILLIAM FRAZER) Dorothy was born on December 5, 1915 in Wheeling, West Virginia where she lived her early years. Dorothy married Bruce McCleaf (1910 – February 1, 1973) January 12, 1935. They lived in Pennsylvania and later moved to Maryland. Dorothy died on June 26, 2002 in Hagerstown, Maryland. Dorothy and Bruce are buried at Germantown Bethel Cemetery, 16924 Raven Rock Road, Cascade, Frederick County, Maryland.[391]

F.2.3.   **CARL LAWRENCE FRAZER** (February 19, 1919 – June 15, 1998) (Son of ARTHUR WATSON FRAZER, SR., BENJAMIN FRANKLIN RENICK FRAZER, ROBERT ADDISON FRAZER, ADDISON FRAZER, ANTHONY FRAZER, JAMES BENJAMIN FRAZER, WILLIAM FRAZER) Carl was born on February 18, 1919 in Wheeling, West Virginia. He enlisted in the Navy on November 14, 1944 through October 18, 1945, serving in World War II.[392] His first wife was Mary Elizabeth Bowman (May 3, 1918 – July 6, 1962). Mary died on July 6, 1962 at 44 years old. She is buried at Wellers Cemetery, 101 North Altamont Avenue, Thurmont, Frederick County, Maryland. He married Wilma Pauline Parsons Kline (July 3, 1924 – March 20, 1992) on May 3, 1967 in Clintwood, Virginia.[393] Carl was a widow and Wilma was divorced. He lived for a time in Blue Ridge Summit, Pennsylvania.

---

[391] Dorothy Evalyn Frazer McCleaf, U.S., Find A Grave, 1600s-Current, Memorial ID 53700776.

[392] Carl Lawrence Frazer, U.S. Department of Veterans Affairs BIRLS Death File, 1850-2010.

[393] Marriage of Carl Lawrence Frazer and Wilma Pauline Parsons Kline, Virginia, Marriage Records, 1936-2014.

Carl was instrumental in helping with starting the Pen Mar United Brethren Church in Pen Mar in the 1940s. He owned and operated Frazer Bus Service in Waynesboro, Pennsylvania in the 1940s. He also worked as an inspector for Letterkenny Army Depot in Chambersburg, Pennsylvania. In the 1950s and 1960s, he owned and operated several car lots in the surrounding area of Waynesboro. Carl died at age 79 on June 15, 1998 in Martinsburg, West Virginia from injuries sustained in an auto accident.[394] Carl and Wilma are buried at Germantown Bethel Cemetery, 16924 Raven Rock Road, Cascade, Frederick County, Maryland.[395]

F.2.4.   **RONALD MCCUE FRAZER** (February 9, 1921 – June 14, 1985) (Son of ARTHUR WATSON FRAZER, SR., BENJAMIN FRANKLIN RENICK FRAZER, ROBERT ADDISON FRAZER, JOSEPH ADDISON FRAZER, ANTHONY FRAZER, JAMES BENJAMIN FRAZER, WILLIAM FRAZER) Ronald was born in Wheeling, West Virginia on February 9, 1921. In 1940, he was living with his brother in Washington, D.C. He was a War World II Veteran in the Air Force, enlisting August 20, 1950 and released on April 21, 1967.[396] He married Dolores Ford (1930 – Unknown). By 1950, he lived in Pen Mar, Franklin County, Pennsylvania. He died on June 14, 1985 and is buried at Germantown Bethel Cemetery, 16924 Raven Rock Road, Cascade, Frederick County, Maryland.[397]

F.2.5.   **BETTY JANE FRAZER BROWN** (February 28, 1922 – May 1, 2010) (Daughter of ARTHUR WATSON FRAZER, SR., BENJAMIN FRANKLIN RENICK FRAZER, ROBERT ADDISON FRAZER, ADDISON FRAZER,

---

[394] *The Herald Mail*, Hagerstown, MD, June 17, 1998.

[395] Carl Lawrence Frazer, U.S., Find A Grave, 1600s-Current, Memorial ID 14733374.

[396] Ronald McCue Frazer, U.S., Department of Veterans Affairs BIRLS Death File, 1850-2010.

[397] Ronald McCue Frazer, U.S., Find A Grave, 1600s-Current, Memorial ID 55257351.

ANTHONY FRAZER, JAMES BENJAMIN FRAZER, WILLIAM FRAZER) Betty was born on February 28, 1922. She married James "Jim" L. Brown (April 29, 1922 - Unknown) on November 9, 1941. They made their home in Upper Marlboro, Maryland. Betty died on May 1, 2010 at age 88. Betty and James are buried at Germantown Bethel Cemetery, 16924 Raven Rock Road, Cascade, Frederick County, Maryland.[398]

F.2.6. **PAUL RAY FRAZER** (August 19, 1923 – February 29, 2008) (Son of ARTHUR WATSON FRAZER, SR., BENJAMIN FRANKLIN RENICK FRAZER, ROBERT ADDISON FRAZER, JOSEPH ADDISON FRAZER, ANTHONY FRAZER, JAMES BENJAMIN FRAZER, WILLIAM FRAZER) Paul was born on August 19, 1923 in Wheeling, West Virginia. He served in the United States Army during World War II from February 3, 1941 to September 30, 1945, serving in the 729th Ordinance Division and President of the Ordinance.[399] Paul was President of the Maryland Independent Auto Deal Association. He married Juanita C. Belew. Paul died on February 29, 2008 at age 84, at which time he lived in Gettysburg, Pennsylvania. He is buried at Germantown Bethel Cemetery, 16924 Raven Rock Road, Cascade, Frederick County, Maryland.[400]

F.2.7. **ROBERT JAMES FRAZER, SR.** (August 25, 1924 – January 11, 1996) (Son of ARTHUR WATSON FRAZER, SR., BENJAMIN FRANKLIN RENICK FRAZER, ROBERT ADDISON FRAZER, JOSEPH ADDISON FRAZER, ANTHONY FRAZER, JAMES BENJAMIN FRAZER, WILLIAM FRAZER) Robert was born on August 25, 1924 in Wheeling, West Virginia. He served in World War II from

---

[398] Betty Jane Frazer Brown, U.S., Find A Grave, 1600s-Current, Memorial ID 51768911.

[399] Paul Ray Frazer, U.S., Department of Veterans Affairs BIRLS Death File, 1850-2010.

[400] Paul Ray Frazer, U.S., Find A Grave, 1600s-Current, Memorial ID 24969076.

March 8, 1943 to April 18, 1946.[401] He married Winifred E. (last name unknown). Robert died on January 11, 1996 at age 71 and is buried at Germantown Bethel Cemetery, 16924 Raven Rock Road, Cascade, Frederick County, Maryland.[402]

F.2.8. **ALICE V. FRAZER MELLOTT** (1925-1950) (Daughter of ARTHUR WATSON FRAZER, SR., BENJAMIN FRANKLIN RENICK FRAZER, ROBERT ADDISON FRAZER, JOSEPH ADDISON FRAZER, ANTHONY FRAZER, JAMES BENJAMIN FRAZER, WILLIAM FRAZER) Alice was born in 1925. She married Fred H. Mellott. Alice died at age 24 on May 1950 and is buried at Broadfording Church of God Cemetery, 16109 Broadfording Road, Broadfording, Washington County, Maryland.[403]

F.2.9. **FREDERICK HAROLD FRAZER** (April 7, 1927 – July 4, 1949) (Son of ARTHUR WATSON FRAZER, SR., BENJAMIN FRANKLIN RENICK FRAZER, ROBERT ADDISON FRAZER, JOSEPH ADDISON FRAZER, ANTHONY FRAZER, JAMES BENJAMIN FRAZER, WILLIAM FRAZER) Frederick was born on April 7, 1927 in West Virginia. He was Seaman First Class in the United States Navy and a veteran of World War II.[404] He died by drowning at age 21-22 on July 7, 1949 at a public park. He was single and is buried at Broadfording Church of God Cemetery, 16109 Broadfording Road, Broadfording, Washington County, Maryland.[405]

F.2.10. **BENJAMIN FRANKLIN "FRANKIE" FRAZER** (September 29, 1928 – December 7, 2006) (Son of ARTHUR WATSON FRAZER, SR., BENJAMIN FRANKLIN

---

[401] Robert James Frazer, Sr., U.S., Department of Veterans Affairs BIRLS Death File, 1850-2010.

[402] Robert James Frazer, Sr., U.S., Find A Grave, 1600s-Current, Memorial ID 8645659.

[403] Alice V. Frazer Mellott, U.S., Find A Grave, 1600s-Current, Memorial ID 50720529.

[404] Frederick Harold Frazer, U.S. World War II Navy Muster Rolls, 1938-1949.

[405] Frederick Harold Frazer, U.S., Find A Grave, 1600s-Current, Memorial ID 50721173.

RENICK FRAZER, ROBERT ADDISON FRAZER, JOSEPH ADDISON FRAZER, ANTHONY FRAZER, JAMES BENJAMIN FRAZER, WILLIAM FRAZER) Benjamin was born on September 29, 1928 in West Liberty, Ohio County, West Virginia and later moved to Blue Ridge Summit, where he lived until he entered the United States Army. Benjamin graduated from the University of South Carolina. He lived in various locations for work, including Iowa, Wisconsin and Ohio. In 1976, Benjamin relocated to Dothan, Alabama as plant manager for Gates Power Drive. He retired in 1992 and started his own company, Southland Roofing. Benjamin married Annette of Dothan and they remained living in Dothan, Alabama. He died on December 7, 2006 at age 78 and is buried at Germantown Bethel Cemetery, 16924 Raven Rock Road, Cascade, Frederick County, Maryland.[406] I located conflicting information for burial on Benjamin. He is also listed at a burial location at Bethel Church Cemetery, Chambersburg, Franklin County, Pennsylvania.[407]

F.2.11. **MARY S. FRAZER LOBINGIER** (1930 – January 27, 2020) (Daughter of ARTHUR WATSON FRAZER, SR., BENJAMIN FRANKLIN RENICK FRAZER, ROBERT ADDISON FRAZER, JOSEPH ADDISON FRAZER, ANTHONY FRAZER, JAMES BENJAMIN FRAZER, WILLIAM FRAZER) Mary was born in 1930. She married Roy W. Lobingier (1924-1995). Mary died January 27, 2020 at 89 years old in Pennsylvania. Mary and Roy are buried at Evergreen Cemetery, Gettysburg, Adams County, Pennsylvania.[408]

---

[406] Benjamin Franklin Frazer, U.S., Find a Grave, 1600s-Current, Memorial ID 54669033.

[407] Benjamin Franklin Frazer, U.S., Find A Grave, 1600s-Current, Memorial ID 17006936.

[408] Mary S. Frazer Lobingier, U.S., Find a Grave, 1600s-Current, Memorial ID 113825539.

OSCAR WALLACE FRAZER, SR.

RAILROAD STATION AGENT, TRAVELING SALESMAN AND COAL COMPANY PRESIDENT AND MANAGER BLUEFIELD, WEST VIRGINIA

THE SEVENTH GENERATION

OSCAR WALLACE FRAZER, SR. (September 17, 1880 – February 20, 1931) (Son of BENJAMIN FRANKLIN RENICK FRAZER, ROBERT ADDISON FRAZER, JOSEPH ADDISON FRAZER, ANTHONY FRAZER, JAMES BENJAMIN FRAZER, WILLIAM FRAZER) was born on September 17, 1880 in Beaver Mill, Nicholas County, West Virginia to Benjamin Franklin Renick Frazer and Laura Williams Frazer.[409] It appears Beaver Mill was once a small community that no longer exists. We located Beaver Mill gristmill that was built in 1852 near Craigsville in Nicholas County. Craigsville, according to the United States Census Bureau, is an area of 6.1 square miles, all land. The Beaver Mill gristmill no longer operates but is listed on the *National Register of Historic Places*.[410] The mill is adjacent to Beaver Creek. The post office and general store burned down in 1932.

> . . . This placed Beaver on the migration/settlement routes in the county and a prime location as one of the early

---

[409] Oscar Wallace Frazer, Sr., West Virginia, Births Index, 1804-1938.
[410] *National Register of Historic Places. National Park Service. July 9, 2010.*

settlements. The road that runs through Beaver is one of the early county roads, and was the main route southeast from Summersville.

The historic town of Beaver Mill was an important little village in Nicholas County's early history. It was the location of the post office and predates the one in nearby Craigsville. This hamlet rivaled Craigsville and was located on the road between Summersville and Greenbrier County.

As evidence of its significance as a local rural center of activity, the town contained two blacksmith shops, one at each end of the bridge, a schoolhouse, a large general store, a church and residences.[411]

Oscar was the first child of Benjamin and Laura Frazer. He was three years older than his younger brother Arthur. In 1900, at 19 years old, Oscar and his brother Arthur were living as boarders in the home of the John Cogar family, in Glade, Webster County, West Virginia which is located near Craigsville.[412] John Cogar was a farmer and a preacher. Oscar worked as a telegraph operator for the Baltimore & Ohio Railroad Company, and his brother Arthur, who was 16 years old, worked as a student telegraph operator. Oscar was an operator and station agent for this railroad for twelve years before changing careers.

In 1907, Oscar married Laura Belle Dyer (August 12, 1881 – February 8, 1968) in Charleston.[413] Laura was born in Kentucky and daughter to Margaret Alice "Maggie" Wooddell Dyer (1861-1928) and Morgan Homer Dyer (1855 – January 22, 1946), a farmer.

Oscar changed careers and by 1910, and perhaps earlier, worked as a traveling salesman for the Christian Peper Tobacco Company of St. Louis, Missouri, a manufacturer of cigarettes. Oscar then worked as a traveling

---

[411] United States Department of the Interior National Park Service, National Register of Historic Places Registration Form, NPS Form 10-900, OMB No. 1024-0018, Rev. Oct. 1990.

[412] 1900 United States Federal Census.

[413] Marriage of Oscar Wallace Frazer, Sr. and Laura Belle Dyer, West Virginia, Marriages Index, 1785-1971.

salesman for the F. H. Hammond Notion Company of Charleston, West Virginia, which was a wholesale dealer of notions and dry goods. He and Laura lived in Bluefield, West Virginia where they raised their family.[414] Bluefield is a small mountain city in Mercer County located on the West Virginia/Virginia border.

Laura and Oscar's first child, a daughter named Margaret, was born in 1909 in Bluefield. Two years later, their second child Ruth was born.[415] Their last child born six years later, a son, named Oscar Wallace, after his dad, was born in 1917.

The census for 1920 indicates that Oscar and Laura continued to live in Bluefield at 150 Giles Street.[416] Oscar worked as a Sales Manager in Bluefield for the Abney-Barnes Company stationed in Charleston, West Virginia. The 1920 U.S. Census lists a cook by the name of Adeline Coles living in the Frazer household.

In 1927, Oscar applied for U.S., Sons of the American Revolution Membership No. 44016, State Number 16 as a descendant of Anthony Frazer as a great-great-grandson, which was approved on February 23, 1929. Oscar's membership application indicates he was the son of Benjamin Franklin Frazer and Laura Williams Frazer, grandson of Robert Frazer and Harriet Summerson, great-grandson of Addison Frazer and Fanny Renick and great-great-grandson of Anthony Frazer and Hannah Herndon. Oscar's ancestor's (Anthony Frazer) service is as follows:

> The records of this office show that one Anthony Frazer served in the Revolutionary War as an ensign in Captain Thomas Meriwether's Company, 1st Virginia State Regiment, commanded by Colonel George Gibson, He was Commissioned May 29, 1777; was promoted to 2nd Lieutenant Dec. 1, 1777, in Captain John Camp's Company, same regiment, and resigned February 12,

---

[414] 1910 United States Federal Census.

[415] Ruth Laura Frazer, West Virginia, Births Index, 1804-1938.

[416] Year; 1920; Census Place: Bluefield Ward 6, Mercer, West Virginia; Roll: T625_1963; Page 7B; Enumeration District: 81.

1778. (Signed) Robert C. Davis, Major General, The Adjutant General.[417]

Laura and Oscar were members of the First Presbyterian Church of Bluefield. Laura was also a member of the Bluefield Chapter of the Daughters of the American Revolution and the United Daughters of the Confederacy. Oscar and Laura continued to live in Bluefield, West Virginia.[418] They moved to another home in Bluefield, owning a home at 816 College Avenue, Bluefield.[419]

By 1930 and perhaps earlier, Oscar Sr. was President and Manager of Ulvah Coal Company located in Bluefield, Letcher County, Kentucky. We were able to locate a Bluefield Post Office in Letcher County during these years.

> Letcher lies in the heart of the eastern Kentucky coal country. But until mining began in earnest with mineral rights acquisitions in the early 1900s, the county was one of Kentucky's most isolated and least economically viable areas. Many of its larger communities began as coal towns, while others grew up around rail stations and distribution centers supplying vicinity mines and camps.[420]

For years 1917 - 1928, Ulvah Coal Company had 150 employees.[421] For years 1925-1932, Ulvah Coal Company had an average of 25 employees.[422] The following was printed in *The Mountain Eagle,* "The Way We Were" on November 8, 2017, which printed clips from the paper since 1907. This

---

[417] U.S., Sons of the American Revolution Membership No. 44016, State Number 16, Oscar W. Frazer as descendant of Anthony Frazer.

[418] 1920 United States Federal Census.

[419] Year: 1930; Census Place; Bluefield, Mercer, West Virginia; Page: 1B; Enumeration District: 0004; FHL microfilm: 2342280.

[420] Letcher County - Post Offices, "The Post Offices of Letcher County, Kentucky," Rennick, Robert M., p. 59.

[421] *Coal Mines in Letcher County, Kentucky,* Compiled from Dodrill's 10,000 Coal Company Stores, sites.rootsweb.com.

[422] *Kentucky Coal Education,* Kentucky Coal and Energy Education Project, 1996-2007 Kentucky Foundation.

clip was originally printed on November 10, 1937 and it mentions Ulvah Coal Company:

> The bankruptcy case involving Ulvah Coal Company will continue November 19 when two coal leases executed by Polly Ann Lusk and Margaret Lusk and all of Ulvah Coal's equipment and other properties are sold at auction in front of the Letcher County Courthouse. The mine and leases are located on the North Fork of the Kentucky River at the Bluefield Post Office in Letcher County.[423]

History of West Virginia, Old and New states the following of Oscar Wallace Frazer, Sr.:

> Oscar Wallace Frazer is one of the progressive and influential businessmen of the City of Bluefield, Mercer County, where he is sales manager for the wholesale dry-goods and notion house of the Abney-Barnes Company, of Charleston, West Virginia, and he is also president and general manager in active supervision of the business of the Ulvah Coal Company, Bluefield, West Virginia, with which he has been thus connected since 1918. The mines of the company are situated at Bluefield, Kentucky.
>
> Mr. Frazer was born at Beaver, Nicholas County, West Virginia, September 17, 1880, and is a son of Benjamin F. R. and Laura H. (Williams) Frazer, the former a native of Virginia and the latter of Ohio. The lineage of the Frazer family traces back to Scotch origin, and representatives of the family came to America in the Colonial period of our national history. Benjamin F. R. Frazer became one of the substantial exponents of farm industry in Nicholas County, West Virginia, and while active in public affairs of local order he never consented to accept any official position except that of trustee of his school district.

---

[423] *The Mountain Eagle*, "The Way We Were," November 8, 2017.

Oscar W. Frazer was afforded the advantages of the public schools of Summersville, judicial center of his native county, and thereafter he learned the art of telegraphy, and for twelve years was in the employ of the Baltimore & Ohio Railroad Company as operator and station agent at various points, including Monongah, Marion County. For four years thereafter he was a traveling salesman for the Christian Peper Tobacco Company of St. Louis, Missouri, and he then passed three years as a traveling representative of the F. H. Hammond Notion Company of Charleston, West Virginia. Since severing this connection, he has been continuously identified with the Abney-Barnes Company of Charleston, West Virginia at Bluefield. He is one of the progressive members of the Bluefield Chamber of Commerce, is affiliated with the local York Rite bodies of the Masonic fraternity, including the commandery of Knights Templar, also the Beni-Kedem Temple of the Shrine at Charleston, West Virginia, is a member of the Bluefield Country Club, and he and his wife hold membership in the Presbyterian Church in their home city.[424]

Oscar died on February 20, 1931 in Williamson, West Virginia at age 50 while traveling for work. He is buried at Spring Hill Cemetery, 1555 Farnsworth Drive, Charleston, West Virginia.[425] Laura died after a short illness at age 86 in Beckley, West Virginia and is also buried at Spring Hill Cemetery. Oscar Wallace Frazer, Sr. and Laura Belle Dyer Frazer had three children:

G.1.   MARGARET LUCILLE FRAZER GIBSON (April 12, 1909 - January 21, 1984)

---

[424] History of West Virginia, Old and New, Volume 2, Callahan, James Morton, p.132.
[425] Oscar Wallace Frazer, Sr., U.S., Find A Grave Index, 1600s-Current, Memorial ID 95299998.

G.2. RUTH LAURA FRAZER PAINTER (November 30, 1911 –
      July 25, 2001)

G.3. OSCAR WALLACE FRAZER, JR. (May 11, 1917 – December
      2, 1993)

G.1. **MARGARET LUCILLE FRAZER GIBSON** (April 12, 1909 -
      January 21, 1984) (Daughter of OSCAR WALLACE FRAZER,
      SR., BENJAMIN FRANKLIN RENICK FRAZER, ROBERT
      ADDISON FRAZER, JOSEPH ADDISON FRAZER,
      ANTHONY FRAZER, JAMES BENJAMIN FRAZER,
      WILLIAM FRAZER) Margaret was born in Charleston, Kanawha
      County, West Virginia on April 12, 1909. Margaret grew up in the
      town of Bluefield, West Virginia. She was 21 years old when her
      dad died. After college, Margaret worked as a teacher in Bluefield.
      She married Ralph Brown Gibson (1902-1947) of Bluefield, who
      worked as a bookkeeper at a bank. Ralph died at age 44 in 1947
      in Preston, West Virginia when Margaret was only 38 years old.
      Margaret later moved to Florida. She died at age 74 on January 21,
      1984 in Fort Lauderdale, Florida.

G.2. **RUTH LAURA FRAZER PAINTER** (November 30, 1911 –
      July 25, 2001) (Daughter of OSCAR WALLACE FRAZER, SR.,
      BENJAMIN FRANKLIN RENICK FRAZER, ROBERT
      ADDISON FRAZER, JOSEPH ADDISON FRAZER,
      ANTHONY FRAZER, JAMES BENJAMIN FRAZER,
      WILLIAM FRAZER) Ruth grew up in Bluefield, West Virginia. In
      1941 at the age of 30, Ruth married Graham Fishburne Painter, Sr.
      (November 9, 1912 – December 15, 1981) in Kanawha County.[426]
      Ruth and Graham made their home in Charleston, West Virginia.
      Ruth died on July 25, 2001 at age 89[427] and is buried at Spring Hill
      Cemetery, 1555 Farnsworth Drive, Charleston, West Virginia.[428]

---

[426] Marriage of Ruth Laura Frazer and Graham Fishburne Painter, West Virginia,
Marriages Index, 1785-1971.

[427] Ruth Laura Frazer Painter, U.S., Social Security Death Index, 1935-2014.

[428] Ruth Laura Frazer Painter, U.S., Find A Grave Index, 1600s-Current, Memorial
ID 119453329.

Graham died on December 15, 1981 at age 69 and is also buried at Spring Hill Cemetery.[429]

My first contact with the Frazer family was with Graham Painter, Sr., husband to Ruth Frazer. Fresh out of high school from a small West Virginia town, I accepted a job with the West Virginia Department of Employment Security in Charleston. I worked there while saving money to attend college. Graham Painter, a Management Analyst, was one of my direct supervisors. He was such a kind, thoughtful and well-liked individual by everyone in the department. Little did I know that he was the uncle of the young man that I would marry.

G.3. **OSCAR WALLACE FRAZER, JR.** (May 11, 1917 – December 2, 1993) (Son of OSCAR WALLACE FRAZER, SR., BENJAMIN FRANKLIN RENICK FRAZER, ROBERT ADDISON FRAZER, JOSEPH ADDISON FRAZER, ANTHONY FRAZER, JAMES BENJAMIN FRAZER, WILLIAM FRAZER) See chapter on **OSCAR WALLACE FRAZER, JR.**, the direct ancestor of my children.

---

[429] Graham Fishburne Painter, U.S., Find A Grave Index, 1600s-Current, Memorial ID 119452787.

OSCAR WALLACE FRAZER, JR.

TRAVELING SALESMAN AND RESTAURANT AND INN MANAGER SAINT ALBANS, WEST VIRGINIA

THE EIGHTH GENERATION

OSCAR WALLACE FRAZER, JR. (May 11, 1917 – December 2, 1993) (Son of OSCAR WALLACE FRAZER, SR., BENJAMIN FRANKLIN RENICK FRAZER, ROBERT ADDISON FRAZER, JOSEPH ADDISON FRAZER, ANTHONY FRAZER, JAMES BENJAMIN FRAZER, WILLIAM FRAZER) was the only son and youngest child of Oscar Wallace Frazer, Sr. and Laura Belle Dyer. He was born on May 11, 1917 in the small city of Bluefield, Mercer County, West Virginia. Oscar's sisters, Margaret and Ruth, were eight and six years older. Oscar, Sr. was 37 years old and his mother Laura was 36 years old at his birth.

Bluefield is a small city in a valley between the headwaters of the Bluestone and East Rivers and runs along the Virginia border, neighboring Bluefield, Virginia in Tazewell County. Bluefield, West Virginia, incorporated in 1889, embodied the rapid growth of the smokeless bituminous coalfields. In the years of World War I, when coal smoke raised from chimneys and the taste of coal hung in the mountain air, coal was at its highest. In 1923, when Oscar was only six years old, Bluefield housed the offices of the Baldwin-Felts Detective Agency, the agency so well known in the coal fields as enemy to the miner. Then "The Great Depression" years nearly wiped out the town. During the years of World War II, once again Bluefield bounced back as it transported up to 40 percent of the North American coal supply.[430] During these years while the coal tonnage was good, Bluefield was known as a "Little New York."[431]

By 1935, Oscar was 18 years old and his family home continued to be in Bluefield, West Virginia, but Oscar attended the Greenbrier Military School in Lewisburg, West Virginia during his high school years. His attendance at the private school was considered by the family as an opportunity for a proper education for a young man. Greenbrier Military School was a boys only private military boarding school for high school and junior college. This school, founded in 1812, educated about 350 boys a year from the seventh grade through high school.[432] For a time, it also offered two years of junior college. Local West Virginia boys and those from neighboring states of Virginia, Ohio, Pennsylvania and Maryland attended the school. The students were active in local churches and brought revenue into the town of Lewisburg. Greenbrier was known as "The School of Achievement."[433] It was fully accredited with excellent teachers. The final catalog for the school (1971-72, p. 96) states,

> We believe in Christian education. . . without regard to man-made creeds or denominations. . . . A comprehension of religion reveals the beauty and meaning of life. We think the Bible should be taught as living literature and the revealed word of God.[434]

The 1930-31 catalog describes the school as having two farms of 800 acres and a rented farm of 600 acres. "On these farms are raised almost all the food used in the school."[435] The school was located fourteen miles from the Virginia state line and just off the C&O Railway, making transportation accessible. Cadets went to the well-known and famous Greenbrier Hotel in White Sulphur Springs to play golf or to watch tournaments and swim at the school expense. Formal dances were also held at The Greenbrier. Oscar

---

[430] National Coal Heritage and Coal Heritage Trail, 2020 Coal Heritage.
[431] Ibid.
[432] *The History of Greenbrier Military School*, 1875-1972, Haberfeld, Louise Rawl, p.18-23.
[433] Ibid.
[434] Ibid.
[435] Ibid.

was a member of the school football team. The Greenbrier Military School closed in 1972, and the campus was converted into the West Virginia School of Osteopathic Medicine.

The following is a picture of Oscar in August 1936 while in Greenbrier Military School.

Photo of Greenbrier Military School in 1936
while Oscar attended the school.

Oscar Wallace Frazer, Jr. in 1936.

While in school in Lewisburg, Oscar met his future wife Emily Francis Cole, who attended Southern Seminary in Buena Vista, Virginia. Fran, as she was called by family and friends, was born to Helen Kathryn Nightingale (1895 – January 16, 1968)[436] and Joseph Dyer Cole (June 20, 1882 – January 17, 1931)[437] on August 3, 1920 in Ohio. Fran grew up in Charleston, West Virginia with siblings Mary E. and Joseph Dyer (records at times spelled "Dyar" and "Dyre") Cole, living on Virginia Street in the 1930s. The family had a housekeeper/cook who lived with them named Dela Franklin, who was born in North Carolina.

Fran's dad Joseph died in 1931 at the age of 49 when Fran was only 10 years old. Her mother Helen remarried Henry Franklin Byrnside. With Fran's mother remarried and her father dead, it was thought it would be best for Fran to attend the Southern Seminary during her high school years. I never questioned Fran as to why the family decided it was best for her to attend the private school instead of living with her mother and her new husband in Parkersburg. Was this a convenience for her mother and her new marriage or was it for Fran's educational benefit? Fran never discussed her mother with me.

Southern Seminary for high school and junior college was a private institution located in what was the Buena Vista Hotel. This building is now on the *National Register of Historic Places*. The school was not officially affiliated with a religious faith, but it did embrace the values of The Church of Jesus Christ of Latter-day Saints. This is informally known as the LDS Church or Mormon Church. Fran nor her family was of the Mormon faith. Fran was raised a member of the Catholic Church. The school was originally founded as a liberal arts school for girls but later became a coeducational institution.

---

[436] Helen Kathryn Nightingale, U.S., Find A Grave Index, 1600s-Current, Memorial ID 135510869.

[437] Joseph Dyer Cole, U.S., Find A Grave Index, 1600s-Current, Memorial ID 135511711.

Photo of what was the Southern Seminary, Buena Vista, Virginia.

Photo of what was the Southern Seminary, Buena Vista, Virginia.
Photo taken by Lillian Frazer, March 2020

On September 11, 1937, Oscar and Fran married in Gallipolis, Gallia County, Ohio. Gallipolis was located on the Ohio River, about 58 miles up-river from Charleston, West Virginia.[438]

By 1938, Fran and Oscar had their first child, a son Oscar Wallace "Wally" III, named after Oscar. Oscar and Fran moved to Detroit, Michigan for Oscar's work, living there in 1940 and 1941. In 1940, they had their second child, a daughter, Nancy Jo. They lived in Detroit when the United States declared war on Japan after the attack on Pearl Harbor. By 1942 and at the age of 25, Oscar served in the Army during World War II and Fran moved back to Bluefield, West Virginia. Oscar was discharged in July 1943.[439] By 1943, they had their third child, a son named Hugh Dyer.

Oscar and Fran moved from Bluefield, making their home in Saint Albans, West Virginia, a small city in Kanawha County located about 13 miles from Charleston, the state capital. Oscar worked as a traveling salesman. Here they had their fourth and last child, a son Frederick Cole. Fran and Oscar were happy with children and work. Then, after twenty plus years married, Oscar and Fran separated and later divorced for a short time. In 1963, they remarried.[440]

Oscar who worked in marketing and sales of food products, had visions of owning or managing a restaurant. Years had gone by and their children were grown, most with families of their own. Retirement was at hand for Fran and Oscar, but the dreams of a restaurant still haunted them. Now was the time, they'd decided. The family home in Saint Albans had been sold and children were grown. They took the leap and stepped away from the comfort zone of home and security and the familiar and grabbed onto an opportunity. It was said Oscar in his younger days was too fond of his drink in the evenings but now that had ended along with his traveling jobs. It was as if they were young again and life was full of promises and anticipated delights yet to be lived and adventures to capture.

They stepped into the water slowly by managing a small variety and eat-in market on the edge of town. This was when I first met Fran and Oscar,

---

[438] Marriage of Oscar Wallace Frazer, Jr. and Emily Frances Cole, Ohio, County Marriage Records, 1774-1993.

[439] U.S., Department of Veterans Affairs BIRLS Death File, 1850-2010.

[440] Marriage of Oscar Wallace Frazer, Jr. and Emily Frances Cole, West Virginia, Marriages Index, 1785-1971.

liking them from my first introduction. Oscar, with his barrel of a chest, close cropped hair and good-natured humor, and Fran, with her ruthlessly soft loose curls and quick warm smile, had this shy small-town girl feel as though I was never a stranger to them. Both were friendly and immediately accepting of me as I graciously allowed myself to overcome my shyness and warm to them. Fran and Oscar shared the ability to mingle with folks of all educational levels and interests, giving each person their full attention without being overbearing. It was not until years later when I realized what a wonderful trait they possessed.

The opportunity was presented to Oscar and Fran for management of an intimate private country club and restaurant tucked in the mountains in a nearby county. There was no flutter of panic, no hesitation, just a strong desire to seize the occasion and plunge into the waters which they did. They had a fully functional commercial kitchen, delightful members to cater to and private parties for which they meticulously provided food and service fully enjoyed. Their dreams had been fulfilled. It was at this country club that I played my first golf. The youngest child of seven having grown up in a coal town, I had not attended any country club function and now I could swim and play golf, though I had no idea how to do either. It was at this country club that I received my first complaint. Being young, I followed the fashion dress of young folks, at which time was short shorts. I quickly learned that short shorts and tennis shoes were not the appropriate attire for a country club golf course resort as management was quickly notified by club members that a young girl was playing golf in inappropriate clothing. My birthday was quickly approaching, and I received a new set of golf clubs, golf shoes, and golf attire as Fran shot me a quick and sweet smile, enlightening me that we would have to follow the social protocol. My embarrassment lasted only briefly as I eyed my new gifts with gratefulness, wondering if I would ever play but happy for the experiences.

After a few years, the constant unrelenting tempo necessary for the country club management and catering became physically overly demanding on Fran as she showed obvious weariness with health issues. She was no longer able to maintain the hectic pace.

As often happens, when one thing ends another begins and so it was. Oscar was given an opportunity to manage a restaurant in Stone Mountain, Georgia, so off they went. Fran recovered physically while Oscar stepped up to a more demanding restaurant but with additional support. Fran and Oscar missed her involvement, having enjoyed sharing these special times together. They had now aged into their early 60s but not ready to retire or end that chapter of their life completely. So, they moved to their next venture, the management of a charming Bed and Breakfast in Elkins, West Virginia. Here the work pace was much slower. With the assistance of a cook, Fran returned to the kitchen and Oscar the management. They again shared their dreams. Both were socially friendly and accommodating to the guests and treasured their new home. The inn was almost as if Fran was back into the days of her youth when she visited her aunt at her Bed and Breakfast at Larchmont Inn in Ohio.

We followed the winding, curvy mountain roads with sweeping views to visit them at the Bed and Breakfast in Elkins on several occasions, enjoying the warmth and welcoming appeal of the Victorian style home, matching Fran and Oscar's warmheartedness. On one cold winter visit, the weather was extreme with frequent snowstorms and snow from an earlier storm was piled high on roadsides. As an icy snowstorm dumped on us overnight and the cold wind passed through the trees, we awoke to a beautiful blanket of snow and ice and I almost danced out of our room in excitement as we were left stranded at the lovely Inn for a couple extra days. It was a perfect location to be snowbound.

When Oscar and Fran were physically unable to continue the persistent pace of restaurant and inn management, they retired in Corbin, Kentucky where their daughter Nancy and her husband Truman lived. Oscar took pleasure in his long-awaited retirement days, reading history books that cluttered the table, catching up with his favorite football teams and visits with family. With a sharp mind and creases deepening around eyes still cheerful and alert, Fran spent these years volunteering at the local hospital, being instrumental in the formation of a local volunteer auxiliary and gift shop.

Oscar Wallace Frazer and Emily Frances Cole had four children (dates are omitted for family privacy):

H.1. OSCAR WALLACE "WALLY" FRAZER III
H.2. NANCY JO FRAZER SNODGRASS
H.3. HUGH DYER FRAZER
H.4. FREDERICK COLE FRAZER

H.1.   **OSCAR WALLACE "WALLY" FRAZER III** (Son of OSCAR WALLACE FRAZER JR., OSCAR WALLACE FRAZER SR., BENJAMIN FRANKLIN RENICK FRAZER, ROBERT ADDISON FRAZER, JOSEPH ADDISON FRAZER, ANTHONY FRAZER, JAMES BENJAMIN FRAZER, WILLIAM FRAZER) Wally, as he was called by family and friends, was born in Bluefield, West Virginia. He attended The Greenbrier Military School in Lewisburg, West Virginia as had his father. Wally joined the U.S. Air Force, serving for 20 years as a fighter pilot and instructor earning many commendations and medals during his military career, notably the Distinguished Flying Cross and the Top Gun award. He flew 100 successful missions over North Vietnam in his F-105 Thunder-chief fighter jet. He made his home primarily in San Antonio, Texas area. Wally is buried at Dallas-Fort Worth National Cemetery, 2000 Mountain Creek Parkway, Dallas, Texas. Wife and children are not listed for privacy of the family.

H.2.   **NANCY JO FRAZER SNODGRASS** (Daughter of OSCAR WALLACE FRAZER JR., OSCAR WALLACE FRAZER SR., BENJAMIN FRANKLIN RENICK FRAZER, ROBERT ADDISON FRAZER, JOSEPH ADDISON FRAZER, ANTHONY FRAZER, JAMES BENJAMIN FRAZER, WILLIAM FRAZER) Nancy married Truman Reed Snodgrass. Nancy and Truman are buried at Pine Hill Cemetery, Corbin, Kentucky. Children are not listed for privacy of the family.

H.3.   **HUGH DYER FRAZER** (Son of OSCAR WALLACE FRAZER JR., OSCAR WALLACE FRAZER SR., BENJAMIN FRANKLIN RENICK FRAZER, ROBERT ADDISON FRAZER, JOSEPH ADDISON FRAZER, ANTHONY FRAZER, JAMES BENJAMIN FRAZER, WILLIAM FRAZER) Hugh was a veteran of the U.S. Army, serving in Vietnam. He is buried at Dallas-Fort Worth National Cemetery, 2000 Mountain Creek Parkway, Dallas, Texas. Wife and children are not listed for privacy of the family.

H.4.   **FREDERICK "FRED" COLE FRAZER** (Son of OSCAR WALLACE FRAZER JR., OSCAR WALLACE FRAZER SR., BENJAMIN FRANKLIN RENICK FRAZER, ROBERT ADDISON FRAZER, JOSEPH ADDISON FRAZER,

ANTHONY FRAZER, JAMES BENJAMIN FRAZER, WILLIAM FRAZER) The name "Cole" was a maternal family name. Fred was born in South Charleston, West Virginia and is buried at Stonewall Memory Gardens, 12004 Lee Highway, Manassas, Virginia. Wife and children are not listed for privacy of the family.

Fran's family was influential and significant to her adult life. In her senior years, as memories lingered like a sweet and sophisticated scent, she spoke often of her ancestors, the Cole and Nightingale families, of whom she was extremely proud. Fran relished sharing stories of her family and their active roles in history. Below is a brief introduction of the Cole and Nightingale families.

COLE AND NIGHTINGALE FAMILIES

Emily Frances "Fran" Cole's mother, Helen Kathryn Nightingale, (1894-1968) was born in Bradford, McKean County, Pennsylvania to Mary Ann O'Connor Nightingale (1864-1913) and John "Jack" Henry Nightingale (1862-1934). As a young child, Helen (Fran's mother) lived in Parkersburg, West Virginia with her family. Below is a picture of Helen and family. Helen is the first child on the first row.

Fran's maternal granddad and Helen's dad John "Jack" Henry Nightingale was a native of Bolton, Lancaster County, England.[441] Jack was a registered Republican born on May 26, 1862. He was of English-Scotch-Irish descent. He came to America as a child, living in Bradford, Pennsylvania. He attended public schools and later attended St. Bonaventure College, Alleghany, New York. In 1881, he was elected to represent the Knights of Labor in the British Trades Congress. He worked for 30 years in England and the United States on behalf of working peoples' rights. He organized workers to join the American Federation of Labor and for five years he was the General Organizer. In 1893, he took up residence in West Virginia. In 1902, when the State Federation of Labor was organized, he was elected its Secretary-Treasurer for the State of West Virginia for two terms. He was appointed State Commissioner of Labor in 1914 by Governor H.D. Hatfield and was made Commissioner of Weights and Measures.[442]

Joseph Cole, Fran's dad was employed by Standard Oil Company. In 1907, Joseph owned Elite Laundry in Charleston originally located on Kanawha Street and later moved to the corner of Columbia Boulevard and Virginia Street. Joseph was highly active in civic affairs. In 1917, he married Helen Kathryn Nightingale in Kanawha County.[443] Joseph died in 1931 in an Ohio Hospital in Marietta where he was sick for about two weeks.[444] Joseph is buried at Sunset Memorial Park, 4301 MacCorkle Avenue, S.W, South Charleston, West Virginia.

According to Fran, the Cole family were descendants of James Cole of Plymouth, Massachusetts. His name stands at the head of the Cole family in America. He and his wife Mary Lobel came to Saco, Maine in 1632 and by 1633 lived in Plymouth.[445] We did not research the Cole family but located a fabulous book, *The Descendants of James Cole of Plymouth*

---

[441] England & Wales, Civil Registration Birth Index, 1837-1915.

[442] *West Virginia Handbook and Legislative Manual*, 1916, Harris, John T., p. 770.

[443] Marriage of Joseph Cole and Helen Kathryn Nightingale, West Virginia, Marriages Index, 1785-1971.

[444] Ohio, Death Records, 1908-1932, 1938-2018.

[445] *The Descendants of James Cole of Plymouth 1633*, Cole, Ernest Byron, The Grafton Press Genealogical Publishers, New York, 1908, p.21.

1633 by Ernest Byron Cole which lists ten generations of descendants of James Cole.

Joseph died at age 49 when Fran was only 10 years old.[446] Her mother Helen remarried Henry Franklin Byrnside (1903-1946) and lived in Parkersburg, West Virginia,[447] visiting Charleston often. Fran had an older sister, Mary Elizabeth Cole (Gierhardt) (1919 – 1999), and a younger brother, Joseph "Joe" Dyer Cole, Jr. (January 20, 1922 – December 13, 1991). Joe, Jr. was a World War II veteran, pipefitter, and coal broker. He died December 13, 1991 and is buried at Sunset Memorial Park, 4301 MacCorkle Avenue, S.W., South Charleston, West Virginia.[448] Helen died on January 16, 1968 at age 74 in Parkersburg, West Virginia after a short illness. She is buried at Sunset Memorial Park, 4301 MacCorkle Avenue, S.W, South Charleston, West Virginia.[449]

After her mother remarried, Fran spent years with her aunt Harriett McNeal, (1872-1967) who she called "Auntie" and who was an older sister to Fran's dad. Harriett married Walter McNeal of Charleston, West Virginia. In 1951, Walter NcNeal became General Manager of the Elite Laundry Company. It is this Aunt Harriett that years later announced Fran's marriage to Oscar and the aunt who after her husband Walter died lived with Fran's family. "Auntie" Harriett lived to the age of 95.[450]

During her youth, Fran and her brother Joe spent many summers visiting their Aunt Emma. These were impressionable and memorable years for Fran, who with an inquisitive nature, was ready to learn and explore. Throughout the years I knew Fran, she often spoke of these fun-filled summers and the exuberance of youth with a wide smile and eyes lit up with sheer delight as they were forever etched in her memories. Aunt Emma Safford Cole Cram (April 16, 1878 – October 27, 1973) had a lovely mansion, the Larchmont Inn, on Second Street in Marietta, Ohio. Aunt Emma was Joseph's (Fran's father) sister, five years his elder.

---

[446] Joseph Cole, U.S., Find A Grave Index, 1600s-Current, Memorial ID 135511711.

[447] Marriage of Helen Kathryn Nightingale Cole and Henry Franklin Byrnside, West Virginia, Marriages Index, 1785-1971.

[448] Joseph Cole, Jr., U.S., Find A Grave Index, 1600s-Current, Memorial ID 147849885.

[449] Helen Kathryn Nightingale Cole Byrnside, U.S., Find A Grave Index, 1600s-Current, Memorial ID 135510869.

[450] Harriett McNeal, West Virginia, Deaths Index, 1853-1973.

She married William Johnson Cram (February 2, 1862 – July 18, 1942) in 1901 in Ohio. In 1919, William Cram purchased the property known as the Larchmont House in Marietta, Ohio for $16,000.[451] Aunt Emma, and Uncle William Cram purchased the southern style plantation of Larchmont while it was in total disrepair according to Fran. The mansion, located at 524 Second Street, a short distance from the Muskingum River, sat high above the street and separated by the neighborhood by a blanket of trees. The Crams painstakingly restored the mansion, widened the porch, added a kitchen and butler's pantry, and proudly turned their lovely home into the Larchmont Inn.

Along with Joe, Fran's brother, they explored every nook and cranny of the old mansion, including the secret passageway as they heard stories of the enchanting home and the Larchmont ghosts. It was at this Inn that Fran acquired her love of cooking while discovering the kitchen and watching those at work.

I located a few notes that Fran wrote and left in my care. She often spoke of Larchmont's part in the underground railroad. Fran described Larchmont as:

> The slaves were taken upstairs in the back bedroom. In this room was a sliding door that could not be detected unless you knew of it. Through this opening, they were taken into a small room that had a ladder built on the wall. The ladder extended into a room above the rafters, behind the walls of the third-floor rooms. Here they stayed until a boat or wagon would pick them up. Some stayed on in and around Marietta.
>
> My brother Joe and I spent many summers at Larchmont as children and as such we were in every nook and cranny of the house. Yes, we were even frightened by the Larchmont ghost.

Originally, the mansion was erected in the 1830s for Albigence Waldo Putnam, a lawyer and historian, who had the home built for his

---

[451] *The Marietta Times*, "A Property's Past: Larchmont," Kelly, Michael, January 19, 2019.

southern bride Catherine Ann Sevier, the granddaughter of Tennessee's first governor.[452] His bride never lived in the mansion after learning that she was unable to bring her servants along. In the years to follow, the mansion changed ownership numerous times. This graceful southern mansion carried a mystique air and believed by many to be one of the relay stations in the underground railroad. Supposedly, the slaves fled to these homes and stations for safety prior to their passage to the North.

---

[452] Ibid.

LARCHMONT

This beautiful southern colonial home is now open to people who enjoy resting in the delightful atmosphere possessed only by places of this kind.

Built in 1838 of brick and stone with thick walls, high ceilings and heavy floors of southern pine, it stands today as firm and strong as when erected. Recently the house was completely renovated. Modern tile baths with showers were installed together with electricity.

While every room has an open fire, there is also a complete heating system.

The house surrounded by larch, cypress, maple, and Norway spruce trees planted in its early days, stands well back from the street in large grounds.

A broad flagstone walk leads to the hospitable doorway.

A WARM WELCOME AWAITS YOU AT LARCHMONT INN

Parking space in the private driveway is free and garage space at small cost.

MRS E. C. CRAM
524 SECOND STREET
MARIETTA, OHIO

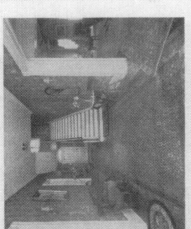

Aunt Emma Cole Cram died on October 27, 1973 and is buried at Union Cemetery, 3349 Olentangy River Road, Columbus, Franklin County, Ohio. Fran loved her summer visits with Aunt Emma and Uncle William and the enchanted home and all its told and untold mysteries. The home stayed within their family for decades. At Larchmont, Fran discovered the joy of gracious dinners with cloth napkins and dreamed of having her own someday. Pride radiated from Fran as in adulthood she told us stories of Larchmont Inn and its part in securing safety and passage to the North for many folks escaping slavery. When researching the validity of the underground tunnel and the elegant mansion's role in slavery, my findings neither documented nor discredited its role. I discovered a newspaper article on the Larchmont with a quote from the current owner of the lovely home stating, *"There's a lot out there that is unverifiable,"*Dernberger (one of the current owners of the home in 2019) said and, *"People like romantic folktales."*[453]

I chose to believe in Fran's love for The Larchmont and its role in history, including assisting slaves to safety to the North. As a non-professional family researcher, I have learned much history has not been documented and cannot be verified as the current owner of Larchmont stated. Myself, I love romantic folktales and old legends, many of which are based on truth or at the very least partial truths and the lovely old home of Larchmont is one of those urban legends passed down from generation to generation. You may come to your own conclusion.

Many of the years prior to Fran and Oscar's retirement, we lived near them and they were always active and supportive in their children's and grandchildren's lives as well as their dreams. In their retirement years, their steps were slow and measured with age and their faces lined with soft creases. They loved the years of their youth and those with their children and family, but in many ways those later years of reaching out for long-awaited dreams were a sheer delight that they shared with one another. Many times, Fran told me these years were among their happiest.

Oscar died on December 2, 1993 at the age of 76 in Corbin, Kentucky.[454] Prior to his death, he had a massive stroke from which he never recovered. Oscar is buried at the Pine Hill Cemetery (also known

---

[453] Ibid.

[454] Oscar Wallace Frazer, Jr., Kentucky, Death Index, 1911-2000.

as Corbin Cemetery or Pine Grove Cemetery), Corbin, Knox County, Kentucky.[455] Eleven years after Oscar's death, Fran died on April 21, 2004 in Corbin Kentucky. She is buried beside Oscar in Pine Hill Cemetery.[456]

It brings a smile and a warmness to me as I think of Fran and Oscar with their generous and adventurous nature and quickness to laugh. They were dreamers, adding spice to our lives and encouraged me to reach for my own dreams. Both touched my life for which I am grateful.

---

[455] Oscar Wallace Frazer (Frazier), Jr., U.S., Find A Grave Index, 1600s-Current, Memorial ID 121094535.

[456] Emily Frances Cole Frazer, U.S., Find A Grave Index, 1600s-Current, Memorial ID 121094551.

A.   **WILLIAM FRAZER** (1701-1734)

B.   **JAMES BENJAMIN FRAZER** (1729-1774/1775)

C.   **ANTHONY FRAZER** (1754-1804)

D.   **JOSEPH ADDISON FRAZER** (1798-1886)

E.   **ROBERT ADDISON FRAZER** (1822-1906)

F.   **BENJAMIN FRANKLIN RENICK FRAZER** (1858-1934)

G.   **OSCAR WALLACE FRAZER, SR.** (1880–1931)

H.   **OSCAR WALLACE FRAZER, JR.** (1917–1993)

This is **NOT** an all-inclusive chart of the William Frazer descendants. My research and concentration involved around the direct ancestors of Oscar Wallace Frazer, Jr. In doing so, many other Frazer ancestors emerged in my findings and those I have included as best and as accurately as possible without in-depth research on each person. I have attempted to include the first generation of each in hopes it may assist others in search of their families or history.

A. **WILLIAM FRAZER** (1701-1734)
   A.1. **JAMES BENJAMIN FRAZER** (1729-1774/1775)
(SEE B. JAMES BENJAMIN FRAZER)

B. **JAMES BENJAMIN FRAZER** (1729-1774/1775)
   B.1. **ANTHONY FRAZER** (March 22, 1754 – March 4, 1804)
(SEE C. ANTHONY FRAZER)
   B.2. JOHN FRAZER (1756 - November 28, 1793)
      B.2.1. THOMAS FOX FRAZER (1783-1841)
         Mary Elizabeth Frazer Chandler (1821- September 9, 1881)
      B.2.2. JOHN FRAZER (1786-1819)
      B.2.3. ANN FRAZER (1788-1792)
      B.2.4. ELIZABETH FRAZER (1790-1873)
      B.2.5. PHILADELPHIA CLAIBORNE FRAZER TURNER (1792-1831)
   B.3. JAMES FRAZER II (December 23, 1758 – December 20, 1798)
      B.3.1. ELIZABETH FRAZER FRAZER (1787-1846)
      B.3.2. MARTHA "BETSY" FRAZER (b. abt. 1789)
      B.3.3. SARAH KENYON "SALLIE" FRAZER HANSFORD (February 10, 1792 – September 3, 1888)
      B.3.4. JAMES FRAZER (b. abt. 1794)
      B.3.5. WILLIAM SMITH FRAZER (November 10, 1795 – January 27, 1850)
   B.4. WILLIAM FRAZER (March 1, 1761 – March 19, 1819)
      B.4.1. REBECCA FRAZER (1788 – October 22, 1851)
      B.4.2. MARY DUERSON FRAZER (1790-1842)
      B.4.3. MARTHA D. FRAZER (1792-1851)
      B.4.4. DR. ROBERT FRAZER (1795-1833)
      B.4.5. WILLIAM FRAZER (January 26, 1797 – 1880)
      B.4.6. LUCY M. FRAZER BARTLETT (1798 - March 6, 1842)
      B.4.7. PHILADELPHIA HERNDON FRAZER (1802-1819)

B.4.8.   DR. WARREN FRAZER (October 6, 1805- November 16, 1884)

B.4.9.   JOHN PEACHY FRAZER (1810-1819)

B.4.10.   VIRGINIA K. FRAZER (Unknown - June 8, 1859)

B.4.11.   ELIZABETH JANE GARNETT FRAZER NOLAN (1814 – May 30, 1852)

B.4.12.   EDMUND FRAZER (Unknown)

B.4.13.   CHILD FRAZER (Unknown)

B.5.   MARTHA FRAZER (abt. 1763 - Unknown)

B.6.   REUBEN FRAZER (1767-1832)

B.6.1.   FREDERICK FRAZER (1807-1863)

B.6.2.   MARTHA FRAZER TURNER (1811 – July 2, 1876)

B.6.3.   CASSANDRA FRAZER (Unknown)

C.   **ANTHONY FRAZER** (March 22, 1754 – March 4, 1804)

C.1.   MARY LEWIS FRAZER (1781-1786)

C.2.   JAMES A. FRAZER (June 7, 1783 – February 11, 1854)

C.2.1.   RICHARD FRAZER (1810-1831)

C.2.2.   JAMES ADDISON FRAZER (July 6, 1812 – March 27, 1860)

C.2.2.1.   William O. Frazer (1839-1889)

C.2.2.2.   Elizabeth Frazer Taylor (1841-1870)
Mary Henry Taylor Randolph (1859-1935)
William Frazer Taylor (1861-1863)
Heyward Gibbons Taylor (1865-1931)
George Edmund Taylor (b. 1867)
Julie Edmond Taylor (b. 1869)

C.2.2.3.   James Frazer (b. 1843)

C.2.2.4.   Major Philip Foulke Frazer (December 22, 1844 – May 5, 1864)

C.2.2.5.   Julia Frazer Edmond (1847-1898)
David Edmond (1868-1952)
Robert P. Edmond (b. 1869/1870)
Philip Edmond (b. 1870)
Mary (Mae) Edmond Bridges (1872-1945)
Julian Edmond (b. 1874)
Mattie Edmond Guthrie (1878-1955)
Bessie Edmond (b. 1879)
John Ducas Edmond (1885-1885)

    C.2.2.6. Martha Frazer Jessel Andrus (Agnes Herndon) (1853-1920)

C.2.3. HANNAH HERNDON FRAZER THOMPSON (February 5, 1815 – January 23, 1889)

C.2.4. WILLIAM HERNDON FRAZER (April 22, 1817 – August 9, 1825)

C.2.5. THOMAS FRAZER (1820)

C.2.6. SARAH THOMAS FRAZER HARRISON (August 1, 1820 – March 3, 1891)

    C.2.6.1. Kitty Heather Harrison (1858-1944)

    C.2.6.2. Margaret Carter Harrison (1860-1937)

C.2.7. MARGARET CARTER FRAZER CALWELL (August 1, 1826 - March 20, 1896)

    C.2.7.1. Mary Elizabeth Calwell Young (1849-1878)

    C.2.7.2. James Lewis Calwell (1852-1895)

    C.2.7.3. Fanny Bedford Calwell (b. 1855)

    C.2.7.4. Sarah Calwell (b.1856)

    C.2.7.5. William B. Calwell

C.2.8. ELIZABETH "BETTIE" TAYLOR FRAZER BEIRNE (February 22, 1829 – November 10, 1908)

    C.2.8.1. Bedford Calwell Beirne (1852-1907)

    C.2.8.2. Patrick Beirne

    C.2.8.3. Harry Heath Beirne, Sr. (1857-1910)

    C.2.8.4. Gordon O. Beirne (1860-1907)

C.3. EDWARD FRAZER (February 4, 1785 – July 25, 1863)

C.4. ELIZABETH FRAZER (February 13, 1787 – December 3, 1803)

C.5. GEORGE FRAZER (March 3, 1790 - November 13, 1830)

C.6. REV. HERNDON FRAZER (August 20, 1792 – July 10, 1877)

    C.6.1. HERNDON "DON" FRAZER (1849 – December 24, 1876)

    C.6.2. HULDAH FRAZER COLEMAN (September 6, 1852 – March 10, 1940)

C.7. MARGARET "PEGGY" FRAZER (1795/1799 – January 9, 1828)

C.8. **JOSEPH ADDISON FRAZER** (May 22, 1798 – March 31, 1886)

(SEE D. JOSEPH ADDISON FRAZER)

C.9. ANTHONY FRAZER (abt. 1801 – February 14, 1839)

C.10. UNKNOWN CHILD

D. **JOSEPH ADDISON FRAZER** (May 22, 1798 – March 31, 1886)

    D.1. **ROBERT ADDISON FRAZER** (1822-1906)

(SEE E. ROBERT ADDISON FRAZER)

D.2. SARAH REBECCA RENICK FRAZER SUMMERSON (abt. 1824 – May 1, 1893)

    D.2.1. WILLIAM FRAZER SUMMERSON (July 21, 1847 – January 28, 1927)

    D.2.2. HENRY EDMUND SUMMERSON (July 12, 1849 – July 13, 1917)

    D.2.3. FRANCES "FANNIE" SUMMERSON BYERS EAKLE (May 25, 1851 – March 4, 1891)

    D.2.4. JUNIUS ROBERT SUMMERSON (June 29, 1853 – December 18, 1909)

    D.2.5. RICHARD PEYTON SUMMERSON (abt. 1856 – March 4, 1879)

    D.2.6. MARY FRAZER (FRAZIER) SUMMERSON HUNTER (September 25, 1858 – February 7, 1931/1932)

D.3. FANNIE FRAZER LINK (abt. 1827-1900)

    D.3.1. IDA FRAZER (FRAZIER) LINK HARRIS (September 16, 1857 – February 6, 1899)

    D.3.2. HERNDON FRAZER LINK (1866 – August 20, 1919)

D.4. LIEUT. JAMES HERNDON FRAZER (abt. 1836 – August 23, 1862)

E. **ROBERT ADDISON FRAZER** (February 11, 1822 – May 4, 1906)

    E.1. RICHARD SUMMERSON FRAZER (December 25, 1849 – July 7, 1938)

        E.1.1. MARY JOSPHINE FRAZER TRENT (April 27, 1871 – July 28, 1953)

        E.1.2. ROBERT FRAZER (abt. 1872 - Unknown)

        E.1.3. HARRIET T. FRAZER (July 23, 1874 – February 12, 1894)

        E.1.4. WILLIAM D. FRAZER (July 8, 1876 – March 5, 1928)

        E.1.5. HANORA ELLEN FRAZER (March 2, 1879 – January 8, 1957)

        E.1.6. GERTRUDE FRAZER (February 11, 1881 – November 29, 1962)

        E.1.7. RICHARD PEYTON (PAYTON) FRAZER (November 15, 1882 - Unknown)

        E.1.8. BENJAMIN F. FRAZER (August 10, 1883 – Unknown)

        E.1.9. FLORENCE ROSELLA FRAZER (August 1885 – October 27, 1967)

    E.2. WILLIAM ADDISON FRAZER (1851- July 7, 1940)

E.2.1.　WILLIE BELLE FRAZER (January 24, 1880 – October 22, 1883)

E.2.2.　JAMES HERNDON FRAZER (October 29, 1881 – May 14, 1944)

E.2.3.　CHARLES EDWARD FRAZER (1883-1968)

E.2.4.　LESLIE BROOKE FRAZER (May 12, 1885 – March 13, 1968)

E.2.5.　ELLA D. FRAZER FISHER (1887-1979)

E.2.6.　LULA E. FRAZER RADER (October 19, 1889 – August 20, 1928)

E.2.7.　STANLEY CLYDE FRAZER (May 10, 1892 – May 9, 1958)

E.2.8.　WILBUR WATSON FRAZER (November 3, 1895 – February 23, 1963)

E.2.9.　HOWARD VIRGIL FRAZER (January 11, 1903 – February 20, 1999)

E.3.　CHARLES HERNDON FRAZER (May 5, 1853 – January 19, 1922)

E.3.1.　HERNDON VEAZEY FRAZER (AUGUST 24, 1880 – JULY 7, 1957)

E.3.2.　MARGARET FRAZER COLEMAN (May 15, 1882 – April 8, 1935)

E.3.2.1.　Charles Bradford Coleman, Jr. (August 14, 1905 - June 29, 1983)

Charles Bradford Coleman III (March 20, 1948 – May 2, 2015)

E.3.2.2.　Caroline Caperton Coleman Myers Hicks (March 27, 1910 – July 14, 1983)

E.3.3.　FELIX ADISON FRAZER (November 19, 1895 – April 26, 1897)

E.3.4.　ROLAND CARTER FRAZER (March 14, 1899 – September 26, 1972)

E.4.　SARAH "SALLIE" FRAZER (abt. 1856-Unknown)

E.5.　**BENJAMIN FRANKLIN RENICK FRAZER** (January 19, 1858 – September 25, 1934)

(SEE F. BENJAMIN FRANKLIN RENICK FRAZER)

E.6.　HANNAH FRAZER (June 22, 1859 - Unknown)

E.7.　ROSABEL FRAZER REYNOLDS (August 31, 1861 - Unknown)

F.　**BENJAMIN FRANKLIN RENICK FRAZER** (January 19, 1858 – September 25, 1934)

F.1.　**OSCAR W. FRAZER, SR.** (September 17, 1880 – February 20, 1931)

(SEE G. OSCAR W. FRAZER, SR.)

>   F.2.   ARTHUR WATSON FRAZER, SR. (September 2, 1882 - May 1947)
>
>>   F.2.1.   ARTHUR WATSON FRAZER, JR. (May 24, 1913 – April 28, 1990)
>>
>>   F.2.2.   DOROTHY EVALYN FRAZER MCCLEAF (December 5, 1915 – June 26, 2002)
>>
>>   F.2.3.   CARL LAWRENCE FRAZER (February 19, 1919 – June 15, 1998)
>>
>>   F.2.4.   RONALD MCCUE FRAZER (February 9, 1921 – June 14, 1985)
>>
>>   F.2.5.   BETTY JANE FRAZER BROWN (February 28, 1922 – May 1, 2010)
>>
>>   F.2.6.   PAUL RAY FRAZER (August 19, 1923 – February 29, 2008)
>>
>>   F.2.7.   ROBERT JAMES FRAZER, SR. (August 25, 1924 – January 11, 1996)
>>
>>   F.2.8.   ALICE V. FRAZER MELLOTT (1925-1950)
>>
>>   F.2.9.   FREDERICK HAROLD FRAZER (April 7, 1927 – July 4, 1949)
>>
>>   F.2.10.   BENJAMIN FRANKLIN "FRANKIE" FRAZER (September 29, 1928 – December 7, 2006)
>>
>>   F.2.11.   MARY S. FRAZER LOBINGIER (1930 – January 27, 2020)

G.   **OSCAR W. FRAZER, SR.** (September 17, 1880 – February 20, 1931)

>   G.1.   MARGARET LUCILLE FRAZER GIBSON (April 12, 1909 - January 21, 1984)
>
>   G.2.   RUTH LAURA FRAZER PAINTER (November 30, 1911 – July 25, 2001)
>
>   G.3.   **OSCAR WALLACE FRAZER, JR.** (May 11, 1917 – December 2, 1993)

(SEE H. OSCAR WALLACE FRAZER, JR.)

H.   **OSCAR WALLACE FRAZER, JR.** (May 11, 1917 – December 2, 1993)
(Dates of children omitted for privacy)

>   H.1.   OSCAR WALLACE "WALLY" FRAZER III
>
>   H.2.   NANCY JO FRAZER SNODGRASS
>
>   H.3.   HUGH DYER FRAZER
>
>   H.4.   FREDERICK COLE FRAZER

CEMETERIES

ARKANSAS

FRIENDSHIP CEMETERY, Springdale, Washington County, Arkansas

BENJAMIN FRANKLIN RENICK FRAZER (January 19, 1858 – September 25, 1934) (Son of ROBERT ADDISON FRAZER, JOSEPH ADDISON FRAZER, ANTHONY FRAZER, JAMES BENJAMIN FRAZER, WILLIAM FRAZER)

KENTUCKY

LEXINGTON CEMETERY, 833 W. Main Street, Lexington, Fayette County, Kentucky (There are many members of the Frazer family buried at this cemetery.)

EDWARD FRAZER (February 4, 1785 – July 25, 1863) (Son of ANTHONY FRAZER, JAMES BENJAMIN FRAZER, WILLIAM FRAZER)

ELIZABETH FRAZER FRAZER (June 24, 1790 – May 10, 1873) (Wife of EDWARD FRAZER, ANTHONY FRAZER, JAMES BENJAMIN FRAZER, WILLIAM FRAZER)

LAURA BROOKING FRAZER (Abt. 1818 – January 18, 1885) (Wife of DR. WARREN FRAZER, WILLIAM FRAZER, JAMES BENJAMIN FRAZER, WILLIAM FRAZER)

DR. WARREN FRAZER (October 6, 1805 - November 16, 1884) (Son of WILLIAM FRAZER, JAMES BENJAMIN FRAZER, WILLIAM FRAZER)

OLD EPISCOPAL THIRD STREET CEMETERY (also known as Christ Church Cemetery), 251 East 3rd Street, Lexington, Kentucky

ELIZABETH JANE GARNETT FRAZER NOLAN (1814 - May 30, 1852), (Daughter of WILLIAM FRAZER, JAMES BENJAMIN FRAZER, WILLIAM FRAZER)

LUCY M. FRAZER BARTLETT (1798 - March 6, 1842) (Daughter of WILLIAM FRAZER, JAMES BENJAMIN FRAZER, WILLIAM FRAZER)

PHILADELPHIA HERNDON FRAZER (October 6, 1770 - September 23, 1830) (Wife of WILLIAM FRAZER, JAMES BENJAMIN FRAZER, WILLIAM FRAZER)

REBECCA FRAZER (1788 – October 22, 1851) (Daughter of WILLIAM FRAZER, JAMES BENJAMIN FRAZER, WILLIAM FRAZER)

VIRGINIA K. FRAZER (Unknown - June 8, 1859) (Daughter of WILLIAM FRAZER, JAMES BENJAMIN FRAZER, WILLIAM FRAZER)

WILLIAM FRAZER (March 1, 1761 – March 19, 1819) (Son of JAMES BENJAMIN FRAZER, WILLIAM FRAZER)

PINE HILL CEMETERY (Also known as Corbin Cemetery or Pine Grove Cemetery), Corbin, Knox County, Kentucky

EMILY FRANCIS COLE FRAZER (FRAZIER) (August 3, 1920 – April 21, 2004) (Wife of OSCAR WALLACE FRAZER JR., OSCAR WALLACE FRAZER SR., BENJAMIN FRANKLIN RENICK FRAZER, ROBERT ADDISON FRAZER, JOSEPH ADDISON

FRAZER, ANTHONY FRAZER, JAMES BENJAMIN FRAZER, WILLIAM FRAZER)

NANCY JO FRAZER SNODGRASS (Dates are private.) (Daughter of OSCAR WALLACE FRAZER JR., OSCAR WALLACE FRAZER SR., BENJAMIN FRANKLIN RENICK FRAZER, ROBERT ADDISON FRAZER, JOSEPH ADDISON FRAZER, ANTHONY FRAZER, JAMES BENJAMIN FRAZER, WILLIAM FRAZER)

OSCAR WALLACE FRAZER, JR. (FRAZIER) (May 11, 1917 – December 2, 1993) (Son of OSCAR WALLACE FRAZER SR., BENJAMIN FRANKLIN RENICK FRAZER, ROBERT ADDISON FRAZER, JOSEPH ADDISON FRAZER, ANTHONY FRAZER, JAMES BENJAMIN FRAZER, WILLIAM FRAZER)

TRUMAN REED SNODGRASS (Dates are private.) (Husband of NANCY JO FRAZER SNODGRASS, OSCAR WALLACE FRAZER JR., OSCAR WALLACE FRAZER SR., BENJAMIN FRANKLIN RENICK FRAZER, ROBERT ADDISON FRAZER, JOSEPH ADDISON FRAZER, ANTHONY FRAZER, JAMES BENJAMIN FRAZER, WILLIAM FRAZER)

MARYLAND

BROADFORDING CHURCH OF GOD CEMETERY, 16109 Broadfording Road, Broadfording, Washington County, Maryland

ALICE V. FRAZER MELLOTT (1925-1950) (Daughter of ARTHUR WATSON FRAZER SR., BENJAMIN FRANKLIN RENICK FRAZER, ROBERT ADDISON FRAZER, JOSEPH ADDISON FRAZER, ANTHONY FRAZER, JAMES BENJAMIN FRAZER, WILLIAM FRAZER)

ARTHUR WATSON FRAZER, SR. (September 2, 1882 – May 1947) (Son of BENJAMIN FRANKLIN RENICK FRAZER, ROBERT ADDISON FRAZER, JOSEPH ADDISON FRAZER,

ANTHONY FRAZER, JAMES BENJAMIN FRAZER, WILLIAM FRAZER)

EVALYN L. MYERS FRAZER (1889-1959) (Wife of ARTHUR WATSON FRAZER SR., BENJAMIN FRANKLIN RENICK FRAZER, ROBERT ADDISON FRAZER, JOSEPH ADDISON FRAZER, ANTHONY FRAZER, JAMES BENJAMIN FRAZER, WILLIAM FRAZER)

FREDERICK HAROLD FRAZER (April 7, 1927 – July 4, 1949) (Son of ARTHUR WATSON FRAZER SR., BENJAMIN FRANKLIN RENICK FRAZER, ROBERT ADDISON FRAZER, JOSEPH ADDISON FRAZER, ANTHONY FRAZER, JAMES BENJAMIN FRAZER, WILLIAM FRAZER)

CHRIST CHURCH EPISCOPAL CEMETERY, 301 South Talbot Street, Saint Michaels, Talbot County, Maryland

JULIA FRAZER EDMOND (1847-1898) (Daughter of JAMES ADDISON FRAZER, JAMES A. FRAZER, ANTHONY FRAZER, JAMES BENJAMIN FRAZER, WILLIAM FRAZER)

MARTHA FRAZER (AGNES HERNDON) JESSEL ANDRUS (1853-1920)[457] (Daughter of JAMES ADDISON FRAZER, JAMES A. FRAZER, ANTHONY FRAZER, JAMES BENJAMIN FRAZER, WILLIAM FRAZER)

GERMANTOWN BETHEL CEMETERY, (Also known as Bethel Cemetery, Germantown Church of God Cemetery) 16924 Raven Rock Road, Cascade, Frederick County, Maryland (located near the Pennsylvania border).

ARTHUR WATSON FRAZER, JR. (May 24, 1913 – April 28, 1990) (Son of ARTHUR WATSON FRAZER, SR., BENJAMIN FRANKLIN RENICK FRAZER, ROBERT ADDISON FRAZER,

---

[457] "West Virginia Births", Index, 1804-1938.

JOSEPH ADDISON FRAZER, ANTHONY FRAZER, JAMES BENJAMIN FRAZER, WILLIAM FRAZER)

BENJAMIN FRANKLIN "FRANKIE" FRAZER (September 29, 1928 – December 7, 2006) (Son of ARTHUR WATSON FRAZER, SR., BENJAMIN FRANKLIN RENICK FRAZER, ROBERT ADDISON FRAZER, JOSEPH ADDISON FRAZER, ANTHONY FRAZER, JAMES BENJAMIN FRAZER, WILLIAM FRAZER) (Records also indicate he was buried at BETHEL CHURCH CEMETERY, Chambersburg, Franklin County, Pennsylvania.)

BETTY JANE FRAZER BROWN (February 28, 1922 – May 1, 2010) (Daughter of ARTHUR WATSON FRAZER SR., BENJAMIN FRANKLIN RENICK FRAZER, ROBERT ADDISON FRAZER, JOSEPH ADDISON FRAZER, ANTHONY FRAZER, JAMES BENJAMIN FRAZER, WILLIAM FRAZER)

BRUCE MCCLEAF (1910 – February 1, 1973) (Husband of DOROTHY EVALYN FRAZER MCCLEAF, ARTHUR WATSON FRAZER SR., BENJAMIN FRANKLIN RENICK FRAZER, ROBERT ADDISON FRAZER, JOSEPH ADDISON FRAZER, ANTHONY FRAZER, JAMES BENJAMIN FRAZER, WILLIAM FRAZER)

CARL LAWRENCE FRAZER (February 19, 1919 – June 15, 1998) (Son of ARTHUR WATSON FRAZER SR., BENJAMIN FRANKLIN RENICK FRAZER,) ROBERT ADDISON FRAZER, JOSEPH ADDISON FRAZER, ANTHONY FRAZER, JAMES BENJAMIN FRAZER, WILLIAM FRAZER)

DOROTHY EVALYN FRAZER MCCLEAF (December 5, 1915 – June 26, 2002) (Daughter of ARTHUR WATSON FRAZER, SR., BENJAMIN FRANKLIN RENICK FRAZER, ROBERT A. FRAZER, JOSEPH ADDISON FRAZER, ANTHONY FRAZER, JAMES BENJAMIN FRAZER, WILLIAM FRAZER)

JAMES "JIM" LESLIE BROWN (April 29, 1922 - Unknown) (Husband of BETTY JANE FRAZER BROWN, ARTHUR WATSON FRAZER SR., BENJAMIN FRANKLIN RENICK FRAZER, ROBERT ADDISON FRAZER, JOSEPH ADDISON FRAZER, ANTHONY FRAZER, JAMES BENJAMIN FRAZER, WILLIAM FRAZER)

PAUL RAY FRAZER (August 19, 1923 – February 29, 2008) (Son of ARTHUR WATSON FRAZER, SR., BENJAMIN FRANKLIN RENICK FRAZER, ROBERT ADDISON FRAZER, JOSEPH ADDISON FRAZER, ANTHONY FRAZER, JAMES BENJAMIN FRAZER, WILLIAM FRAZER)

ROBERT JAMES FRAZER, SR. (August 25, 1924 – January 11, 1996) (Son of ARTHUR WATSON FRAZER SR., BENJAMIN FRANKLIN RENICK FRAZER, ROBERT ADDISON FRAZER, JOSEPH ADDISON FRAZER, ANTHONY FRAZER, JAMES BENJAMIN FRAZER, WILLIAM FRAZER)

RONALD MCCUE FRAZER (February 9, 1921 – June 14, 1985) (Son of ARTHUR WATSON FRAZER SR., BENJAMIN FRANKLIN RENICK FRAZER, ROBERT ADDISON FRAZER, JOSEPH ADDISON FRAZER, ANTHONY FRAZER, JAMES BENJAMIN FRAZER, WILLIAM FRAZER)

WILMA PAULINE FRAZER (July 3, 1924 – March 20, 1992) (Second wife of CARL LAWRENCE FRAZER, ARTHUR WATSON FRAZER SR., BENJAMIN FRANKLIN RENICK FRAZER,) ROBERT ADDISON FRAZER, JOSEPH ADDISON FRAZER, ANTHONY FRAZER, JAMES BENJAMIN FRAZER, WILLIAM FRAZER)

WELLERS CEMETERY, 101 North Altamont Avenue, Thurmont, Frederick County, Maryland

MARY ELIZABETH BOWMAN FRAZER (May 3, 1918 – July 6, 1962) (First Wife of CARL LAWRENCE FRAZER, ARTHUR

WATSON FRAZER SR., BENJAMIN FRANKLIN RENICK FRAZER,) ROBERT ADDISON FRAZER, JOSEPH ADDISON FRAZER, ANTHONY FRAZER, JAMES BENJAMIN FRAZER, WILLIAM FRAZER)

OHIO

UNION CEMETERY, 3349 Olentangy River Road, Columbus, Franklin County, Ohio

EMMA COLE CRAM (April 16, 1878 – October 27, 1973) (Aunt to EMILY FRANCIS COLE FRAZER wife of OSCAR WALLACE FRAZER, JR.)

PENNSYLVANIA

BETHEL CHURCH CEMETERY, Chambersburg, Franklin County, Pennsylvania.

BENJAMIN FRANKLIN "FRANKIE" FRAZER (September 29, 1928 – December 7, 2006) (Son of ARTHUR WATSON FRAZER, SR., BENJAMIN FRANKLIN RENICK FRAZER, ROBERT ADDISON FRAZER, JOSEPH ADDISON FRAZER, ANTHONY FRAZER, JAMES BENJAMIN FRAZER, WILLIAM FRAZER) (Records also indicate he was buried at Germantown Bethel Cemetery, (Also known as Bethel Cemetery, Germantown Church of God Cemetery) 16924 Raven Rock Road, Cascade, Frederick County, Maryland.)

EVERGREEN CEMETERY, Gettysburg, Adams County, Pennsylvania (Many members of Frazer family buried in this cemetery.)

MARY S. FRAZER LOBINGIER (1930 – January 27, 2020) (Daughter of ARTHUR WATSON FRAZER, SR., BENJAMIN FRANKLIN RENICK FRAZER, ROBERT ADDISON FRAZER, JOSEPH ADDISON FRAZER, ANTHONY FRAZER, JAMES BENJAMIN FRAZER, WILLIAM FRAZER)

ROY W. LOBINGIER (1924-1995) (Husband to MARY S. FRAZER LOBINGIER)

TEXAS

DALLAS-FORT WORTH NATIONAL CEMETERY, 2000 Mountain Creek Parkway, Dallas, Texas

> **HUGH DYER FRAZER** (Dates are private.) (Son of OSCAR WALLACE FRAZER JR., OSCAR WALLACE FRAZER SR., BENJAMIN FRANKLIN RENICK FRAZER, ROBERT ADDISON FRAZER, JOSEPH ADDISON FRAZER, ANTHONY FRAZER, JAMES BENJAMIN FRAZER, WILLIAM FRAZER)

> **OSCAR WALLACE (WALLY) FRAZER III** (Dates are private.) (Son of OSCAR WALLACE FRAZER JR., OSCAR WALLACE FRAZER SR., BENJAMIN FRANKLIN RENICK FRAZER, ROBERT ADDISON FRAZER, JOSEPH ADDISON FRAZER, ANTHONY FRAZER, JAMES BENJAMIN FRAZER, WILLIAM FRAZER)

VIRGINIA

BEREA CHRISTIAN CHURCH CEMETERY, Spotsylvania Courthouse Road (Rt. 208), Spotsylvania County, Virginia

> **MARY ELIZABETH FRAZER "FRAZIER" CHANDLER** (1821 – September 9, 1881) (Daughter of THOMAS FOX FRAZER, JOHN FRAZER, JAMES BENJAMIN FRAZER, WILLIAM FRAZER)

> **THOMAS COLEMAN CHANDLER** (1798 – February 1890) (Husband of MARY ELIZABETH FRAZER "FRAZIER" CHANDLER)

CHANCELLOR FAMILY CEMETERY, (Also known as Fairview Cemetery), Chancellorsville, Spotsylvania County, Virginia

JOHN THOMAS FRAZER (April 12, 1820 – May 18, 1881) (Son of THOMAS FOX FRAZER, JOHN FRAZER, JAMES BENJAMIN FRAZER, WILLIAM FRAZER)

MARY EDWARDS CHANCELLOR FRAZER (May 7, 1827 – October 22, 1922) (Wife of JOHN THOMAS FRAZER, THOMAS FOX FRAZER, JOHN FRAZER, JAMES BENJAMIN FRAZER, WILLIAM FRAZER)

FREDERICKSBURG CEMETERY, (CITY CEMETERY), Washington Avenue, Fredericksburg, Virginia

MARY ELIZABETH (CONSTANCE) CALWELL YOUNG (1849 – October 27, 1878) (Daughter of MARGARET CARTER FRAZER CALWELL, JAMES A. FRAZER, ANTHONY FRAZER, JAMES BENJAMIN FRAZER, WILLIAM FRAZER)

HOLLYWOOD CEMETERY, 412 South Cherry Street, Richmond, Virginia

MAJOR PHILIP FOULKE FRAZER (December 22, 1844 – May 5, 1864) (Son of JAMES ADDISON FRAZER, JAMES A. FRAZER, ANTHONY FRAZER, JAMES BENJAMIN FRAZER, WILLIAM FRAZER)

LONGWOOD CEMETERY, Bedford, Virginia

JUNIUS ROBERT SUMMERSON (June 29, 1853 – December 18, 1909) (Son of SARAH REBECCA RENICK FRAZER SUMMERSON, JOSEPH ADDISON FRAZER, ANTHONY FRAZER, JAMES BENJAMIN FRAZER, WILLIAM FRAZER)

NORTH PAMUNKEY CEMETERY, 15109 Pamunkey Lane, Orange, Virginia

REV. HERNDON FRAZER (August 20, 1792 – July 10, 1877) (Son of ANTHONY FRAZER, JAMES BENJAMIN FRAZER, WILLIAM FRAZER)

HERNDON "DON" FRAZER (1849 – December 24, 1876) (Son of REV. HERNDON FRAZER, ANTHONY FRAZER, JAMES BENJAMIN FRAZER, WILLIAM FRAZER)

MARTHA L. RAWLINGS FRAZER (June 24, 1812 – November 28, 1880) (Wife of HERNDON FRAZER)

STONEWALL MEMORY GARDENS, 12004 Lee Highway, Manassas, Virginia

FREDERICK COLE FRAZER (Dates are private.) (Son of OSCAR WALLACE FRAZER JR., OSCAR WALLACE FRAZER SR., BENJAMIN FRANKLIN RENICK FRAZER, ROBERT ADDISON FRAZER, JOSEPH ADDISON FRAZER, ANTHONY FRAZER, JAMES BENJAMIN FRAZER, WILLIAM FRAZER)

NICOLE "NIKKI" LEIGH FRAZER (Dates are private.) (Daughter of FREDERICK COLE FRAZER, OSCAR WALLACE FRAZER JR., OSCAR WALLACE FRAZER SR., BENJAMIN FRANKLIN RENICK FRAZER, ROBERT ADDISON FRAZER, JOSEPH ADDISON FRAZER, ANTHONY FRAZER, JAMES BENJAMIN FRAZER, WILLIAM FRAZER)

THORNROSE CEMETERY, 1041 West Beverley Street, Staunton, Virginia

FRANCES "FANNIE" RENICK FRAZER (August 28, 1799 – April 12, 1884) (Wife of JOSEPH ADDISON FRAZER, ANTHONY FRAZER, JAMES BENJAMIN FRAZER, WILLIAM FRAZER)

FRANCES "FANNIE" SUMMERSON BYERS EAKLE (May 25, 1851 – March 4, 1891) (Daughter of SARAH REBECCA RENICK FRAZER SUMMERSON, JOSEPH ADDISON FRAZER,

ANTHONY FRAZER, JAMES BENJAMIN FRAZER, WILLIAM FRAZER)

HENRY EDMUND SUMMERSON (July 12, 1849 – July 13, 1917) (Son of SARAH REBECCA RENICK FRAZER SUMMERSON, JOSEPH ADDISON FRAZER, ANTHONY FRAZER, JAMES BENJAMIN FRAZER, WILLIAM FRAZER)

LIEUT. JAMES HERNDON FRAZER (abt. 1836 – August 23, 1862) (Son of JOSEPH ADDISON FRAZER, ANTHONY FRAZER, JAMES BENJAMIN FRAZER, WILLIAM FRAZER)

JOSEPH ADDISON FRAZER (May 22, 1798 – March 31, 1886) (Son of ANTHONY FRAZER, JAMES BENJAMIN FRAZER, WILLIAM FRAZER)

RICHARD SUMMERSON (1820 – November 20, 1880) (Husband of SARAH RENICK FRAZER SUMMERSON)

RICHARD PEYTON SUMMERSON (abt. 1856 – March 4, 1879) (Son of SARAH REBECCA RENICK FRAZER SUMMERSON, JOSEPH ADDISON FRAZER, ANTHONY FRAZER, JAMES BENJAMIN FRAZER, WILLIAM FRAZER)

SARAH REBECCA RENICK FRAZER SUMMERSON (abt. 1824 – May 1, 1893) (Daughter of JOSEPH ADDISON FRAZER, ANTHONY FRAZER, JAMES BENJAMIN FRAZER, WILLIAM FRAZER)

WILLIAM FRAZER SUMMERSON (July 21, 1847 – January 28, 1927) (Son of SARAH REBECCA RENICK FRAZER SUMMERSON, JOSEPH ADDISON FRAZER, ANTHONY FRAZER, JAMES BENJAMIN FRAZER, WILLIAM FRAZER)

WOODLAND CEMETERY, Ashland, Hanover County, Virginia

LUCY CHANDLER PENDLETON (1851-1943) (Daughter of MARY ELIZABETH FRAZER CHANDLER, THOMAS FOX FRAZER, JOHN FRAZER, JAMES BENJAMIN FRAZER, WILLIAM FRAZER)

WEST VIRGINIA

CAMPBELL CEMETERY, Bethany, West Virginia

MARTHA FRAZER TURNER (1811 – July 2, 1876) (Daughter of REUBEN FRAZER, JAMES BENJAMIN FRAZER, WILLIAM FRAZER)

GEORGE TURNER (1793-1880) (Husband to MARTHA FRAZER TURNER)

CUNNINGHAM MEMORIAL PARK, 815 Cunningham Lane, Saint Albans, Kanawha County, West Virginia

HERNDON VEAZEY FRAZER (August 24, 1880 – July 7, 1957) (Son of CHARLES FRAZER, ROBERT ADDISON FRAZER, JOSEPH ADDISON FRAZER, ANTHONY FRAZER, JAMES BENJAMIN FRAZER, WILLIAM FRAZER)

ROLAND CARTER FRAZER (March 14, 1899 – September 26, 1972) (Son of CHARLES FRAZER, ROBERT ADDISON FRAZER, JOSEPH ADDISON FRAZER, ANTHONY FRAZER, JAMES BENJAMIN FRAZER, WILLIAM FRAZER)

FAIRVIEW-CURRY CEMETERY, Nicholas County, West Virginia (There are many other Frazer family buried in this cemetery.)

CHARLES EDWARD FRAZER (1883-1968) (Son of WILLIAM ADDISON FRAZER, ROBERT ADDISON FRAZER, JOSEPH ADDISON FRAZER, ANTHONY FRAZER, JAMES BENJAMIN FRAZER, WILLIAM FRAZER

HOWARD VIRGIL FRAZER (January 11, 1903 – February 20, 1999) (Son of WILLIAM ADDISON FRAZER, ROBERT ADDISON FRAZER, JOSEPH ADDISON FRAZER, ANTHONY FRAZER, JAMES BENJAMIN FRAZER, WILLIAM FRAZER)

JAMES HERNDON FRAZER (October 29, 1881 – May 14, 1944) (Son of WILLIAM ADDISON FRAZER, ROBERT ADDISON FRAZER, JOSEPH ADDISON FRAZER, ANTHONY FRAZER, JAMES BENJAMIN FRAZER, WILLIAM FRAZER)

LESLIE BROOKE FRAZER (May 12, 1885 – March 13, 1968) (Son of WILLIAM ADDISON FRAZER, ROBERT ADDISON FRAZER, JOSEPH ADDISON FRAZER, ANTHONY FRAZER, JAMES BENJAMIN FRAZER, WILLIAM FRAZER)

STANLEY CLYDE FRAZER (May 10, 1892 – May 9, 1958) (Son of WILLIAM ADDISON FRAZER, ROBERT ADDISON FRAZER, JOSEPH ADDISON FRAZER, ANTHONY FRAZER, JAMES BENJAMIN FRAZER, WILLIAM FRAZER)

WILBUR WATSON FRAZER (November 3, 1895 – February 23, 1963) (Son of WILLIAM ADDISON FRAZER, ROBERT ADDISON FRAZER, JOSEPH ADDISON FRAZER, ANTHONY FRAZER, JAMES BENJAMIN FRAZER, WILLIAM FRAZER).

FRAZER CEMETERY, Tioga, Nicholas County, West Virginia

EMILY FRANCES BABER FRAZER (October 14, 1857 – January 7, 1948) (Wife of WILLIAM ADDISON FRAZER.)

WILLIAM ADDISON FRAZER (1851 - July 7, 1940) (Son of ROBERT ADDISON FRAZER, JOSEPH ADDISON FRAZER, ANTHONY FRAZER, JAMES BENJAMIN FRAZER, WILLIAM FRAZER)

WILLIE BELLE FRAZER (January 24, 1880 – October 22, 1883) (Son of WILLIAM ADDISON FRAZER, ROBERT ADDISON

FRAZER, JOSEPH ADDISON FRAZER, ANTHONY FRAZER, JAMES BENJAMIN FRAZER, WILLIAM FRAZER)

HANSFORD CEMETERY, Hansford, Kanawha County, West Virginia

CARRIE VINCENT HANSFORD SMITH FRAZER (1859 – November 16, 1940) (Wife of CHARLES HERNDON FRAZER, ROBERT A. FRAZER, JOSEPH ADDISON FRAZER, ANTHONY FRAZER, JAMES BENJAMIN FRAZER, WILLIAM FRAZER)

CHARLES HERNDON FRAZER (May 5, 1853 – January 19, 1922) (Son of ROBERT A. FRAZER, JOSEPH ADDISON FRAZER, ANTHONY FRAZER, JAMES BENJAMIN FRAZER, WILLIAM FRAZER)

FELIX ADISON FRAZER (November 19, 1895 – April 26, 1897) (Son of CHARLES HERNDON FRAZER, ROBERT ADDISON FRAZER, JOSEPH ADDISON FRAZER, ANTHONY FRAZER, JAMES BENJAMIN FRAZER, WILLIAM FRAZER)

FELIX GILBERT HANSFORD, SR. (December 12, 1795 – May 27, 1867) (Husband of SARAH KENYON "SALLIE" FRAZER HANSFORD)

MAJOR JOHN SAMUEL F. SMITH (1820-1896) (Father of CARRIE VINCENT HANSFORD SMITH FRAZER)

MARGARET FRAZER COLEMAN (May 15, 1882 – April 8, 1935) (Daughter of CHARLES HERNDON FRAZER, ROBERT ADDISON FRAZER, JOSEPH ADDISON FRAZER, ANTHONY FRAZER, JAMES BENJAMIN FRAZER, WILLIAM FRAZER)

MARTHA JANE HANSFORD SMITH (December 12, 1824 – December 27, 1906) (Mother of CARRIE VINCENT HANSFORD SMITH FRAZER)

SARAH KENYON "SALLIE" FRAZER HANSFORD (February 10, 1792 – September 3, 1888) (Daughter of JAMES FRAZER II, JAMES BENJAMIN FRAZER, WILLIAM FRAZER)

JARRETT FARM CEMETERY, Alta, West Virginia

ROBERT RENICK II (1757 – February 9, 1835) (Father to FRANCES "FANNIE" RENICK FRAZER, Wife of JOSEPH ADDISON FRAZER, ANTHONY FRAZER, JAMES BENJAMIN FRAZER, WILLIAM FRAZER)

MONTGOMERY MEMORIAL PARK, 9619 Dupont Avenue, London, Kanawha County, West Virginia

CHARLES BRADFORD COLEMAN, SR. (March 13, 1880 – June 13, 1958) (Husband to MARGARET FRAZER COLEMAN, CHARLES HERNDON FRAZER, ROBERT ADDISON FRAZER, JOSEPH ADDISON FRAZER, ANTHONY FRAZER, JAMES BENJAMIN FRAZER, WILLIAM FRAZER)

OLD STONE PRESBYTERIAN CHURCH CEMETERY, 644 Church Street, Lewisburg, West Virginia

ANTHONY FRAZER (abt.1801 – February 14, 1839) (Son of ANTHONY FRAZER, JAMES BENJAMIN FRAZER, WILLIAM FRAZER)

BEDFORD CALWELL BEIRNE (October 31, 1852 – March 27, 1907) (Son of ELIZABETH "BETTIE" TAYLOR FRAZER BEIRNE, JAMES A. FRAZER, ANTHONY FRAZER, JAMES BENJAMIN FRAZER, WILLIAM FRAZER)

ELIZABETH FRAZER FRAZER (August 1, 1781 – December 14, 1846) (Wife of JAMES A. FRAZER, ANTHONY FRAZER, JAMES BENJAMIN FRAZER, WILLIAM FRAZER)

ELIZABETH "BETTIE" TAYLOR FRAZER BEIRNE (February 22, 1829 – November 10, 1908) (Daughter of JAMES A. FRAZER, ANTHONY FRAZER, JAMES BENJAMIN FRAZER, WILLIAM FRAZER)

GORDON O. BEIRNE (August 10, 1860 – January 1907) (Son of ELIZABETH "BETTIE" TAYLOR FRAZER BEIRNE, JAMES A. FRAZER, ANTHONY FRAZER, JAMES BENJAMIN FRAZER, WILLIAM FRAZER)

HANNAH HERNDON FRAZER THOMPSON (February 5, 1815 – January 23, 1889) (Daughter of JAMES A. FRAZER, ANTHONY FRAZER, JAMES BENJAMIN FRAZER, WILLIAM FRAZER)

HARRY HEATH BEIRNE, SR. (December 1, 1857 – July 12, 1910) (Son of ELIZABETH "BETTIE" TAYLOR FRAZER BEIRNE, JAMES A. FRAZER, ANTHONY FRAZER, JAMES BENJAMIN FRAZER, WILLIAM FRAZER)

MAJ. HARRY HETH HARRISON (1820 – August 11, 1893) (Husband of SARAH THOMAS FRAZER HARRISON)

JAMES A. FRAZER (June 7, 1783 – February 11, 1854) (Son of ANTHONY FRAZER, JAMES BENJAMIN FRAZER, WILLIAM FRAZER)

JAMES ADDISON FRAZER (July 6, 1812 – March 27, 1860) (Son of JAMES A. FRAZER, ANTHONY FRAZER, JAMES BENJAMIN FRAZER, WILLIAM FRAZER)

KITTY HETH (HEATHER) HARRISON (October 17, 1858 – January 22, 1944) (Daughter of SARAH THOMAS FRAZER HARRISON, JAMES A. FRAZER, ANTHONY FRAZER, JAMES BENJAMIN FRAZER, WILLIAM FRAZER

MARGARET "PEGGY" FRAZER (April 4, 1799 – January 9, 1828) (Daughter of ANTHONY FRAZER, JAMES BENJAMIN FRAZER, WILLIAM FRAZER)

MARY FRAZER (FRAZIER) SUMMERSON HUNTER (September 25, 1858 – February 7, 1931/1932)[458] (Daughter of SARAH REBECCA RENICK FRAZER SUMMERSON, JOSEPH ADDISON FRAZER, ANTHONY FRAZER, JAMES BENJAMIN FRAZER, WILLIAM FRAZER)

SAMUEL SINGLETON THOMPSON (March 28, 1801 – March 3, 1877) (Husband of HANNAH HERNDON FRAZER THOMPSON)

SARAH THOMAS FRAZER HARRISON (August 1, 1820 – March 3, 1891) (Daughter of JAMES A. FRAZER, ANTHONY FRAZER, JAMES BENJAMIN FRAZER, WILLIAM FRAZER)

WILLIAM HERNDON FRAZER (April 22, 1817 – August 9, 1825) (Son of JAMES A. FRAZER, ANTHONY FRAZER, JAMES BENJAMIN FRAZER, WILLIAM FRAZER)

RIVERVIEW CEMETERY, Ronceverte, West Virginia

FANNIE FRAZER (FRAZIER) LINK (abt. 1827-1900) (Daughter of JOSEPH ADDISON FRAZER, ANTHONY FRAZER, JAMES BENJAMIN FRAZER, WILLIAM FRAZER)

FRANKLIN "FRANK" HASKELL LINK (October 25, 1825 – May 22, 1889) (Husband of FANNIE FRAZER "FRAZIER" LINK)

HERNDON FRAZER LINK (1866 – August 20, 1919) (Son of FANNIE FRAZER LINK, JOSEPH ADDISON FRAZER, ANTHONY FRAZER, JAMES BENJAMIN FRAZER, WILLIAM FRAZER)

---

[458] Virginia Department of Health; Richmond, Virginia; Virginia Deaths, 1912-2014.

IDA FRAZER (FRAZIER) LINK HARRIS (September 16, 1857 – February 6, 1899) (Daughter of FANNIE FRAZER LINK, JOSEPH ADDISON FRAZER, ANTHONY FRAZER, JAMES BENJAMIN FRAZER, WILLIAM FRAZER)

SAINT JOHN'S CATHOLIC CHURCH CEMETERY, Summersville, Nicholas County, West Virginia

FLORENCE ROSELLA FRAZER (August 1885 – October 27, 1967) (Daughter of RICHARD SUMMERSON FRAZER, ROBERT ADDISON FRAZER, JOSEPH ADDISON FRAZER, ANTHONY FRAZER, JAMES BENJAMIN FRAZER, WILLIAM FRAZER)

GERTRUDE FRAZER (February 11, 1881 – November 29, 1962) (Daughter of RICHARD SUMMERSON FRAZER, ROBERT ADDISON FRAZER, JOSEPH ADDISON FRAZER, ANTHONY FRAZER, JAMES BENJAMIN FRAZER, WILLIAM FRAZER)

HANNORA "NORA" O'MEARA FRAZER (January 14, 1853 – December 4, 1920) (Wife of RICHARD SUMMERSON FRAZER, ROBERT ADDISON FRAZER, JOSEPH ADDISON FRAZER, ANTHONY FRAZER, JAMES BENJAMIN FRAZER, WILLIAM FRAZER)

HANORA ELLEN FRAZER (March 2, 1879 – January 8, 1957) (Daughter of RICHARD SUMMERSON FRAZER, ROBERT ADDISON FRAZER, JOSEPH ADDISON FRAZER, ANTHONY FRAZER, JAMES BENJAMIN FRAZER, WILLIAM FRAZER)

HARRIET T. FRAZER (July 23, 1874 – February 12, 1894) (Daughter of RICHARD SUMMERSON FRAZER, ROBERT ADDISON FRAZER, JOSEPH ADDISON FRAZER, ANTHONY FRAZER, JAMES BENJAMIN FRAZER, WILLIAM FRAZER)

RICHARD SUMMERSON FRAZER (December 25, 1849 – July 7, 1938) (Son of ROBERT ADDISON FRAZER, JOSEPH ADDISON

FRAZER, ANTHONY FRAZER, JAMES BENJAMIN FRAZER, WILLIAM FRAZER)

SPRING HILL CEMETERY, 1555 Farnsworth Drive, Charleston, West Virginia

GRAHAM FISHBURNE PAINTER, SR. (November 9, 1912 – December 15, 1981) (Husband of RUTH LAURA FRAZER PAINTER)

LAURA BELLE DYER FRAZER (August 12, 1881 – February 8, 1968) (Wife of OSCAR WALLACE FRAZER SR., BENJAMIN FRANKLIN RENICK FRAZER, ROBERT ADDISON FRAZER, JOSEPH ADDISON FRAZER, ANTHONY FRAZER, JAMES BENJAMIN FRAZER, WILLIAM FRAZER)

MORGAN HOMER DYER (1855 – January 22, 1946) (Father of LAURA BELLE DYER FRAZER)

OSCAR WALLACE FRAZER, SR. (FRAZIER) (September 17, 1880 – February 20, 1931) (Son of BENJAMIN FRANKLIN RENICK FRAZER, ROBERT ADDISON FRAZER, JOSEPH ADDISON FRAZER, ANTHONY FRAZER, JAMES BENJAMIN FRAZER, WILLIAM FRAZER)

RUTH LAURA FRAZER (FRAZIER) PAINTER (November 30, 1911 – July 25, 2001) (Daughter of OSCAR WALLACE FRAZER SR., BENJAMIN FRANKLIN RENICK FRAZER, ROBERT ADDISON FRAZER, JOSEPH ADDISON FRAZER, ANTHONY FRAZER, JAMES BENJAMIN FRAZER, WILLIAM FRAZER)

SUNSET MEMORIAL PARK, 4301 MacCorkle Avenue, S.W., South Charleston, West Virginia

HARRIETT COLE MCNEAL (February 4, 1872 – July 13, 1967) (Aunt to EMILY FRANCIS COLE FRAZER the wife of OSCAR WALLACE FRAZER, JR.)

HELEN KATHRYN NIGHTINGALE COLE BYRNSIDE (1895 – January 16, 1968) (Mother to EMILY FRANCIS COLE FRAZER the wife of OSCAR WALLACE FRAZER, JR.)

JOSEPH DYRE COLE, JR. (January 20, 1922 – December 13, 1991) (Brother to EMILY FRANCIS COLE FRAZER the wife of OSCAR WALLACE FRAZER, JR.)

JOSEPH DYRE COLE, SR. (June 20, 1882 – January 17, 1931) (Father to EMILY FRANCIS COLE FRAZER the wife of OSCAR WALLACE FRAZER, JR.)

Printed in the United States
By Bookmasters